VOICES OF AMERICA

SAN ANTONIO

in the 1920s and 1930s

VOICES OF AMERICA

SAN ANTONIO

in the 1920s and 1930s

Mary E. Livingston
Illustrated and edited by Frances R. Pryor

ARCADIA
PUBLISHING

ISBN 978-0-7385-0152-9

Published by Arcadia Publishing
Charleston, South Carolina

Printed in the United States of America

For all general information contact Arcadia Publishing at:
Telephone 843-853-2070
Fax 843-853-0044
E-mail sales@arcadiapublishing.com
For customer service and orders:
Toll-Free 1-888-313-2665

Visit us on the Internet at www.arcadiapublishing.com

Contents

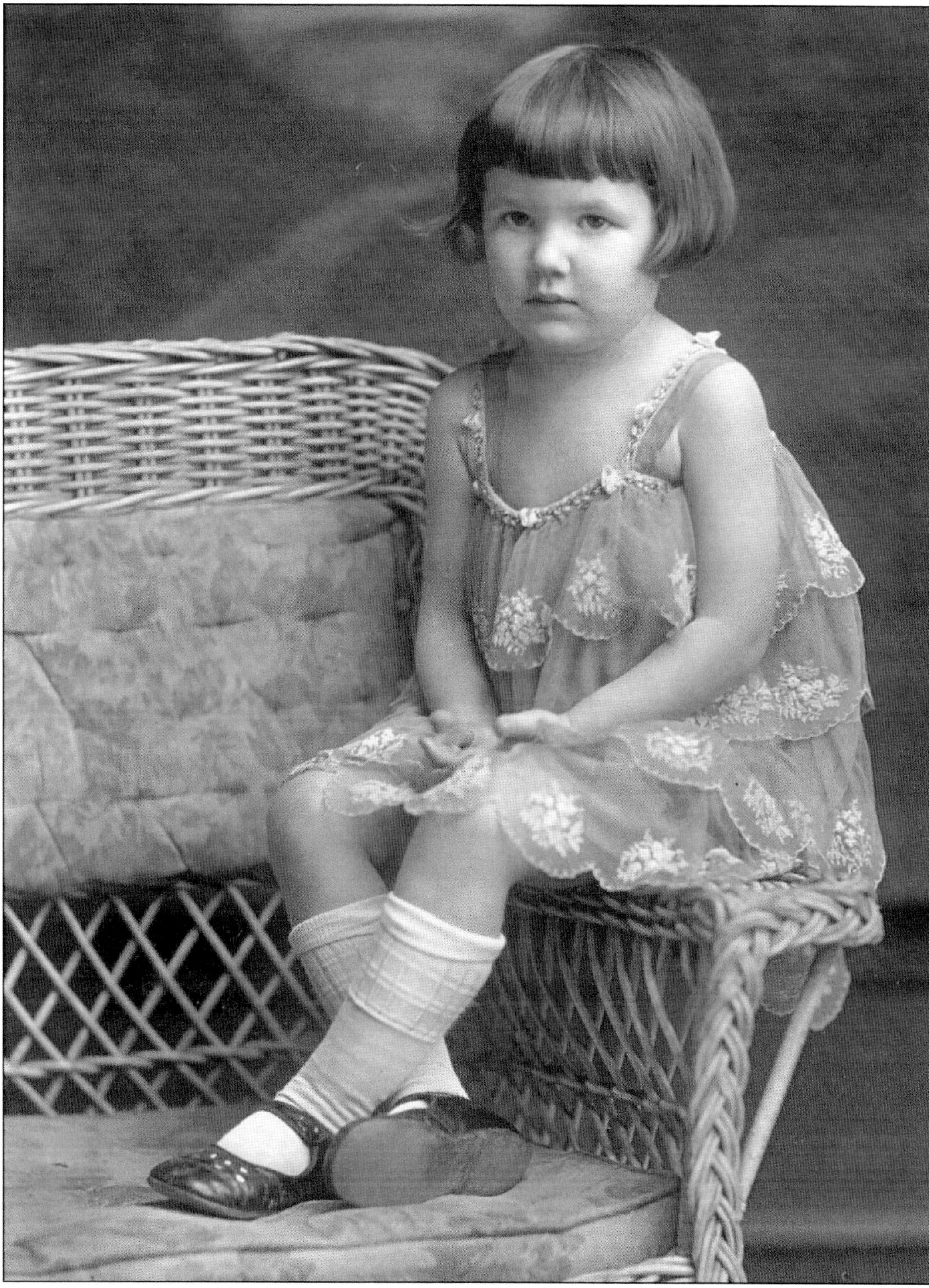

In the 1920s and '30s, Mary Elizabeth Rife (the author) enjoyed a life of peace and tranquility in the "green meadows of childhood," the term being symbolic of a life filled with everything to nurture a body and soul.

Prologue

A few months ago while watching my little granddaughters at play, I found myself wondering if I could remember the games I played when I was a little girl. And suddenly a feeling of peace and tranquillity came over me as I returned once again to the Green Meadows of childhood, the phrase Green Meadows being symbolic of a life filled with an abundance of everything needed to nurture body and soul.

I started thinking back to what I did with my time when I was a child over 60 years ago, and the first thing that came to my mind was the social atmosphere I grew up in, not the games I played. In many ways, it was entirely different from today.

The era of my childhood (1923-1935) was a time of gentility and innocence. It was a period when women and children were respected and protected by the men in their lives and a time when men tipped their hats to ladies, stepped aside to allow ladies and children first, opened doors for them, and helped them in and out of cars. Men certainly never swore or told off-color stories or jokes around women and children. Husbands were, generally speaking, the sole breadwinners, and the wives were busy homemakers and mothers. The few married women I knew who worked outside the home did so by choice.

My first confrontation with the unpleasant, seamier side of reality was in the newsreels that were run in theaters right after the movies. Most of the ones that I remembered were about the sadness of the Depression, but others concerned a crime of some sort and happenings in foreign countries. Many times Mother took me to the restroom during a particularly unpleasant news report to spare me from hearing it. It was her theory that a person wouldn't be influenced or disturbed by something he or she had never seen or heard in the first place, and that it would serve no purpose whatsoever to expose her daughters to such things. Father certainly agreed with her.

Memory tells me that the most stressful situations I encountered in my daily existence were, for the most part, things like "How many butterflies will I see before sunset?" or "Will I finally get to see a bud on one of Mother's flowers open into a bloom today?" Or "Will Mother make waffles, pancakes, or biscuits for breakfast?"

Did all of this protection have an adverse effect on me as an adult? I certainly can't say that it did; instead, I firmly believe it made for a much better life all-around. In fact, it is my contention that I grew up in a time when the world at large respected and yearned for innocence and gentility.

But what did a child do with himself in the 1920s and 1930s? Wasn't there an unlimited amount of time to kill, in which there was nothing to do, without a television around to look at and an endless array of games to play?

Well, there were a few things available at that time to entertain children: first, there was the Victrola, which had to be cranked and then it played music for only about ten or fifteen minutes before it had to be cranked again. Later came the radio, which didn't offer much until the early 1930s, and then mostly at night. Of course, we had baby dolls, Lincoln Logs, Lionel electric trains, and some of the standard toys, but nothing like the assortment offered now.

To a young person of the 1990s, all this probably sounds like a very boring era in which to live, wherein there was not a lot to do. But when I looked back and started remembering that period of my life, I couldn't recall a single moment when I was bored. On the whole, there was always too much to do and never enough time.

Then I started writing down the highlights of some of the things I remembered with the hope that my granddaughters would read about them and see what childhood was like in a different era. At the same time, I hoped they might learn a little about some of their immediate relatives who lived and died in an earlier time.

My childhood memories are separated into different categories according to where I lived. For my first five years it was at 630 East Park Avenue in San Antonio. For the next almost eight years, it was at 3701 Pleasanton Road, in what was then called "Mayfield Park," on the south side of San Antonio. Thus, all of my formative years were spent in and around the "Alamo City."

This book covers many topics such as family activities, fun and games, learning experiences, medical problems, happy times and sad times, my hometown, the effects of the Depression, and then just some things that I remembered.

There are two things in particular that I have gleaned from my reveries. First, the fact that (family and acquaintances notwithstanding) my very bestfriend and constant companion has always been my imagination. Second, the realization that my greatest aid in learning has always been an inquiring mind. I am now, and forever will be, grateful that television and other forms of entertainment available today were not around when I was a child to interrupt and stint either my imagination or my inquiring mind.

Chapter One

Life at 630 East Park Avenue

Before I get to what I remember about life on East Park Avenue, I will first tell how it all began.

In December 1921, my father, T.D. Rife, suddenly realized that soon he would be 30 years old and still single. Until that time he had delayed thoughts of marriage for many reasons. First, he had spent several years helping his parents send his older brother through Texas A&M College, then, he had sojourned in West Texas for several years buying and selling cattle, sheep, and goats. During World War I, he had been in the army, and then he spent a couple of years establishing himself in the real estate business in San Antonio. Last, but not least, he hadn't found "the right girl."

After thinking about all of this, Father decided to take time out and find himself a wife. "The Templeton girl," whom he had noticed at a Baptist Young People's Union (BYPU) meeting in the First Baptist Church, immediately came to mind, and he told a friend of his who knew her that he would like to make her acquaintance. His friend introduced him to both of the Templeton girls and he made arrangements to visit with them in their home the following week.

Mary Templeton, the younger of the two, was only about 20 years old and very attractive. She had jet-black hair and big brown eyes that held a look of surprise most of the time. Grandmother kept her outfitted in the latest and most fashionable clothes of that time. She wasn't allowed to do anything around the house that might damage her beautiful hands. She was considered by her peers to be very eligible for marriage.

Jean Templeton was about 27 years old, had light brown hair, a flawless ivory complexion, and never wore any makeup, not even lipstick. Her eyes were a deep shade of blue that sparkled when she smiled, revealing her sense of humor and zest for life. She had a natural beauty that made one overlook the plain, drab dresses that Grandmother compelled her to wear until they were worn out. Instead of protecting her hands, Grandmother had her do all the household chores.

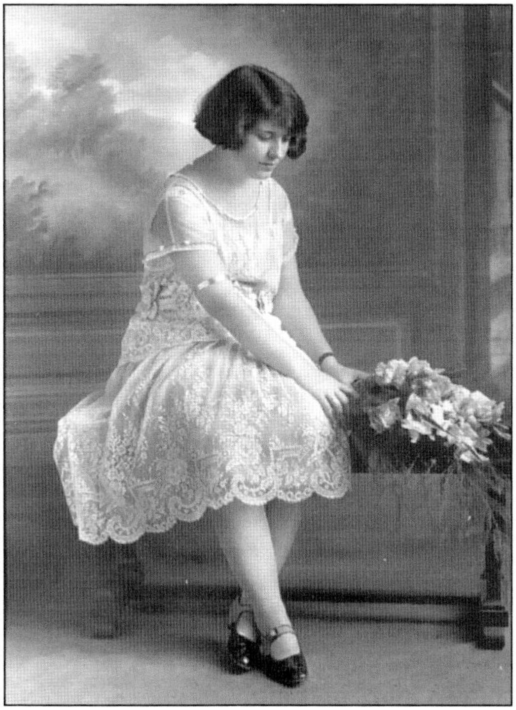

Mary Templeton was the youngest of the two Templeton girls and considered the one most eligible for marriage.

Father was very handsome, with a strong build, lots of black wavy hair, dark brown eyes, fair complexion, and a manner about him that gave the impression he knew what he wanted and was in a hurry to get it. He had a vibrant sense of humor and a true zest for life.

It was taken for granted by Father's friend and everyone else that his interest was in Mary, the younger of the two sisters, as Jean, the older one, was already considered by most people to be a confirmed spinster lady. But once in the Templeton home, Father immediately surprised everyone by spending all his time with "plain" Jean. After visiting a while, Father made a date to see Jean again in a day or so.

Father told us that his friend immediately told him he was after the wrong girl, that Mary was the one he should marry. Father said his reply was, "No way. Jean is the one for me. I like everything about her." Father also told us in later years that he knew, before he ever went to her home that day to meet her, Jean was the one with whom he wanted to spend his life. After a whirlwind courtship of about six weeks, filled with stumbling blocks Grandmother put in their way, he proposed to Jean and she accepted. Whenever they told the story, Mother and Father always made it sound more like a fairy tale "Cinderella" romance than a story from real life.

When they announced their intentions to marry, Grandmother was immediately filled with shock and disbelief that her daughter would even consider leaving her to marry anyone, let alone a "man she hardly knew." And what in the world could any man, especially one as debonair and handsome as T.D. Rife, see in her "plain" Jean? Grandmother had planned for Mother to live with her, keep her company, help her with the household chores, and do the sewing for as long as Grandmother lived. In those days, it was not uncommon for a daughter to do just that. Since Mother was in her early teens, Grandmother had been preparing her to be the spinster daughter who filled that bill. She started by teaching Mother how to cook and care for the house, then how to sew. She gradually turned more and more duties over to Mother, who always did her best to please Grandmother.

Mother completed her education at the Mulholland School for Girls. It was San Antonio's most prestigious finishing school, attended by daughters of socially prominent wealthy families. It was taken for granted that upon graduation each would make her formal debut into society with a debutante ball.

Mother was only allowed a limited wardrobe, which got sparser as she matured. She told me many times that she went to school everyday for the entire year wearing the same dress that she had made. She washed and starched it on

Saturday, wore it to church on Sunday and for the next five days to school. When she broached the subject of making herself another dress, as the other girls had quite a few, Grandmother replied, "The one you have isn't worn out yet. Just see to it you keep it clean enough to last out the week." She did as she was told without complaining.

She didn't even think it wrong that she had to stay home and work when her classmates (who liked her right off in spite of her lack of wardrobe) asked her to their parties and informal after-school gatherings. She merely told them, "Mother needs me at home." The school year finally ended and Mother heard her classmates plan their resplendent debutante balls. She asked Grandmother when her own ball would be held and was told, "You don't need one, you don't have time to socialize and you're not going to get married, so it would be a waste of money." Mother wondered why she had been sent to the Mulholland School in the first place.

When Mother received invitations to her classmates' coming-out parties, Grandmother replied, "You don't have anything to wear and it would be foolish to make a dress to wear one time." Mother never objected or argued with Grandmother.

I don't believe Grandfather ever knew Mother was unhappy about the situation; she never bothered him with "such unpleasant trivialities." But Grandfather must have had a special feeling for Mother, as he presented her with a diamond ring on her 21st birthday. Grandmother immediately forbade her to wear it except during meals when Grandfather was present and to church.

When Father came along, he literally liberated her from a very severe situation, giving Mother a newfound freedom and happiness. Grandmother's exacerbation about the impending wedding grew, and she did everything humanly possible to stop it. She even refused to buy Mother a wedding dress.

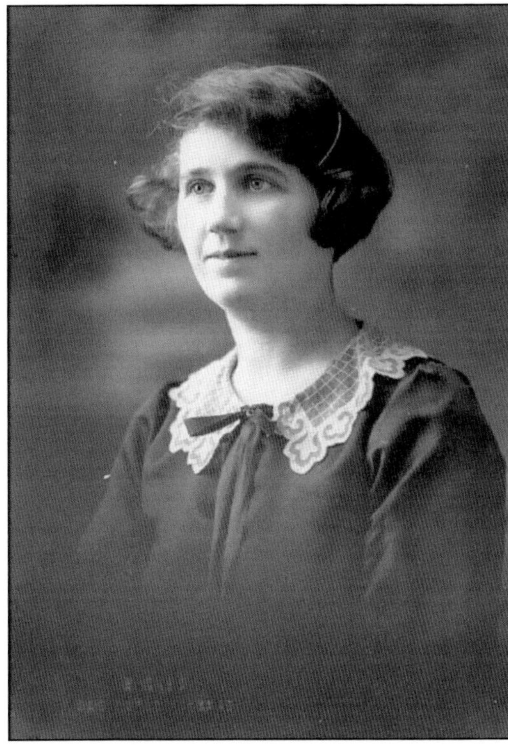

Jean Templeton, who was much older and well on her way to becoming a spinster, was the one Father preferred.

Grandmother insisted the wedding would never take place and if it did, Mother would have to wear the dark brown taffeta dress that she had bought her years ago for special occasions. She also insisted that there would be absolutely no pictures taken of the wedding, and none were. All this for spite, as it certainly wasn't due to lack of funds. Grandfather was a very wealthy man, and he gave Grandmother unlimited access to his bank account.

On March 18, 1922, 90 days after Father and Mother were formally introduced, they became man and wife, dark brown wedding dress and Grandmother's protestations notwithstanding. The wedding took place in the pastor's study in the First Baptist Church with Dr. Gates, the

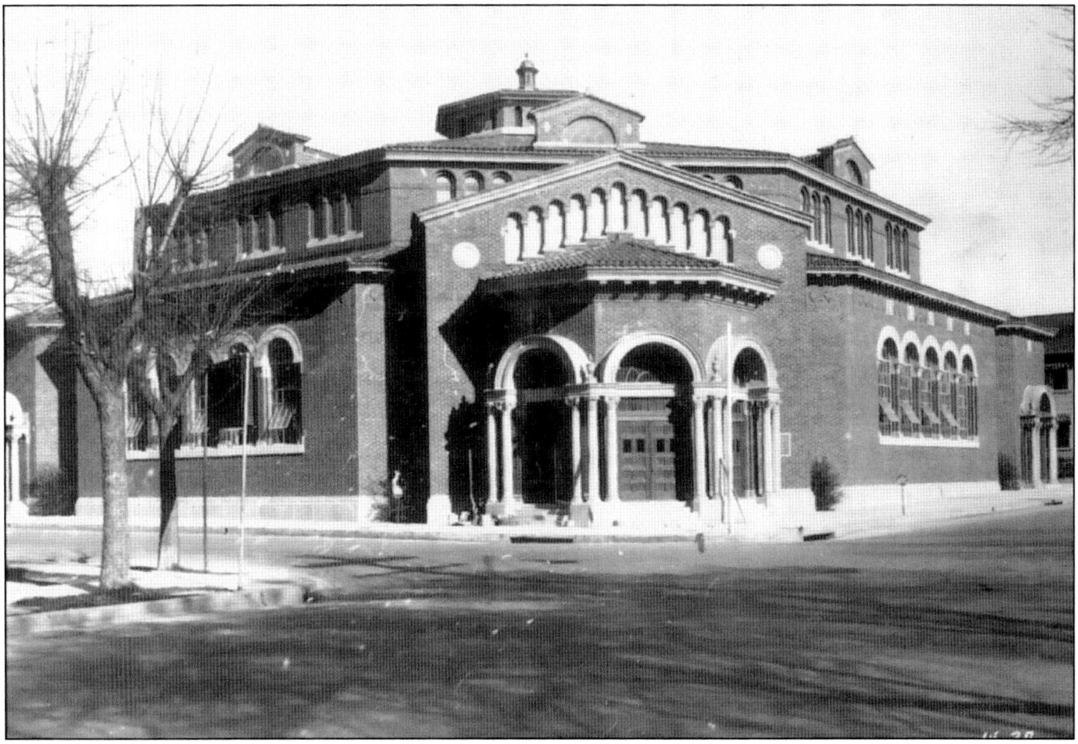

This is San Antonio's First Baptist Church, where Mother and Father first met and were later married. (Photo courtesy of the University of Texas Institute of Texan Cultures at San Antonio.)

pastor, officiating. Mother and Father were both members in good standing of that church.

A sparse reception followed the ceremony, and then Cinderella and Prince Charming got in Father's Model T Ford and rode off "into the sunset" to start a fairy tale life together filled with love, happiness, and a lot of work.

I don't think Grandmother ever forgave Father for taking her daughter away from her, but Grandfather, being very realistic about everything, found a house still under construction about 20 blocks from his home and purchased it as a wedding present for the couple. Even though Grandmother's contempt for Father never changed, he ignored it and stayed away from her. Mother, on the other hand, felt duty bound to visit her at least once a week. They made small talk and avoided the subject of her marriage.

Finally, it was time to move into their new home at 630 East Park Avenue. The architecture of the house was very unique. It was the only one in that part of town with three large French doors spaced evenly across the front opening onto a roofed verandah which spanned the entire front of the house. The columns, which extended from the floor to the roof on the outer edge of the verandah, brought to mind a home you might see on a Southern plantation.

Everything was perfect for the newlyweds. Soon after they moved into their new home, Mother found she was expecting a baby, probably sometime in March of the following year. This pleased Mother and Father immensely as they were very eager to have children. The baby, of course, proved to be me.

Mother made my layette from scratch. The many items displayed her expertise in various kinds of needlework. She cut out the baby clothes and then sewed them partly by hand and partly on her treadle sewing machine. One of the little dresses she made had a border of hand-crocheted lace on the sleeves and hem with roses embroidered all around the yoke and the lower part of the skirt. There were plainer dresses with tatting on the edges of the sleeves, collars, and skirts, and embroidery on the yokes. Even the white flannel receiving blankets had crocheted edging on them. Every garment was decorated with Mother's embroidery, crochet, tatting, or fancy needlework.

Mother told me a little about my birth. Labor started late in the evening on March 12, 1923, and lasted into the night in the front bedroom of her home. Yes, at that time women were still having their babies at home, barring unusual circumstances or an excess of wealth that caused the mother to want to show off by going to a hospital.

The nurse Dr. Bates sent to assist in the birth held onto Mother when it seemed necessary or she started to pass out with pain. She managed to smother any cries of discomfort due to the throes of childbirth because she didn't want to startle her husband. She was determined that she would do all humanly possible to make the delivery of her child seem a normal, not too painful occurrence so that he would not have an aversion to the baby because of the pain it caused her. He was fooled, too, by her show. Father paced around from room to room, stopping now and then to ask, "Is the baby here yet?"

The labor was a long, hard, trying time for Mother, and I was only the first of three children she was to bear in her lifetime. She said that just when the pain had become unbearable, the doctor said he could see my head. He said, "It won't be long now," and she took another breath of pain and waited, not knowing what was happening or what to expect next. I finally cried and Mother let out a sigh of relief and went to sleep for a few hours. The nurse bathed and dressed me in some of the baby clothes, and then she put me down to sleep also.

Father and Dr. Bates had a long talk in the living room, during which he told the doctor my name and paid him $25 for the delivery. Mighty cheap baby! I believe that was the going rate at the time.

Mother wrote in my baby book that I was born Wednesday, March 13, 1923, at 3:10 a.m. and weighed eight pounds, eight ounces. Mother and Father named me Mary Elizabeth after my two grandmothers. Mother immediately started recording important events in my baby book as they occurred, such as my first outing to visit

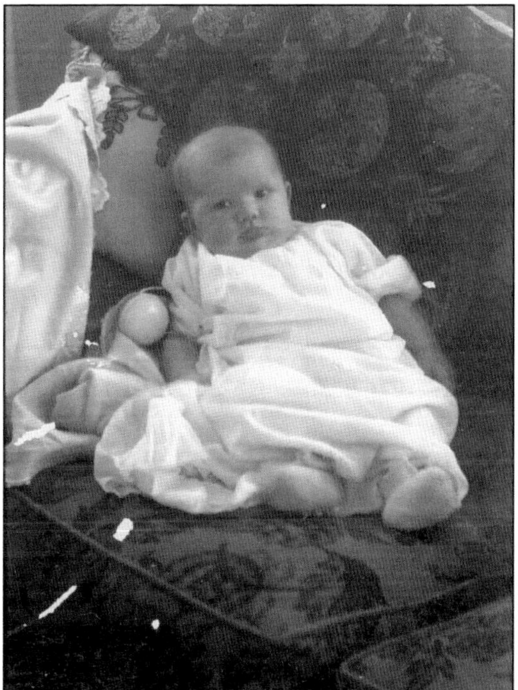

Just six weeks old, Mary Rife reclines on the comfortable sofa at their new home at 630 East Park Avenue.

Mother's parents, and when I attended church for the first time at the age of five weeks. Mother's sister Mary (from here on referred to as "Aunt Sissie") married Atwood Wells on January 29, 1924, which marked my first wedding attendance. It was quite a surprise to note that I spent my first night away from home with Grandmother Templeton when I was only 13 months old.

The earliest memory of any kind, of which I am sure of the date, concerns (unlikely as it may seem) the nurse who came to stay with us when my sister Jean was born on May 16, 1925. I may have been only a little over two years old at the time, but I definitely remember she was quite tall, very large, and extremely cold and unfriendly toward me. She stayed seven days and it was a happy day when she left. She had been like a dark cloud hovering between Mother and me.

Maybe Grandmother didn't approve of the marriage, but that didn't keep her from becoming completely captivated by the fruit thereof. In no time at all, Mother began to enjoy her visits with Grandmother with me in tow. However, Grandmother never did forgive Father for stealing her daughter.

At the early age of three, my tonsils and adenoids were removed. The anesthetic used was ether, and I have never forgotten its hideous smell. Whooping cough attacked me when I was four years old. I remember the days and days of strangling coughs. I am really glad that we have a vaccination for it today and children no longer have to go through it.

In the middle of January 1928, I contracted scarlet fever and ran a temperature of 104 degrees for about four days. The doctor came out again and this time he hung a quarantine sign on the front door. After he left, Mother drew a white line across my bedroom floor with chalk and told me not to cross it (of course, I was too ill to leave my bed) and told Jean to stay on her side of the line. Jean was almost two and a half years old and every time Mother lost sight of her for even a moment, she wound up in bed with me jumping around, trying to get me to play.

After a couple of days my fever went down a little, and I can still remember the white chalk line, Jean being all over me, and Mother carrying her away all day. Mother was exasperated by the time my fever finally broke. She steeled herself for what she thought was the inevitable—Jean's having scarlet fever too—but she didn't get it. Even the doctor was puzzled as to why Jean didn't contract scarlet fever from me.

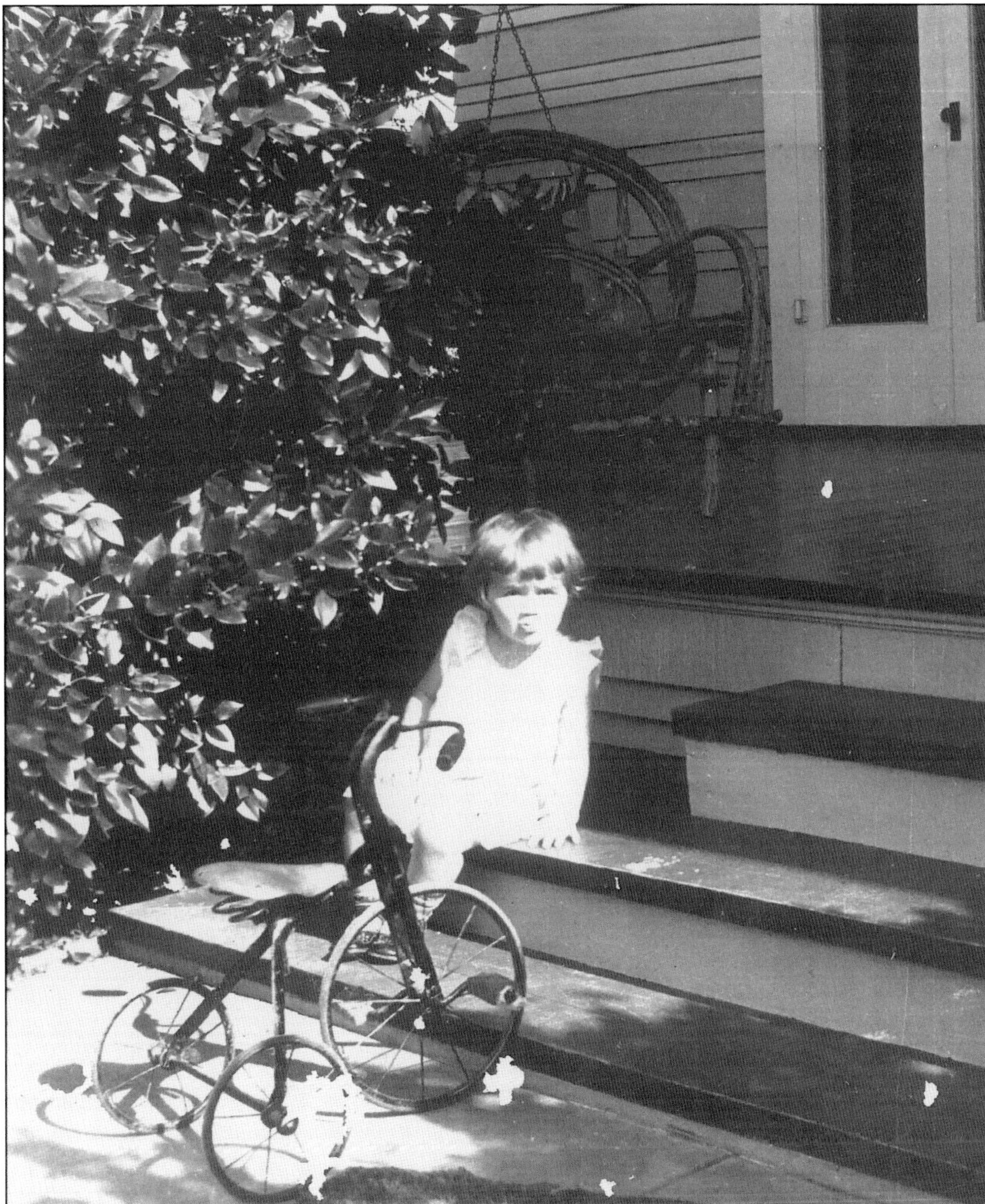

After a fall, Jean had to have her tongue sewed back together. She tried (successfully) to work the stitches out and had to have it sewed back together again.

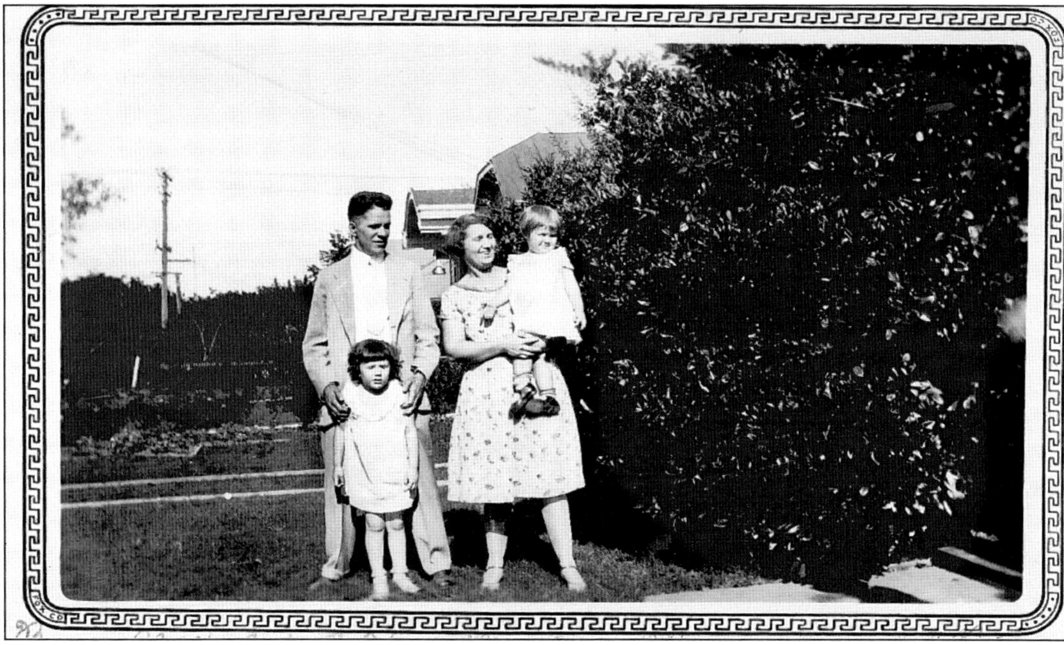

Just a few years later there were four of us. Father, Mother, sister Jean, and I are pictured in the front yard of our beautiful new home.

Chapter Two

The World Around Me

Every time it rained, Mother got out her car, picked up Aunt Sissie, and took us riding in the rain. We laughed and giggled and sometimes just sat on the side of the road and watched the rain come down.

Mother really loved to ride around in the rain. I think it had something to do with the fact that she had spent the first twenty some-odd years of her life with a horse and buggy, and a traveler usually got wet in a buggy when it rained. Then she found that you could stay dry in a car, and it fascinated her.

If it rained really hard for awhile, Mother took us to the Olmos Dam. We rode across it to look at the water and marvel at the dam holding it back. Mother had never forgotten the torrential rains that flooded all the downtown department stores in San Antonio before the dam was built. We rode over that dam many times in the rain.

Another fun thing we did with Aunt Sissie concerned Mother's penchant for following fire wagons. Whenever she heard one clanging through the neighborhood she picked up Aunt Sissie and we were off to follow the fire engine. Several times we watched the firemen put out a fire. We weren't the only sightseers following the fire trucks, but no one seemed to mind. In the late 1920s, there wasn't a traffic problem like there is today.

Mother must have started taking me on those adventurous rides the first time that it either rained or she heard a fire wagon, because it seems that they were always a welcome part of my life. I wonder how many other little girls could boast of riding over the Olmos Dam in a torrential downpour just for fun, or chasing red fire engines, with her well-bred and otherwise sedate mother and aunt. It was exciting! Such capers would not be feasible in the large metropolis that San Antonio has come to be at this time. However, if I lived in Olmos Park, east of the dam, I would be tempted to ride over it once more during a rainstorm.

Shortly before reaching my fourth birthday, I experienced a very exciting weather happening: it snowed on Park Avenue! I remember standing at the window watching the snowflakes as they

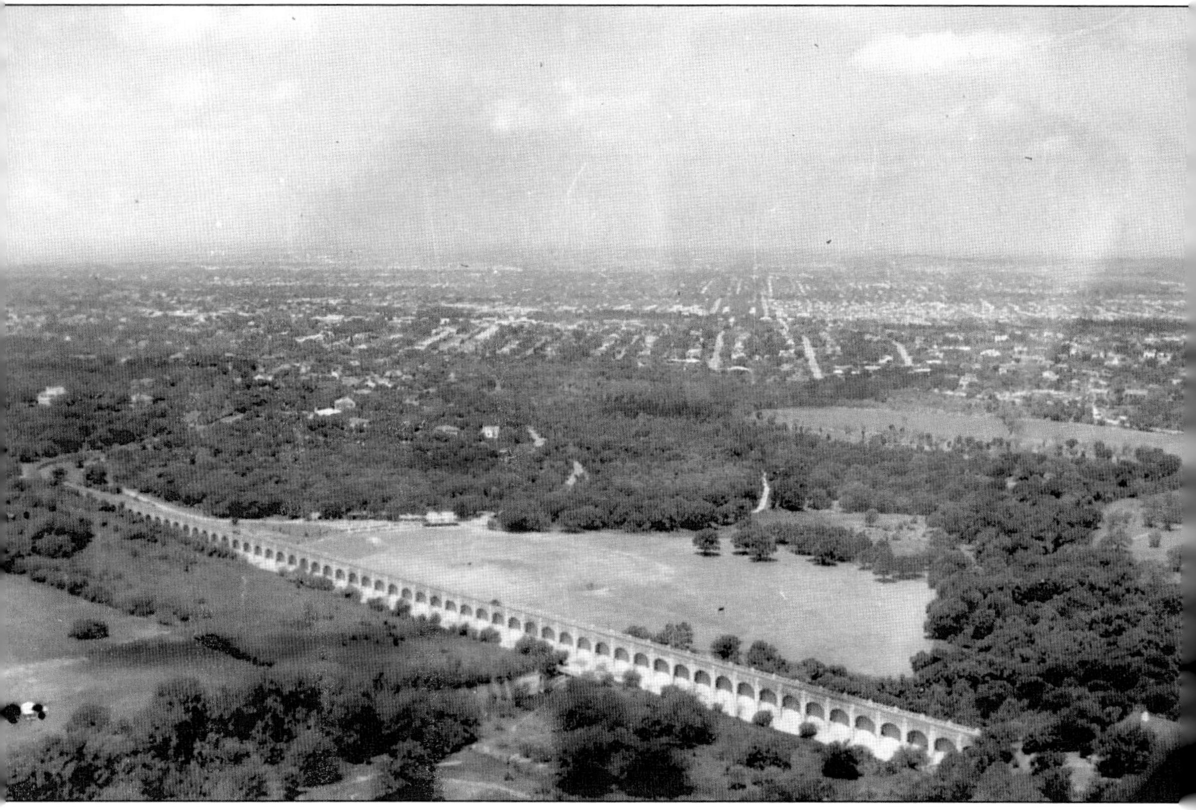

The Olmos Dam was built to assure that the flooding did not occur again. Mother loved to ride across it during a rainstorm. (Photo courtesy of the UT Institute of Texan Cultures.)

floated down from the sky and finally landed on the ground, until there was a three- or four-inch blanket of the beautiful white snow everywhere. As soon as it stopped falling, Mother bundled us up in our heavy winter clothing and took us outside to "play in the snow," as she put it.

Going down the front steps was a slippery mushy mess, but walking down the sidewalk was intriguing as I left a four-inch-deep footprint after each step. Mother immediately started picking up handfuls of snow to roll into a snowball. I did likewise.

My hands and feet started to ache so much from the cold that I began to cry. Mother said we would have to go back into the house and warm up, but I wanted to stay outside a little longer, in spite of the cold. I insisted on going back out into the beautiful, white, winter wonderland.

Mother was ecstatic, as she rarely saw snow in San Antonio. Later in the day she said, "Let's make some snow ice cream." Then she took a large mixing bowl outside and filled it with snow. Next she went into the kitchen and mixed the snow with some sweetened whipped cream and vanilla and, voila! snow ice cream! We sat there in the kitchen giggling while we ate snow ice cream. That was the first time I had ever seen snow in my life, and the first and last time I ever ate snow ice cream.

On the east side of our house, the Pfeiffers had a lovely home and several

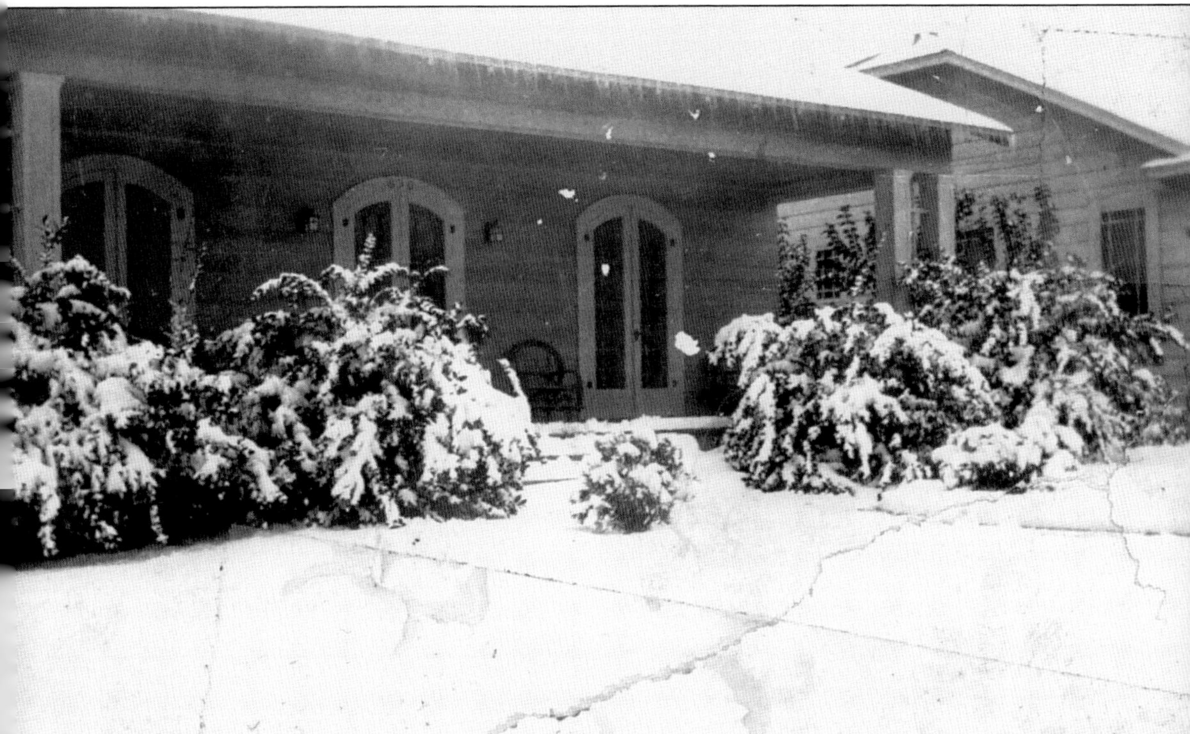

A rare snowstorm covered our yard in snow and we got the chance to make "snow ice cream."

children. One of them was a girl named Rita with whom I enjoyed playing. On the west side of Aunt Sissie's house, the Lozanos lived in a very luxurious home built on about three city lots. I believe Mr. Lozano owned the *La Prensa* newspaper. They had a daughter my age, named Maria Alicia, with whom I played. Since they had another home in Mexico, they weren't at Park Avenue all the time. I remember playing in Maria's large, beautifully decorated home and in their artistically landscaped yard.

I played with the neighborhood children sometimes, but all in all, with visiting Grandmother Templeton, Grandmother Rife, Aunt Sissie, following Mother around, going to kindergarten and church, and doing all the little things I could dream up to do around the house, I was quite busy. I was only on Park Avenue until I was five years old.

By going to Sunday school, kindergarten, and knowing neighbors, I eventually became acquainted with quite a few little boys and girls and it seemed that we were always going to somebody's birthday party. During one particularly memorable birthday party, for a friend named Judy Sallings, I saw someone faint for the first time ever.

It was supposed to be the best of days, as Judy was having a birthday party. She was six years old. Mother dressed Jean and I in our best dresses. They were made alike out of ecru pongee, a type of fabric that was very fine and dressy when I was a little girl. I helped Mother wrap a small gift for Judith, and then we got into our Buick and went to the party.

I wondered what it would be like to be six years old. I was only four and a half at that time, but I can remember it very well, just like it happened yesterday. But then, I suppose certain things do stand out in one's mind more than others, like seeing a lady faint for the first time.

Shortly after we arrived, we started playing games such as Pin the Tail on the Donkey and Musical Chairs. We were all having fun, gathered in a circle in their large and very beautiful living room. All of a sudden Mrs. Sheen jumped up and shouted, "I'm going to faint, I'm going to faint, I know I am, because I always do." Then, believe it or not, just after we had all focused our attention on her, Mrs. Sheen said very clearly, "Going, going, gone!" And she swooned lithely down toward her chair finally coming to rest on the floor in the middle of our little game circle

Well, that did it! It practically ruined Judy's sixth birthday party, and she would never be six years old again to celebrate another one. All of us children were herded into the adjoining dining room as soon as possible while several of the ladies hovered over Mrs. Sheen and brought her around with something, probably spirits of ammonia.

After all that excitement, I'm sure that even Judy's opening the gifts was nothing but an anticlimax. All we could do was stand around in a sort of awestruck manner not even talking amongst ourselves. To a four, five, or six year old, it was a terrifying thing to suddenly have a grown woman stand up, announce that she was going to faint, and then proceed to count herself down.

Mother always wondered but never knew whether or not Mrs. Sheen really fainted, or whether some devious trick of the mind made it seem convenient for her at that moment to stage the event. Nevertheless, Judy Sallings's sixth birthday party was a birthday party I never forgot and never will as long as I live. By the way, I have never seen anyone "faint" in that manner again.

Judy Sallings's father built the large grocery store on San Pedro a few blocks north of Romano Plaza. It was huge and almost regal looking on the outside. It appeared to be finished in stucco in a sort of pinkish color.

The inside of the store was a dream come true for shoppers who appreciated good taste in architecture and decor, and had been longing for a complete variety of every kind of foodstuff imaginable as well as all sorts of household and cleaning supplies. We shopped there often.

Sallings Grocery Store was an "ultra" supermarket of its era and I don't believe there was any other grocery store in San Antonio at that time that even came close to it in size, service, and class. Years later when the store was closed for some reason, Studer's bought the building and turned it into a photograph studio. It still had that regal look on the outside.

As a child, I enjoyed attending numerous other birthday parties, all of which were conducted more or less the same as Judy Sallings's. The guests all brought nice gifts to the honoree and for the most part, we played the same little party games. The mothers always attended with their children, and seemed to consider the parties major social events at which each one tried to outshine the other, which included trying to have herself and her child adorned in the most beautiful attire there.

The serving of the cake was always the highlight of the party for the children. That's because the cake always contained a dozen or so sterling silver trinkets that had been stirred into the batter before it was baked and every child wanted to find one. Thus, the excitement began as each guest gingerly bit into his or her piece of cake, hoping to find a trinket. Now, that really was fun. At Maria Alicia Lozano's birthday party, I found a sterling silver wishbone in my piece of cake, at Marjorie Biard's party I found a heart, and at another party I found a harp. No two trinkets were alike, and none of them were much over a half-inch in size. They were always made out of sterling silver. In addition to the wishbone, heart, and harp, there were also things like a silver spoon, a baby shoe, a butterfly, and a fish. Those birthday parties really were occasions that highlighted the lives of all involved.

There was never a lack of interesting things going on around me. About once a month I heard a clippety-clop, clippety-clop coming up the street and ran to the window to see a horse-drawn delivery wagon coming slowly toward our house.

The wooden wagon was enclosed on all sides and covered with a flat roof. It had a wooden door in the back and an opening in the front behind the driver's head. It was obvious it had once been painted white, but the paint was peeling off and what was left had faded to a muggy grayish-white. The bread advertisement on the sides of the wagon had long since become illegible.

A thin little man, at least fifty or sixty years old, sat on the wooden seat in the front of the wagon holding the reins loosely, sort of letting the horse take the lead. The horse was thin and scraggly, a dirty brown color. The little man shouted out, many times in each block, a sing-song phrase that I can still remember: "Homemade Boston steam-baked brown bread!"

Once in a while a housewife walked out to flag him down and buy a loaf of bread. When the little man got down from the wagon, I could see that he wore a frayed coat and trousers that had once been white, but were now a very tattletale gray. An old light gray felt hat that had seen better days was planted squarely on top of his head. He looked very fragile, as if just being there was a struggle.

I once got close enough to see some of that bread. It was the color of dark molasses and about the size of a medium-sized coffee can. Mother never bought any as she said it wasn't sanitary. But that didn't keep me from getting a thrill out of his visits to our neighborhood, rushing out to see him and hearing him call out. I would still like to taste that bread just once.

I loved our backyard on Park Avenue and spent a lot of time there. One day while I was making a sand castle in the sand pile, Mother came out all excited about someone flying across the Atlantic Ocean all alone in an airplane. I didn't know what she was talking about so she went into great detail trying to explain it. She must have been successful, because years later when we studied in school about Lindbergh's solo flight across the Atlantic Ocean, I remembered plainly that Mother had told me about it the day it happened. From then on, I spent a lot of time in the backyard looking up for a glimpse of an airplane.

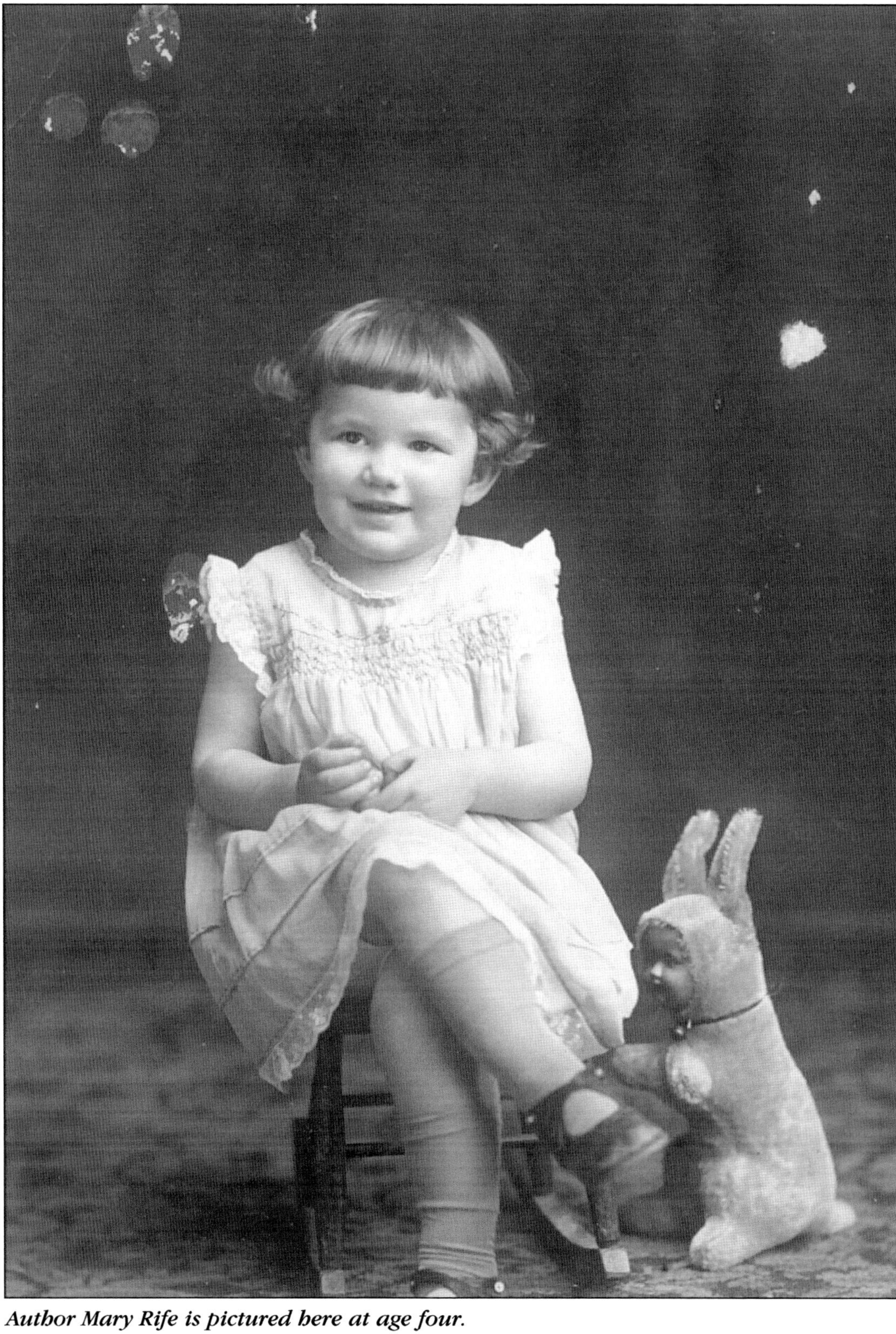

Author Mary Rife is pictured here at age four.

Chapter Three

Family

Aunt Sissie

Aunt Sissie, my favorite aunt, was married to Atwood Wells, a southern gentleman, born and raised on his father's tobacco plantation in Virginia. He had an average build, light brown hair, and gray eyes. He was relaxed and casual of manner and spoke with a delightful southern drawl, indigenous to the elite of Virginia. He was eight years older than Aunt Sissie. Aunt Sissie met and dated him several times during World War I while he was a serviceman stationed at Fort Sam Houston, and they corresponded once or twice after he went overseas. Uncle Atwood was one of the numerous soldiers who contracted the terrible influenza that plagued servicemen during the war. He told me years later that he spent his entire overseas tenure in an army hospital in England due to the flu.

After he returned home from the army, Grandmother suggested that she and Aunt Sissie go to Virginia and visit with him, as he was still weak from his bout with the flu. Mother said it was more because Grandmother thought Aunt Sissie should be married and had decided Atwood would be a perfect son-in-law as he was a quiet, agreeable man who would always do her bidding.

Aunt Sissie reluctantly boarded a train to Virginia with Grandmother to visit a man eight years her senior, whom she felt she hardly knew. Furthermore, at the tender age of 20, her naivete concerning life in general, especially a romantic attraction for the opposite sex, rendered her totally unprepared for ensuing events. In plain words, she had never experienced a sexual attraction toward a man and wouldn't know what to do about it if she did.

Their visit completely charmed Uncle Atwood, who immediately fell in love with Aunt Sissie. He, of course, thought she reciprocated, or she wouldn't have traveled all the way to Virginia to see him. Being the perfect Southern gentlemen, he made no physical advances other than holding hands at times.

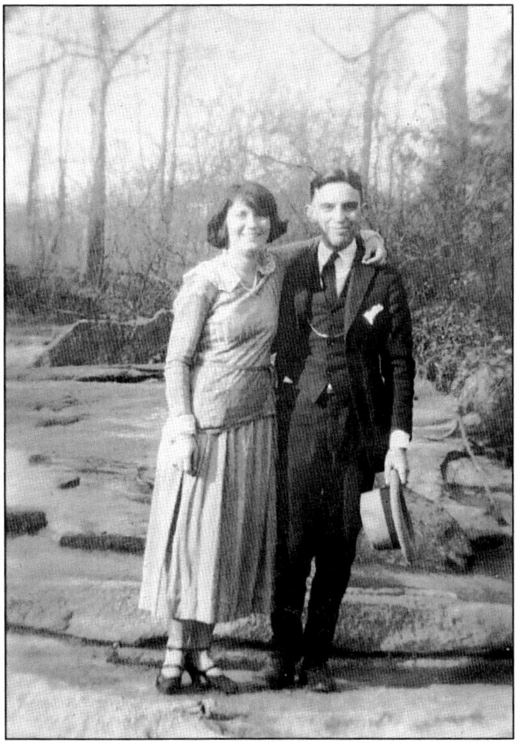

Mother's sister Mary eventually became known to us as Aunt Sissie. She is pictured here with her husband, Atwood Wells.

After feeling she had accomplished her goal, Grandmother took Aunt Sissie back home. Sure enough, her absence brought Uncle Atwood to San Antonio on the next train, to pursue a polite period of restrained courtship. He secured a position with the Strauss Frank Company and proposed. Aunt Sissie, in a state of bewilderment, filled with tacit questions, felt compromised into accepting his proposal. After all, maybe she was in love; she didn't know.

Mother always said Grandmother maneuvered Aunt Sissie into the marriage as she thought Uncle Atwood, as a son-in-law, would be putty in her hands. Grandmother was right about that.

Uncle Atwood left his family and Virginia behind and relocated in San Antonio, adopting Aunt Sissie's family as his own. After staying with the Strauss Frank Co. for many years, he left for health reasons and later obtained a position in the City Water Board office, where he remained until he retired. Our fondness for Uncle Atwood grew stronger throughout the years. Aunt Sissie resigned herself to a dull life with a man who was stodgy beyond his years. Aunt Sissie found her excitement in all kinds of things around her. Atwood didn't mind.

Sometimes Aunt Sissie and Uncle Atwood took me with them when they went places with other married couples. Mother and Father didn't have any interest in running around like that, but they did let me go with Aunt Sissie and Uncle Atwood. On several occasions, Aunt Sissie and Uncle Atwood took me with them to a dance at the San Antonio Country Club. I sat at a table on the side of the dance floor and watched them dance. Uncle Atwood didn't care much for dancing, so he would sit there with me while Aunt Sissie danced with other men.

Aunt Sissie's first and foremost pleasure in life was playing the piano, and I loved the music she made. Grandmother said before she was two years old she was at the piano picking out tunes. By four, she was playing everything she heard by ear.

When she was ten, Grandmother locked the piano and said she couldn't play again until she learned to read music. She was sent to a music teacher and within a few months she could play any music set before her.

That made her a very unique accomplished musician. She could read notes and sight-read perfectly, and also play by ear. In fact if she had ever heard a song played all the way through at one time, she could sit down at the piano and play it perfectly, melody and bass accompaniment both. Some of the songs I liked most that she played were: "Nola," "Parade of the Wooden Soldiers,"

"Glowworm," "Country Gardens," "Up A Lazy River," and "Tea For Two." Aunt Sissie played a kiddie song, just for me, that was popular at that time titled, "I Faw Down An' Go Boom!" I enjoyed hopping around the living room with a broom, making believe it was my stick horse, singing the song while Aunt Sissie played it over and over again on the piano. She also played things just for the novelty of it, such as "Yankee Doodle" with the left hand and "Dixie" with the right hand, at the same time.

Aunt Sissie was a flashy dresser, and I loved the clothes she wore. She didn't dress anything at all like Mother, who was always very conservative and mature in her choice of apparel.

For dress wear, Aunt Sissie frequently chose clothing made in the style and fashion of the flapper era. One silk dress I remember was powder blue with a navy blue trim, had a sleeveless, low-necked, long-waisted, unbelted top that came halfway down the derriere, and was finished off with soft pleats for a skirt that barely reached the knees.

Most of her better dresses were rather loose, giving the effect of sort of being slung over the shoulders on a shapeless body. The young ladies of that era were noted for binding their bosoms tightly in an effort to conceal, or camouflage them so they wouldn't show at all. It was also desirable at that time to downplay the waistline, preferring to conceal it as well. Aunt Sissie had dresses made out of linen, cotton, rayon, satin, pongee, and silk trimmed with lace or velvet. These dresses were either bold prints or solid colors.

For ordinary everyday wear, she wore one-piece cotton dresses that had short sleeves, a collar, and wide belts. They came in various solid colors and small prints.

Aunt Sissie's underwear was especially fascinating. The only undergarment she wore besides a breast confiner, was a cute little thing she called a "teddy." It seemed to be something new at that time and Aunt Sissie gave the impression she was really doing something to wear it in the first place. As I remember it, the teddy resembled a shouldered slip with slip length, wide-legged, slit-sided panties at the bottom of it, all of which was cut from the same piece of material. I don't remember how in the world she got in and out of the thing. The teddies came in various exotic pastel colors and were made out of batiste, rayon, satin, or silk trimmed with all sorts of lace. She wore rayon or silk stockings, which were held up with garters.

Her shoes, which usually matched her dress, were made from patent leather, suede, or satin, in all colors. I loved the ornamental clips she put on some of her shoes, such as beaded or jeweled buckles and bows.

Her hats were funny-looking things. They resembled a snood more than a hat and came straight down on the crown of the head far enough to cover her forehead and reach her eyes. Some had a narrow floppy brim that stood out somewhat at that point shading the eyes. They were all color coordinated to match a certain dress. When she was dressed to go some place special she wore long strings of glass "flapper beads" which hung down below the waist.

She had several kinds of handbags. The ones for everyday use weren't so special, being more like a starched lunch sack with a drawstring at the top, which she dangled around her wrist. But her evening bags were fabulous. One was an envelope style bag that was completely covered with crystal beads of many colors; the other was made of soft flexible pieces of sterling silver meshed together with a sterling silver chain on a wire frame at the top and metal fringe at the bottom. Those two bags were my favorites of all her clothing items.

Aunt Sissie's wardrobe was the only one of its kind that I had firsthand contact with, and although she didn't actually

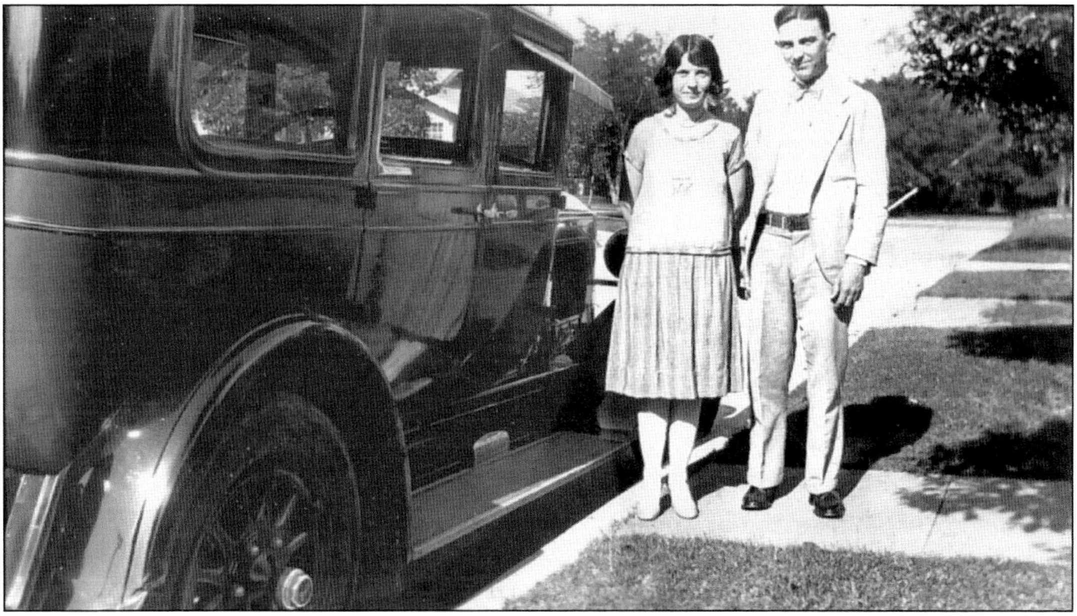

Aunt Sissie and Uncle Atwood did enjoy running around a lot.

have dozens and dozens of dresses, the ones she did have were well worth seeing. Wherever she was, Aunt Sissie struck quite a beguiling figure as she flitted here and there in her charming little outfits, and I basked in the pleasure of the attention they drew whenever I was with her. One might say she was a veritable fashion plate of the above average young lady of that time. And when the fashion changed, she changed her wardrobe to conform to it, always remaining in style. But the clothing she wore in the 1920s continued to be my favorites.

Aunt Sissie derived much excitement from her wardrobe and having fun, but as I said earlier, her most favorite thing in the whole world was playing the piano. Since the radio didn't really exist yet, and the Victrola just didn't compare, there was nothing then that took the place of live music. Since the piano was the most complete musical instrument, there were hundreds of piano teachers all over the country with thousands of pupils who were trying to learn to play well enough to enjoy music in their homes.

Consequently, any business offering sheet music for sale wanted a skilled pianist in its music department to play anything the prospective customer wanted to hear, from Bach, Beethoven, and Chopin to jazz, popular, or church music, or most any other selection. It was hard to find a pianist versatile enough to fill this order.

However, Aunt Sissie was overqualified, if anything, and therefore could always find a place to work anytime she chose. All the music stores and dime stores (which had also gotten into the act of having a music department with a pianist) wanted her to play for them. They appreciated Aunt Sissie's talent for playing even more than I did.

It just so happened that during one of those periods in which she chose to work at the most prestigious music store in San Antonio, Thomas Goggins Music Company, my father brought home a big brown box with a lid that opened and a handle for turning on one side. When he put a flat black thing called a record in it, it made music. I eventually discovered that the brown box was a Victrola, but for a long time I just called it "the music box." I always loved music, so I listened to the Victrola over and over, learning the melodies and words to lots of songs.

Since Aunt Sissie had daily access to records at the Thomas Goggins Music Company, whenever Father wanted another record he asked her to bring it to us. She used to bring home records of Gene Austin, Al Jolson, and Sir Harry Lauder, a Scottish man who was a craze in the United States at the time. I can still remember the sound of his voice as he sang, "Oh, It's Nice to Get Up in the Morning, but It's Nicer to Stay in Bed."

Through the years, we all had a lot of happy times and fun with Aunt Sissie. She was indisputably my favorite aunt.

Mother arranged for me to take piano lessons from Mrs. Springall also. Mrs. Springall was a very unique person; she must have been about 50 years old, had long, silver-gray hair coiled around her head in the same manner as Grandmother Templeton, a beautiful complexion, and was always immaculately dressed in something fashionable. Her voice was clear and filled with instructions and authority.

When I arrived for my lesson, I was ushered into her large living room, which had a grand piano at the end of it and chairs scattered all over the room. Her home was beautifully decorated and there was always another student either finishing a lesson or waiting to begin.

While teaching a student, Mrs. Springall would run back and forth to the kitchen to check on the cook and the maid, supervising their progress on cooking meals and preparing for social events. She would call instructions out to the students from the other room and correct them if they hit a wrong note. If they weren't keeping proper time, she would suddenly appear from nowhere and start a metronome clicking the right time for the students to play. I didn't see how she could keep up with all of that and still be so calm and collected on top of everything her students did.

Mrs. Springall had a keyboard upstairs with no sound on it that students were made to practice on if they had an ear for music, and she suspected they might be learning from the way the music sounded rather than by reading the notes. I usually fell into that "dummy piano," as I called it, because she said I fell into that category. I hated that "dummy piano," but sure enough, I actually learned to read the notes during that summer with Mrs. Springall. She was quite an experience.

Mrs. Springall periodically gave a piano recital in which each of her pupils played a little piece. She frequently had the grand piano moved out onto her front porch and set up folding chairs in rows for those recitals. About 30 or 40 guests usually attended. After everyone had played his or her presentation, Mrs. Springall served refreshments.

I played *Melody in F* at my recital. My sister Jean once played Chopin's *Minute Waltz* in one minute at another recital. Jean took lessons long enough to master quite a few piano classics.

I remember one of those porch recitals very well. It was held at night, and there was a large table set with a linen tablecloth, crystal punch bowl and cups, sterling silverware, and fine china. The punch bowl was filled with pink punch and topped with scoops of lime sherbet. There were salted mixed nuts and mints in sterling silver bowls. She also served a yellow cake with white icing that was beautifully decorated with dainty pink roses and lime green leaves. It was delicious.

Mrs. Springall gave one recital featuring Aunt Sissie only. After she walked out and took a bow, she played a number of classical selections. Then she ended by playing, from memory, exactly as written, the original piano score of Paul Whiteman's Rhapsody in Blue. That was one time she deliberately followed the music exactly.

Mrs. Springall was a marvel to me and I must say that I learned a lot about music and the piano in those short three months that summer. When school started, it wasn't practical for me to continue with the lessons. By the next summer, my interest had turned to other things. I didn't study the piano again until the summer of 1936, when I returned to Mrs. Springall for four or five lessons. After that, I never took another piano lesson again.

Grandmother Templeton (My Second Mother)

My maternal grandparents, Judge and Mrs. Howard Templeton, were financially independent; in fact they were very wealthy. They lived in a large two-story home at 120 East Cypress Street.

Grandmother Templeton was a very complex person, so much so that describing her isn't simple. For one thing, she immediately made Father's visits in her home so unpleasant that he stopped visiting altogether. But he encouraged Mother to visit her anytime she wished, as she had always been very close to her family and he didn't see why that should change. At the same time, Grandmother welcomed Mother's visits alone and even though she ceased to openly rebuff her for marrying Father, Mother never failed to sense her tacit disapproval.

Then I came along and from the moment she laid eyes upon me, she was completely smitten. She insisted that Mother bring me over every day for an hour or so. By the time I was a year and a half, she convinced Mother to let me spend at least one night a week with her. Her house became my second home and she became my second mother. I called her "Mama Templeton" and she called me "Mary Elizabeth," enunciating every syllable. She treated me like a little grownup person instead of a child, which certainly encouraged me to conduct myself accordingly. I followed her around and tried to mimic whatever grownup thing she was doing. I don't ever remember playing games, dolls, or with toys at her house like I did at home.

Grandmother's house was oh-so-different from Mother's home, filled with an endless recurrence of scheduled happenings and interruptions, which never ceased to interest and captivate me. I found the way she managed her house to be very unique. Because of all the time I spent in her home, I knew her daily routine by heart.

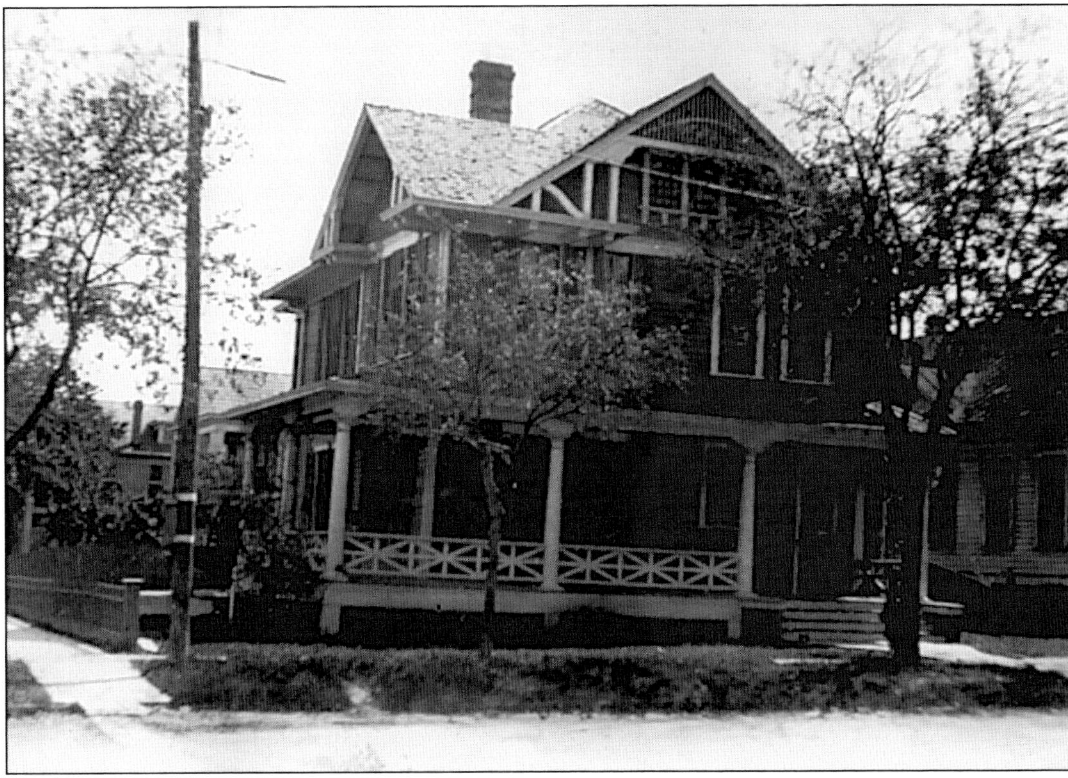

This is the Templeton home at 120 East Cypress Street, where I spent a lot of time as a child.

Grandmother's days were completely regimented, as the same things happened regularly at about the same time on a daily, weekly, or monthly basis, except on Saturday and Sunday, which had their own repetitive agendas. Grandmother was always out of bed at 6:30 a.m. and downstairs before seven, with a morning dress on and her hair a little rumpled from sleeping. Alex, the family butler and chauffeur, had breakfast started, and Grandmother helped finish and serve it.

After breakfast, Grandfather walked about two miles downtown to his law office. He enjoyed the walk and thought he needed the exercise. Right after he left, I can remember trade-people coming and going, without knocking. They entered through the back door and had to go through the room Grandmother was sitting in to accomplish their mission. She had it planned this way.

The iceman usually started the "parade." Each customer had a large square card indicating "amount of ice wanted" to place in a window where it would be visible by the iceman from his truck. Ice was sold in 12 1/2, 25, 50, and 100-pound blocks. The number standing straight up at the bottom of the side of the card facing the street was the amount of ice ordered. It was a simple way of letting the iceman know before he left the truck how much ice to chop off and carry to the ice box. After the ice was delivered, the customer took down the card until he needed more ice.

The man called out "Iceman" as he came laboring in the back door, carrying a heavy block of dripping ice in the amount

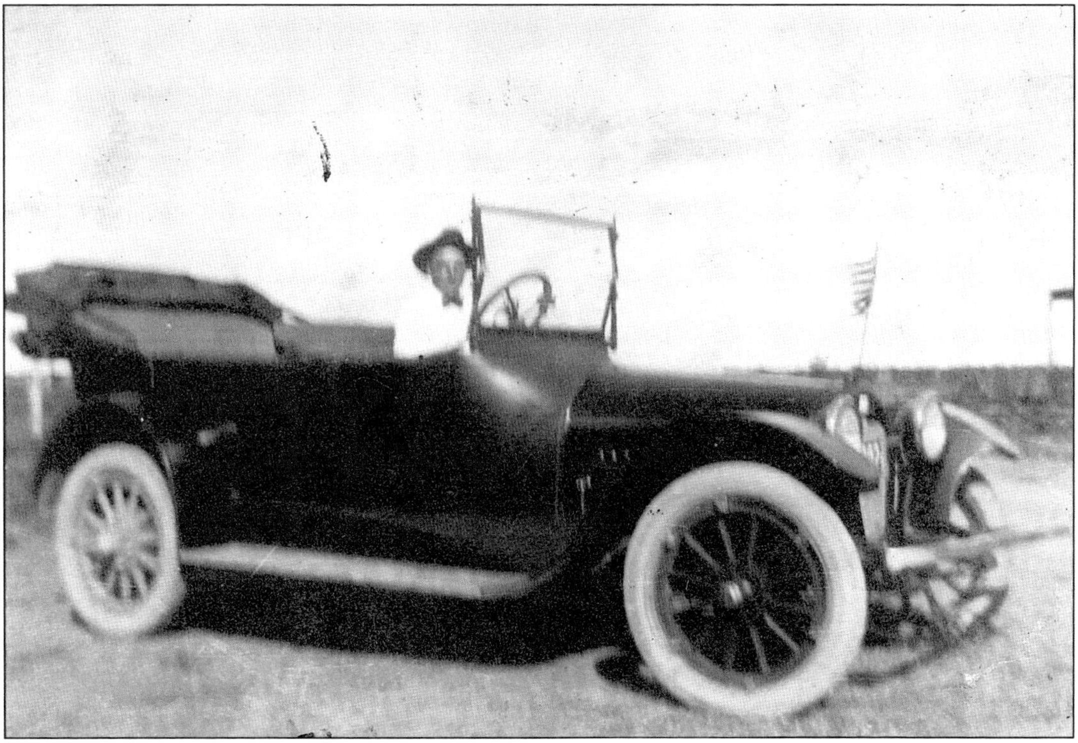

When Grandfather Templeton purchased his first car, he hired Alex Krisch to be his chauffeur. This is one of his first cars.

ordered, with huge metal ice tongs. After he put the ice in the box, Alex paid him. Then he returned to the ice truck and went on to the next house.

Right on the iceman's heels the milkman was usually heard announcing his arrival as he came running in the back door carrying a compartmentalized wire rack filled with milk bottles. He wore a white work coat, trousers, and a white visor cap—the uniform of the company for which he worked. The milkman first went to the icebox and put in the milk and other dairy products ordered, such as half and half, cream, chocolate milk, orange juice, and cottage cheese. Then he picked up all the empty milk bottles Alex had set out for him and rushed back to the milk truck to continue his route. The dairy items were paid for at the end of each month.

About twice a week, around 9:00 a.m., a large vegetable truck lumbered in the driveway, and a round little man with an old brown felt hat on one side of his head got out and started pacing up and down beside it. He loudly sang out "A-bra-ham" over and over, while shaking an old-fashioned school bell until Grandmother and Alex came out to look over his wares.

A rush of excitement went through me when I heard him arrive and I couldn't wait to get out there to see him show off his wares. He was entertaining in many ways: his dress, his accent, his disarming smile. On his truck he had all kinds of vegetables in season: shelled lima beans, tomatoes, carrots, turnips and greens, mustard greens, green beans, potatoes, onions, cabbage, and others. He also stocked various fruits in season, such as strawberries, apples, oranges, plums, peaches, pineapples, grapes, and coconuts. There was a large stalk of bananas hanging from the top of the truck. He also had large covered glass jars filled with various kinds of pastries and homemade candies sold by the piece, but Grandmother never once let me taste them. She said they weren't sanitary.

Grandmother looked everything over carefully and chose vegetables and fruits to last for a couple of days. She didn't seem to pay much attention to the sales pitch, but made up her own mind as to what she wanted. The items she chose were either counted or weighed on an old scale that was hanging in the truck and then Alex paid him. Abraham and his colorful vegetable truck didn't come to our neighborhood, so I only saw him at Grandmother's.

We all paraded back into the house, and Grandmother and Alex discussed lunch and supper. After serious planning, Grandmother told Alex what other food items she needed for that day. Alex then called Flores Bros. Grocery Store on the telephone and ordered everything, including the exact cut of meat she had stipulated, bread, other staples, and a cake of some kind made by the Colonial Cake Company. About 10:00 a.m. the grocery order was delivered by a boy calling out "Flores Brothers" as he came in the back door to leave the order on the kitchen table. The groceries were charged and paid for on the first of each month.

By 11:00 a.m., vegetables for that day had been prepared and put on the stove to cook for an hour or two. Then, after arranging how the meat for supper would be prepared and cooked, Grandmother was ready to go upstairs for awhile.

Grandmother had dark black-brown hair with red shadows in it. Scissors never touched her hair, not even one time in her whole life. It was so long that it touched the floor when she stood up straight. Once she was upstairs, she took her hair down and brushed and groomed it for about 45 minutes. It was fascinating to watch her methodically take her hands and twist and turn and wind her hair around and around on her head, and finally secure it in place with large tortoise-shell hairpins. She really had a knack for this as it pretty much stayed in place until the next day. After finishing with her hair, she used a scant amount of makeup and powder on her face. Finally, she put on a dress for the day.

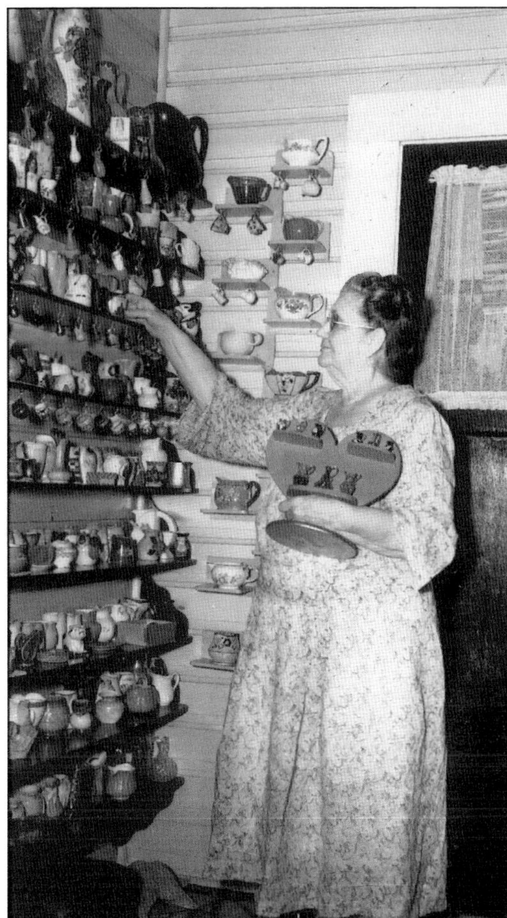

Grandmother Templeton had a special pitcher room built onto her home, where she eventually made room for a collection of over three thousand. (Photo courtesy of the UT Institute of Texan Cultures.)

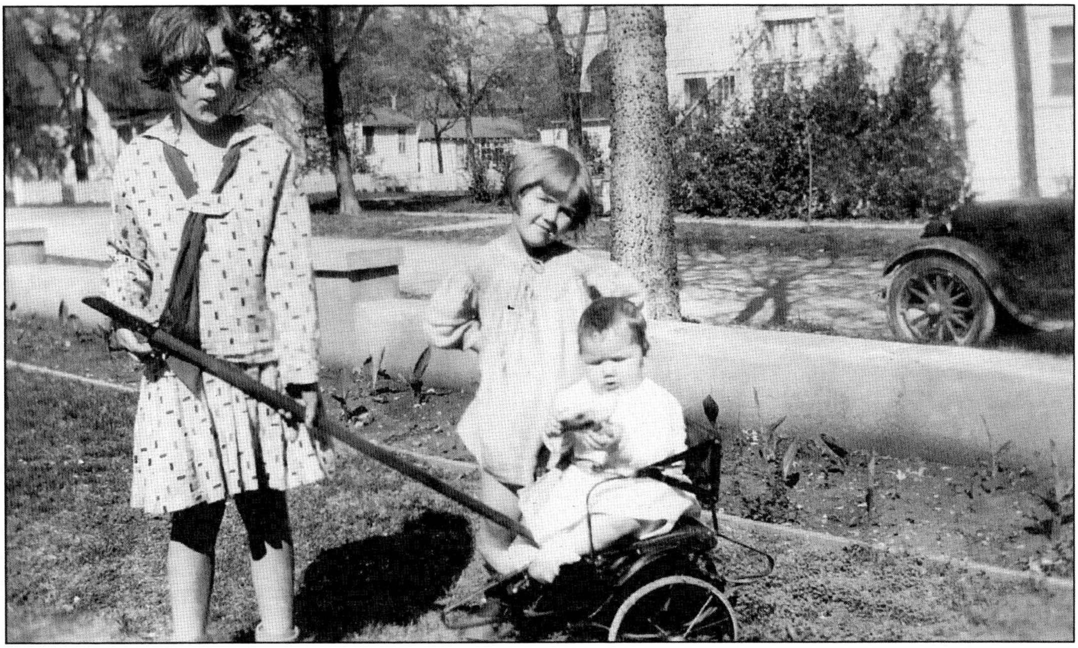

We visited Grandmother Templeton once a week. Here we are in her backyard.

Once a week, the beds were changed and the laundry was put into bags. Around 11:00 or 11:30, the laundry man came in the back door crying out, "Laundry Man" as he dashed up the back stairs taking two or three steps at a time. He left the clean clothes packed in large flat paper bundles and picked up the bags of dirty ones. After that, Grandmother and a servant put fresh linen on the beds and in the bathrooms. Then the fresh, clean laundry was sorted and put away. At our house, we certainly didn't have a laundry man. Mother washed our clothes in a new electric washing machine Father had bought for her.

After the morning business was completed upstairs, we went downstairs for lunch, which was served in the kitchen. I remember many a time that she served cabbage or turnips and greens with ham hocks that had been cooking about two hours. I never ate those vegetables. She also had meat and potatoes and other things left from the night before. Everyone then helped get the kitchen in order, and Grandmother went to the downstairs back parlor. Mother always saw to it I had a proper lunch, but she didn't have a table full of foods and it wasn't an "occasion" like at Grandmother's.

She had two pairs of reading glasses, one pair in a sewing basket upstairs, and another in a basket downstairs. She forevermore had some handwork she was working on such as crocheting a rug, knitting a blanket, or embroidering a pillowcase. She didn't have time to do much though, as there was something different lined up for almost every day.

Once a week Dr. Kasten, the chiropractor, came to Grandmother's home to adjust her back for an hour. He drove a very interesting car made by the Hudson Company. Dr. Kasten was a very nice-looking man with a cheerful personality. During the hour-long adjustment, he tried to move first one vertebra and then another. If they didn't do what they were supposed to, he continued the massage routine until they either moved or one hour had

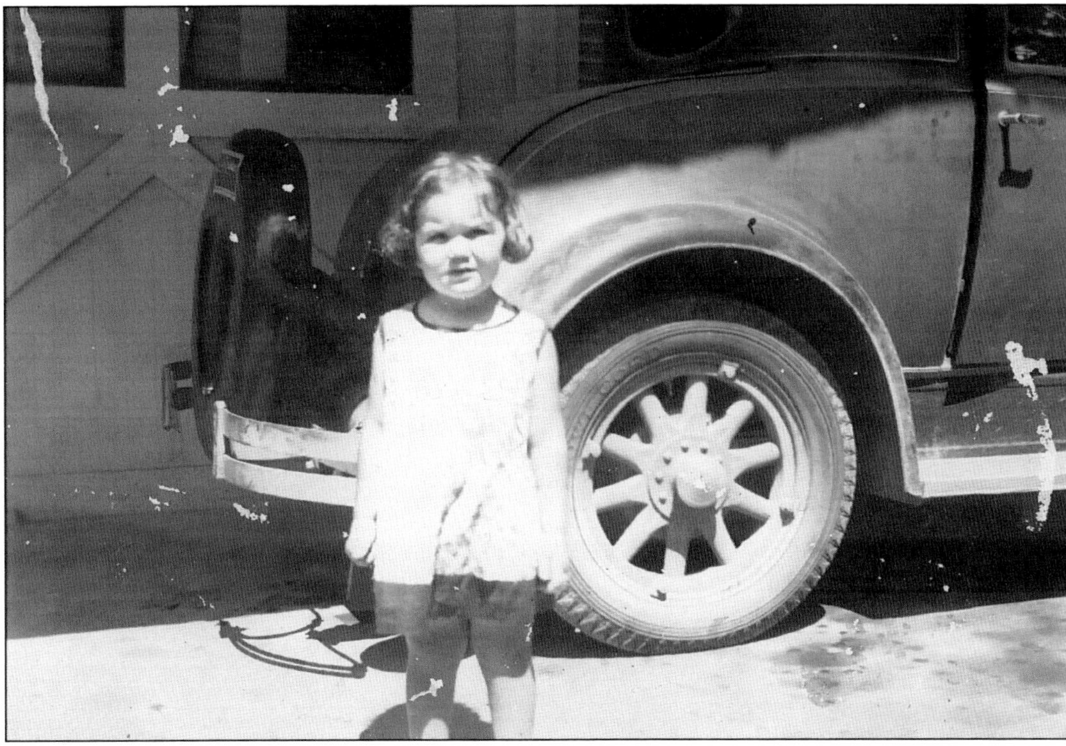

This was Alex's car, which we called a roadster. Baby sister Frances stands in front of it about 1931.

passed; then he stopped until next week. On the days when I was there, he did the same thing to me, but only for about 15 minutes. The adjustment was really a treat for me. I was always glad when I was at Grandmother's the day he came. I am sure he would have come to our house if Mother called him, but no one in our family ever needed an adjustment.

A yardman came around once a week, and every Friday the entire house was cleaned, polished, and dusted. If we visited Grandmother on "Winn's Day," she took us to Winn's with her. The clerks met her at the door with a stool to sit on, and Grandmother told each of us to pick out something to wear, such as socks, or underpants, or something else practical, for ourselves. In fact, just before Christmas each year, Grandmother took my sister Jean and me to Winn's and told each of us to pick out gifts for all the family members who would be at her Christmas party, so we could put them under her Christmas tree. After Grandmother paid for our things, we went back to her home.

Another daily ritual I love to remember was that everyday about 5:00 p.m., we all got into the limousine and Alex drove us downtown to pick up Grandfather. He was almost always in front of the bank waiting, and he got in the front seat with Alex. Alex asked, "Where to, Judge Templeton?" and Grandfather answered, "Anyplace." Then we took about an hour's joyride through various sections of town.

Supper was the next event. All family members were present dressed for dinner, which was served in the dining room on a linen tablecloth (napkins to match), with fine china and tableware

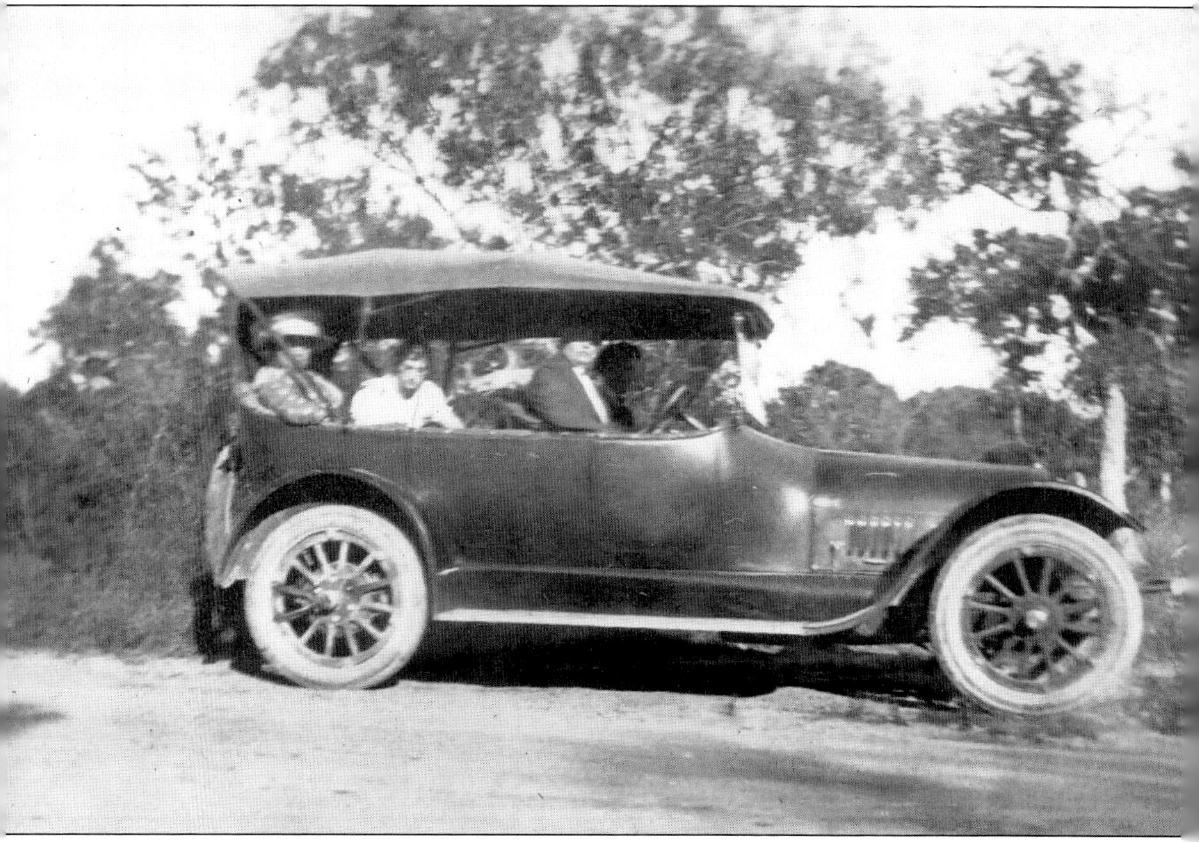

Here's the Templeton family in one of Grandfather's never-ending supply of automobiles. Grandmother Templeton is sitting in the back seat.

and pretty little hand-painted crystal water glasses. It was a grandiose event consisting of various meats such as ham, roast, steak (sometimes all at once), three or four vegetables, mashed potatoes, and frequently macaroni with oodles of cheese. Cornbread was almost always a staple at suppertime, and for dessert we had cake from the Colonial Cake Company. The event was so different from supper in my home. We ate in the kitchen with everyday china and tableware, and only had one type of meat.

One did not have to spend much time at Grandmother's house to learn that every meal was an event to take full advantage of, as she frowned on anyone eating anything between meals except an occasional ice-cream cone at the corner drugstore. She never served anything to drink between meals except water, drunk only in the kitchen and with permission.

After supper everyone except Grandfather helped put the dining room and kitchen in order, and then retired to the back sitting room to visit and do handwork until bedtime. Grandfather always went into the study to work on legal briefs until he retired. Shortly after dark we would go upstairs, bathe, and get in bed for the night. Sleep always came swiftly. The next morning about 6:30 a.m., everything started all over again.

It's hard to believe that Grandmother found time to see many other tradesmen and servicemen during the day, but I do remember that a Fuller Brush man came periodically and showed us different kinds of brushes, combs, and other things to order. There was also a Watkin's man who came to sell extracts, spices, and cooking herbs. Grandmother always found another brush or comb to order, and some kind of flavoring or spice to buy for the kitchen. I enjoyed examining the brushes and combs, and smelling all the Watkins extracts and spices.

Also, it was not unusual to find Grandmother and Alex grinding up fresh pork and making pan sausage in her kitchen. From time to time, she also got hog fat to make lye soap. She made the soap in a wash-pot, over a wood fire, under a walnut tree in her backyard. When the soap was cooked to suit her, she had Alex help her pour it into trays to set.

Off and on during the day, the front doorbell rang and Alex found a panhandler there asking for a handout. This was a common practice because so many people were out of work during the Great Depression. They never left Grandmother's home without at least the price of a meal. Alex said he knew that they had the house marked somehow to show each other there was a handout available there. Answering the door and taking care of them annoyed him, so he kept looking for the mark so he could remove it. I also spent lots of time looking for it, though I didn't know what it was supposed to look like. We never found it.

Even as a small child, I found my grandmother's clothing a fascinating oddity. She seemed to live in a fashion world of her own. She had two seamstresses. One of them came to the house and stayed all day using Grandmother's machine. We called her "Miss Annie" and she made all of Grandmother's underclothing, nightgowns, some of her plain everyday dresses, and Grandfather's nightshirts. And she did all of the darning and sewing repair as needed. The other seamstress owned her own sewing machine and quite a lot of equipment. She came to Grandmother's house to get instructions and take measurements, and then went back to her own home to do the work. These two women made everything Grandmother wore, except shoes, hosiery, and perhaps a corset.

Grandmother's underclothes were something else! I have never seen any like them in my life, even to this day. They were made from white cotton like the percale used in sheets, only softer. The underpants were knee length, gathered at the waist to a band, and buttoned in the front. Her camisole was made from the same material, gathered to a band, which fit her around the waist, and was buttoned in the front. Her slip was an abbreviation of the pattern used for her dresses: low neck, no sleeves, and enlarged armholes.

Her dresses were all basically made from the same pattern, with only a change in the color or decoration in the front. They all had straight, full sleeves that came halfway between elbow and wrist, and some had a little lace at the bottom of the sleeves. They had button openings in the front from the neck to down below the waist, and they came almost to the ankle. Each dress had a belt made from the same material.

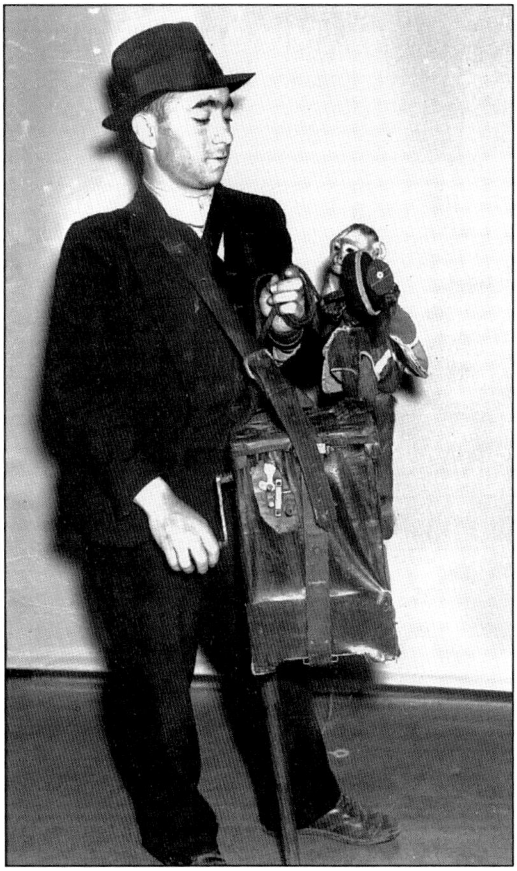

Tony Library, pictured here with his monkey, Jimmie, was one of San Antonio's eight organ grinders. We were always excited when we heard them in our neighborhood. (Photo courtesy of the UT Institute of Texan Cultures.)

One of my fondest memories of impromptu happenings at Grandmother's is of the organ grinder (or Monkey Man, as we called him). He came down the street playing an accordion with a cute little monkey on a leash skipping along beside him. When the neighborhood children heard him, they all came running with nickels, dimes, and pennies. As soon as a number of them were gathered around, the organ grinder signaled to the little monkey to dance while he played a tune on his small music box.

The monkey was dressed so cute in a little red vest and blue pants, and he had a little red-and-black hat sitting on the side of his head. After the show, the monkey went to the children and took the coins they held out for him.

I still remember numerous other things I did throughout the years at Grandmother's house: taking a nickel to Houck's Drug Store for an ice cream cone, learning to roller skate in the Twin Parks across the street from her home, going with her to the lock box at her bank to clip coupons on Treasury Bills, and using finger bowls while dining out at the St. Anthony Hotel in San Antonio or at the Nimitz Hotel in Fredericksburg. I could write forever about my many visits to my grandmother's home, but these are some of the ones I remember the most.

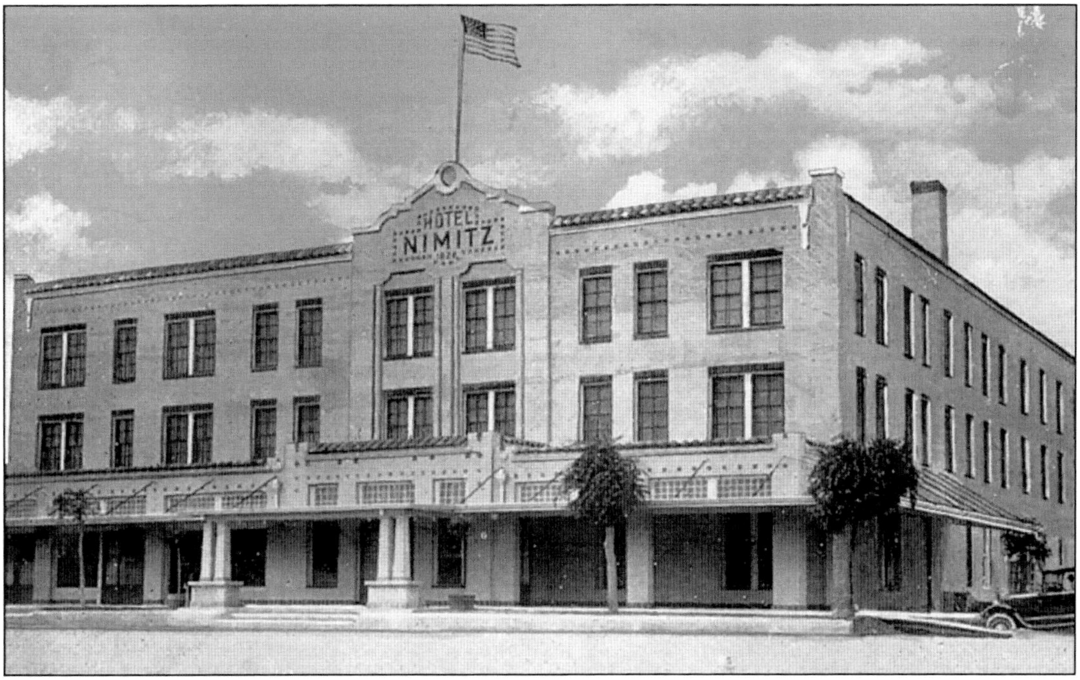

Grandmother Templeton loved to visit the Nimitz Hotel in Fredericksburg. We went there from time to time and usually stayed overnight.

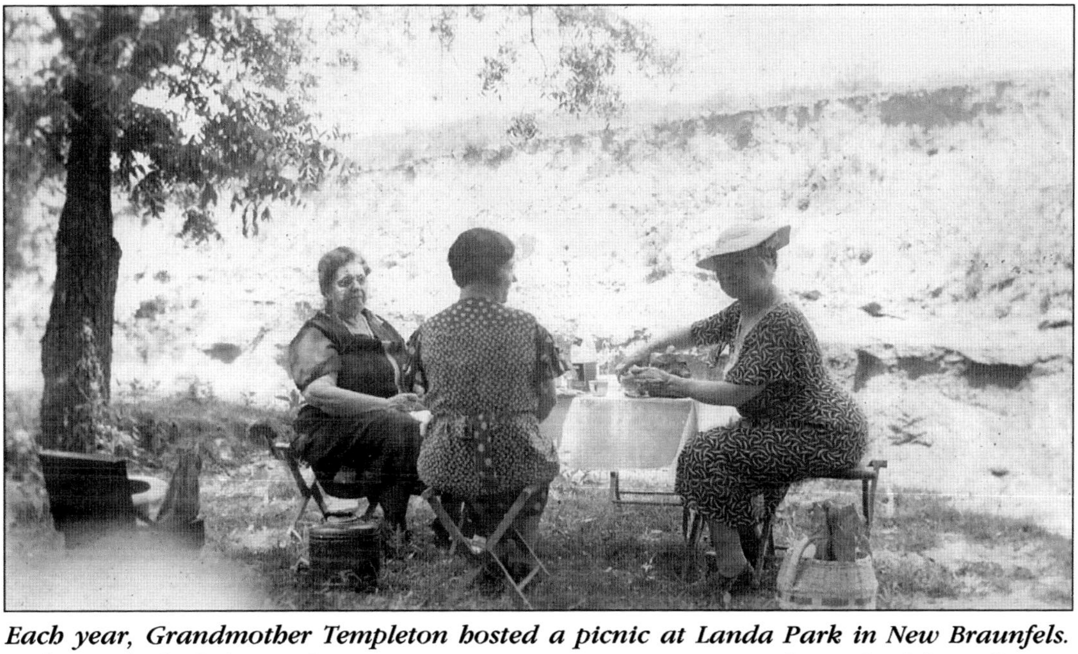

Each year, Grandmother Templeton hosted a picnic at Landa Park in New Braunfels. I always looked forward to it, as it was quite an event. We always had lots of crisp, golden-brown fried chicken, potato salad, deviled eggs, fruit, and one of Mother's delicious homemade three-layer chocolate cakes with seven-minute icing. Those picnics were a lot of fun.

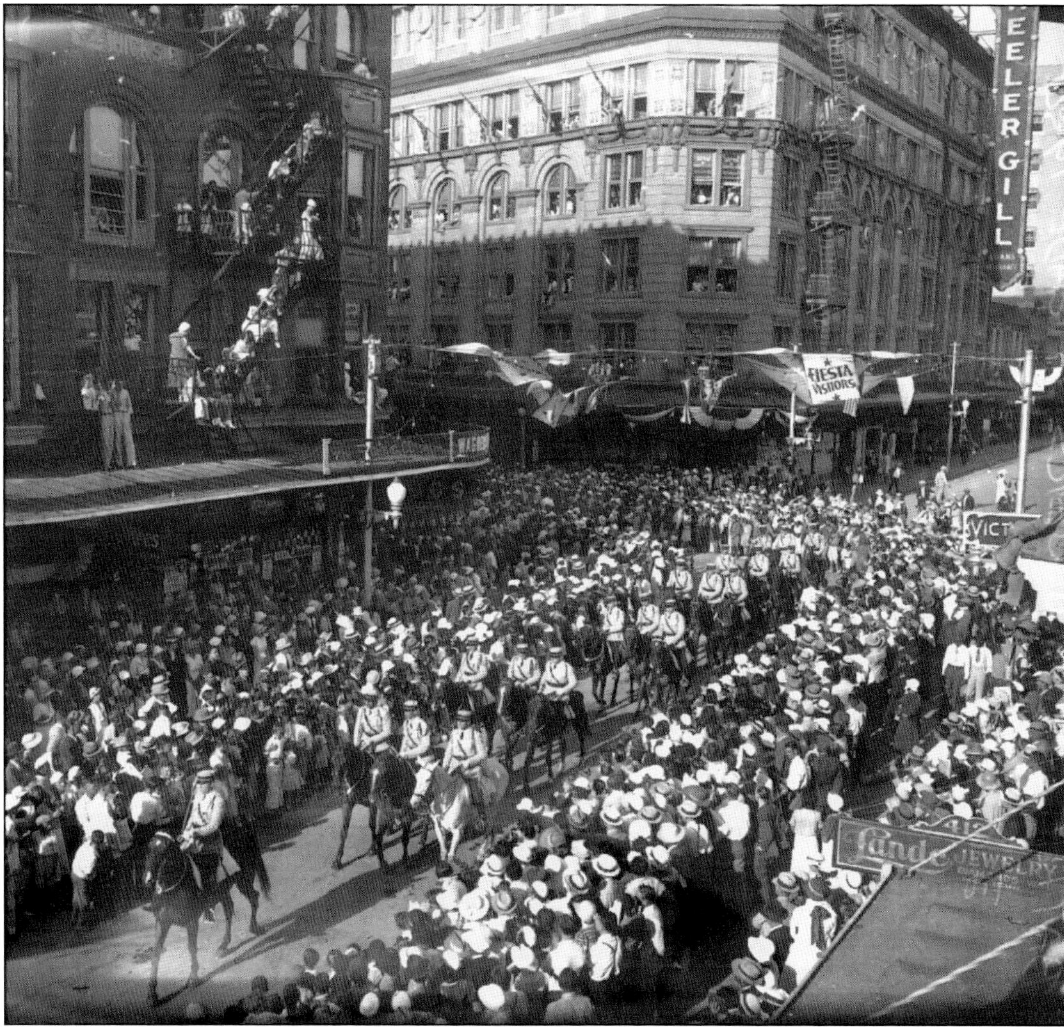

The 1934 Battle of the Flowers Parade is pictured at the intersection of Houston Street and Broadway. Father's office was nearby in the Bedell Building. We never missed a parade, so I suspect we were in that crowd. (Courtesy of the UT Institute of Texan Cultures.)

Chapter Four

Outings In and Around Town

The Battle of the Flowers Parade

The annual Battle of the Flowers Parade was one of the colorful San Antonio events Father always wanted to see with his family. Many a time he practically dragged Mother and us down there to stand for over an hour waiting for the parade to start and then wouldn't let us leave until the last float had passed. He loved parades.

The week after the parade, Father took us downtown to see all the gowns that the queen and her court had worn in the parade. They were always on display in the showcase windows of Joske's, Frost Bros., and the Vogue department stores. Those gowns were so beautiful! We could stand there and admire each one as long as we wished. There was usually a lavish display in the window with the queen's gown, which included the flower girl and some of the other members of her party's attire.

The Kendall County Fair in Boerne

Mother and Father started talking about the Kendall County Fair each year as soon as they learned the date it would be held. They looked forward to it eagerly and discussed all their plans in great detail. They lived in avid anticipation of the fun they would have there. It wasn't very long before I was all excited too, at the thrill of a picnic and the mystique surrounding the fair.

Fair day came and we arose with the sun, got ready, and left home about 8:00 a.m. The car ride to the fair was like taking a trip in the country. The trees got taller and more colorful as we rode along. It only took about an hour to get there, but it always seemed like much longer.

The fair was held on a strip of undeveloped land well out of town with extremely tall trees. There were picnic tables under some of the trees, which we passed on the way to a large wooden building where the ladies' contributions to the fair were displayed. I remember there were a number of different displays of handwork and food items. In one section Mother was engrossed in admiring jars of peach, plum, fig, and strawberry preserves, various jams, marmalades, and jellies.

There was a whole section of home-canned fruits, such as peaches, pears, pineapple, and figs. Mother had never canned any fruit, as she didn't like the idea of the water-bath method available to her for home canning at that time. Another section contained all sorts of cucumber pickles: dill pickles, sweet pickles, bread-and-butter pickles, sour pickles, and pickles with onions, carrots, and cauliflower. There were also pickled peaches, pears, tomato relish, chow-chow, and beets.

The handwork section had quite a few homemade quilts hanging on display on the wall. Mother stopped and examined the pattern in each one of them. Sometimes she sketched a design for a quilt and then went home and made a quilt square like it to use as a pattern in the future. The quilts made a very colorful covering on the wall, and I remember being captivated by their beauty.

After we left the quilt section, Mother examined all of the crocheted and knitted handwork and embroidered items on display. There were all kinds of crocheted doilies, tablecloths, bedspreads, blankets, knitted sweaters, foot warmers, tea cozies, baby clothes, embroidered tablecloths, handkerchiefs, and table runners.

The entire display of foodstuffs and handwork at the fair was a testimony to Mother of the unlimited challenges of creativity available to a lady who lived on a farm. I could see that she was anxious to get involved.

Father followed Mother around until we had looked over all the food items and handwork, and then we all deployed to the livestock area where Father "had his day." He could have spent hours looking over all the animals that were shown at the fair. Father just wanted to look at, touch, examine, and ask questions about all the different animals. I was very curious about the animals also, as I rarely saw some of them anywhere else when I was that young.

In retrospect, I must say that after having attended many small town fairs and livestock exhibits through the years (including the annual livestock shows held in the Coliseum in San Antonio), none of them had as many different things on display as that small Kendall County Fair at Boerne, Texas. We enjoyed attending the fair for many years.

The Circus Comes to Town

When the circus came to town, Father didn't have to see every show, but he did have to see what he thought was the main event: the early morning "raising of the Big Top," as he called it. So it follows that every year when he thought the Barnum and Bailey Circus was due, Father started checking on the time of arrival of the circus train, which came all the way to the circus grounds on a railroad spur.

Father finally came home from work one night all excited saying, "Tomorrow's the big day!" He got us out of bed in the dark the next morning and we rushed to the circus grounds, hoping to get there before the circus train pulled in. Because Father always checked with the railroad ahead of time for the time of arrival, we usually got there in time to watch the train clang, clang, clang into place at the circus grounds.

As soon as the train stopped, circus people started emerging from coaches, Pullman cars, and boxcars and started unloading everything. They put ramps in front of the animal cars and rolled the animal cages down. The colorful cages were filled with all kinds of animals such as gold-and-black-striped tigers, yellowish tan lions with big shaggy manes, cute little dogs, horses and ponies, chocolate-colored bears, sometimes seals, and now and then maybe some other animals. The humongous gray elephants came lumbering down ramps and were immediately put to work lifting tent poles and other heavy things with their trunks. I marveled at the way the elephants seemed to do anything the men led them to do. They appeared to be slow and cumbersome, but they did a lot of lifting that couldn't have been done without them.

There were men everywhere running around like ants and they all seemed to know exactly what to do, and right before our eyes an entire circus was being erected.

Father just sat waiting in great anticipation for the "Raising of the Big Top," which was strictly an elephant show, not excluding the trainers. We watched them use their trunks to raise the giant outer poles that held up the Big Top. Then they outlined the perimeter of the tent and set up three giant rings inside it that would all have their own spectacular events going on at the same time that afternoon. Next they unrolled the giant tent across the rings and checked the ropes.

Then suddenly, Father said, "This is it. They're going to raise the Big Top!" We watched in spellbound silence as the elephants and men raised the huge canvas tent up into the air with the gigantic center poles, stretching it outward over the huge side poles, and then tying it down at regular intervals to large pegs that had been driven into the ground.

It was a sight worth getting up in the dark to see. There it was, a complete circus all set up and ready for the afternoon performance right after lunch. Father was especially exhilarated, as he said he always watched the circus set up when it came to his hometown when he was a boy. There were only a few other people around who appeared to be watching at all, and I never saw any of them stay very long, but Father never left until he had seen "the whole show." It still is a treasured memory of my childhood.

The Original Mexican Restaurant

Once in a while Father took us to the Original Mexican Restaurant for a Mexican supper. Ordinarily Father didn't want to eat anything unless Mother had cooked it because he didn't think anyone else could cook anything that was "sanitary." (I don't know how he survived before they were married.) But he loved that Mexican food. I think they had him fooled into thinking their food was sanitary by the immaculate manner in which an order was taken and served.

First, the maitre d' led us to a table. Next, a male waiter wearing black trousers and a white coat buttoned down the front came over with a white-starched towel folded lengthwise, draped over his left arm. Then he proceeded to put the clean, snow-white tablecloth he carried with him on our table, and laid out a napkin for each of us. After that he brought polished, shining silverware and laid it out. Next, spotlessly sparkling clear glasses of ice water were distributed. The waiter handed out flawless menus, which looked as if they had never been touched before, and Father placed our orders.

When the food came, each item was served in its own individual snow-white china container such as one enchilada on an oblong white dish, chili, rice, and beans, each in its own little round bowl, a taco or a chalupa on its own little plate, and steaming hot tortillas between two hot china plates. After distributing our orders, the waiter stood by at a respectable distance with the towel over his arm and waited on no one else until we finished! He was at our beck and call during the entire meal.

We never saw the kitchen, but I really believe all the pomp and show in their serving of the meal lulled us into believing the kitchen was spotless and everything was sanitary.

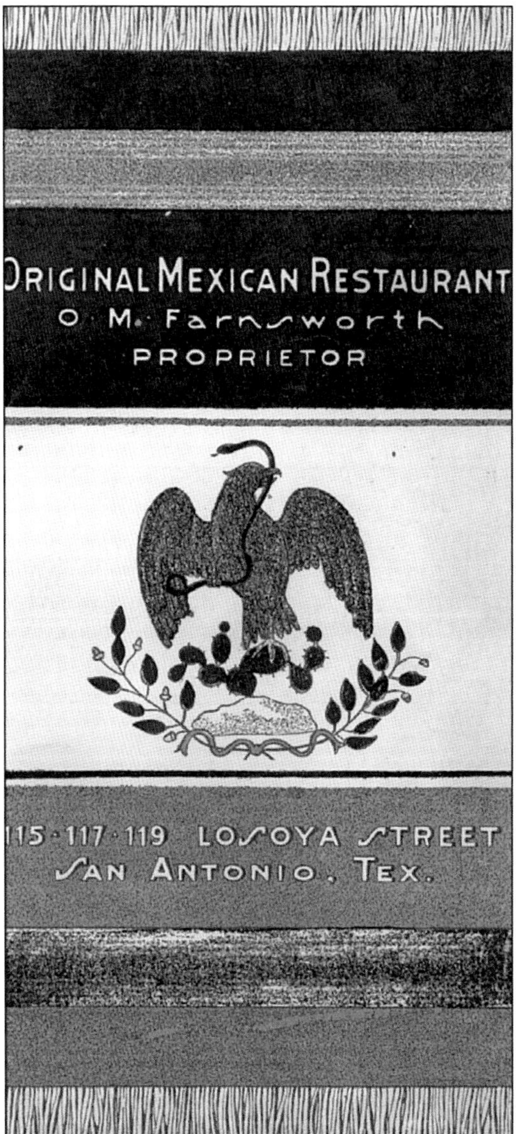

The Original Mexican Restaurant was everybody's favorite.

Around Town in the Essex

Once in a while Father took us to San Marcos to visit his sister and brother-in-law, Aunt Ada and Uncle Ed. Uncle Ed had the Hudson-Terraplane car dealership in San Marcos. We were visiting with them right after the Hudson people put the Essex car on the market, probably about 1930, and Uncle Ed talked Father into buying and driving one of his new cars home.

The Essex gave us trouble from the word "go." Anytime we had to stop for a light, or anything else, the motor died, and when it came time to go it didn't; in fact, it wouldn't start until something pushed it.

It was sheer misery to go anywhere in that car. I can remember it like it was yesterday. Every time we came home we had to follow a streetcar which was powered by electricity and ran on a track in the middle of the street. The streetcar was San Antonio's means of public transportation in those days. It stopped at every corner, and the law was that all cars had to stop too.

Each time the streetcar stopped, and Mother put the brake on to stop the Essex, the motor died. When the streetcar started up again, persons driving cars that would go would try to pass it before it stopped at the next corner. But since the Essex wouldn't start when the streetcar started up again, we found ourselves just sitting there, high and dry. And we didn't go until someone either took pity on us (or just wanted to get us out of their way) and pushed us a little ways. Then it ran fine to the next corner where we had to stop for the streetcar again to repeat the same embarrassing mess. We went through this every time we ventured out in that Essex. It was terrible!

We often shopped at a Chinese grocery store. It had an array of food staples in barrels that the owner weighed out and sold in brown paper sacks in any amount a person wanted. Mother and Father both liked to shop there often for things like lard, sugar, flour, salt, various dried fruits, and many more items. They had everything in large tins or barrels and the clerk did the measuring; customers never touched the scoops. When we got through, Mother started trying to get someone to push us in the Essex and sometimes we had to wait a while until a car moved from in front of us before we could go. We really didn't have all that much trouble finding someone to push us, as cars in general weren't that trustworthy in those days, all of them having trouble of one kind or another once in a while. It was sort of an unspoken courtesy of the road to help each other; after all, many of the older drivers still remembered the days of the horse-and-buggy. Shopping in the Chinese grocery store in that Essex presented quite a challenge. Mother had to plan before the fact where she would park that would position the car in a manner that she could ask someone to push her to start it when she was ready to leave.

I don't think that any car ever gave as much predictable repetitious trouble as that Essex did. Even though mechanics tried, no one ever managed to improve it at all. Finally, after about a year of that, Grandfather Templeton decided to purchase a new limousine and he gave Mother his 1928 Buick four-door luxury sedan, which ran so beautifully it caused us to forget all about that Essex.

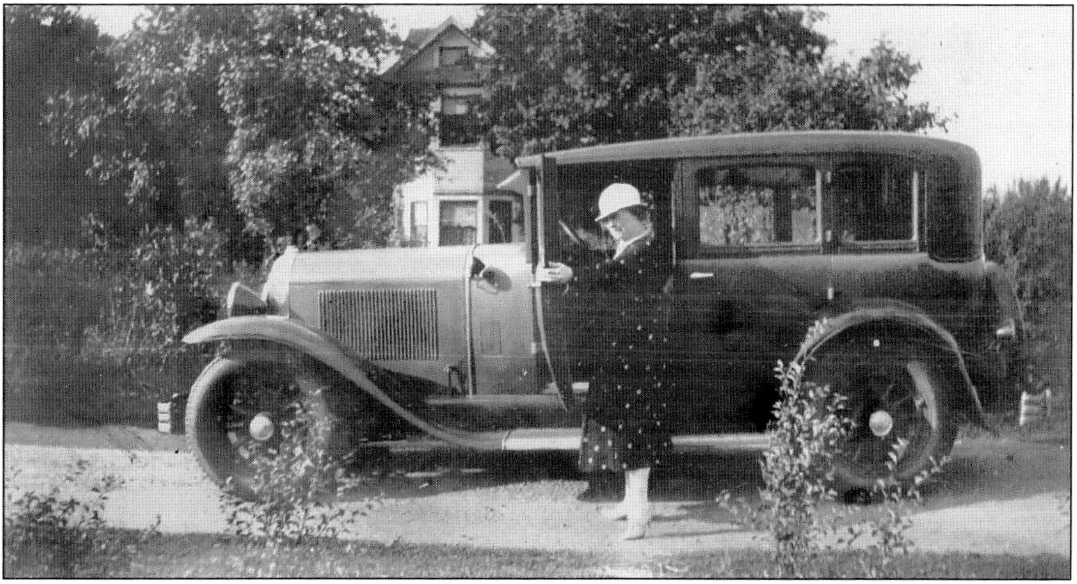

One of our neighbors is pictured here with what was probably another one of Grandfather Templeton's endless supply of cars.

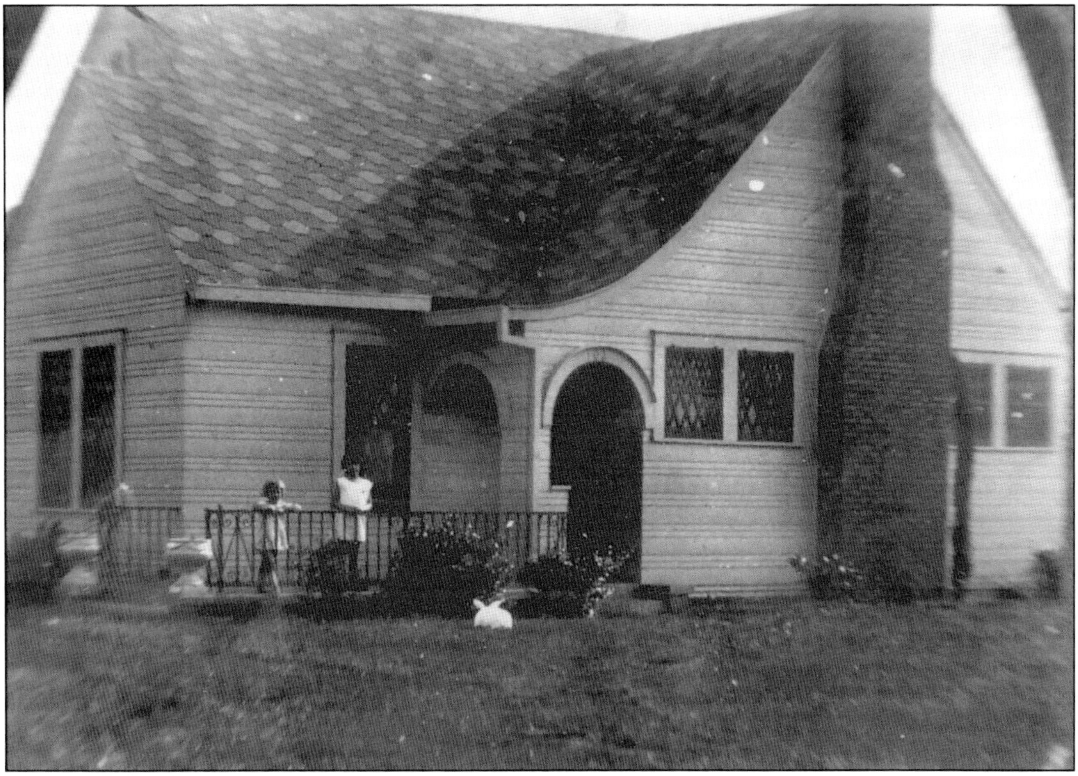

Our home at Mayfield Park was Mother's new dream home. Designed by an architect, it had every modern amenity imaginable.

Chapter Five

A New Home and Baby Sister

(Mayfield Park and Frances)

When Father returned from the Army at the end of World War One, he set up a real estate and loan brokerage business in San Antonio, with the goal of saving as much money as possible so he could eventually go out west and buy a four-thousand-acre ranch. Two years later his plans were put on hold when he married Mother.

In 1927, Thurman Barrett, one of his business friends, was developing a subdivision on the south side of San Antonio, which he dubbed "Mayfield Park." Mr. Barrett urged Father to branch out and purchase a seven-acre tract in that new subdivision. He took Father out to look it over and pointed out the proximity of it to Father's office (seven miles).

The area had a public water supply, city sewage, and electricity and had been surveyed and platted into large tracts with graveled paved streets throughout. Mother immediately fell in love with the idea of having her own vegetable and flower gardens and a new dream house that she and Father had planned together.

Using the house Grandfather gave them as a down payment, cash Father had saved up, and a loan from a business acquaintance, they started on the venture by buying the seven-acre tract and hiring an architect to draw up the plans for their custom-built home.

When Grandmother found out what was happening, she was furious that "that thing" (my father) was selling the house Grandfather had given to Mother, and "moving her way out in the middle of nowhere, to live in who knows what." I heard her say we'd be so far away she'd never see us again.

Grandmother was so distraught she didn't even try to be discreet around me (as was customary where Father was concerned), but blared out all sorts of expletives, short of cursing, showing her intense jealousy and hatred towards Father. But Grandmother's agony was ignored by all concerned and moving arrangements went on as planned. The house was sold almost immediately, the loan was in place, and the contractor was on the site starting construction.

Mother and Father were so anxious to live on their rural property, they had the contractor build the two-car garage with an apartment attached first so they could move into it, and watch their new home being built. We moved into it in February of 1928.

Their excitement and enthusiasm overflowed to me, and before long I was so filled with the anticipation of a new home that I didn't have time to even think about the home I had left behind. When Father returned from his office each evening, we examined the progress made that day on our home. Watching the construction, some things I saw made a stronger impression than others, for instance, watching the carpenters line our front bedroom closet with cedar. It smelled just like the inside of Mother's cedar chest and still had the same aroma over 50 years later. Finally, our new home was finished and we moved in. With all its new furniture, rugs, and beautiful drapes, it felt like a castle in a fairy tale.

Father immediately had the garage apartment converted into a hatchery, and the other buildings on the property were completed. There were three large hen houses for laying hens, one brooder house, a large storeroom and feed house combined, and at the other end of the property there were a cowshed and feed house. There was also a small house for a hired hand and his family, as well as two cars in the garage and a pick-up truck under the car shed.

Eventually the hen houses were filled with laying hens, and the incubators in the hatchery were hatching eggs. Father decided he couldn't operate the chicken farm and his real estate business both so he hired a man with a family to handle the chicken and egg business. He moved them into the house built for hired help, with the understanding the man's wife would help Mother whenever she needed her around our house. But operating his real estate business in downtown San Antonio didn't keep Father from overseeing and directing the chicken farm.

We met our next door neighbors, Mr. and Mrs. Oehler, and their children, Bernice, Harris, and Phyllis, while our house was being built at the same time as theirs on the west end of our block. They had a baby girl named Doris about the same time my Mother had my sister Frances. After a couple of years, we began to visit each other often, having a lot of fun. Mother gave us lots of old clothes to play dress-up in and we used the garage apartment when it was empty to change in. If it was occupied, we dressed behind the ligustrum bushes; by that time, they were quite large and offered full cover.

Soon after we moved into the house, Father brought "Old David" home and put a cot in one corner of the storeroom and made a place for him to stay for a couple of weeks at a time. "Old David" wasn't really old to Mother and Father, but he was to Jean and me and that's what we called him.

David was a black man who had been taking care of our lawn on Park Avenue. As Mother really liked David, she let him come into our house and cook, and he would do anything she asked him to do. He once had a career as a head porter on the Southern Pacific Railroad, but after about 15 years he had to quit because, as he put it, he was an alcoholic who had been getting gradually worse until it interfered with his work.

He could leave alcohol alone for periods of two or three weeks at a time, then he would drink anything he could get his hands on for four or five days, then stay off of it for two or three weeks, and then start the cycle all over again. Since it was during prohibition, this was especially hard on him. At this time it was not at all easy to get liquor; the only thing he could drink was what they called "bootleg whiskey."

David was kept pretty busy and before long he was trimming bushes and mowing the large lawn. Jean and I loved to follow David around while he mowed the lawn. David could last without liquor about two weeks at a time, and sometimes even three, but then he asked Father to take him back to his apartment so he could find something to drink for four or five days. Father always paid him for the work he had done and took him back whenever he wanted to go, with arrangements to pick him up in about a week.

Then, just before the repeal of prohibition, a tragedy occurred. Father went to pick David up at a prearranged time and found him lying in his apartment dead. Father called the authorities and they told us later that David had drunk some bad liquor, and it had killed him.

We were all very sad and we missed David very much, but we had a beautiful yard to remember him by forever. He had planted our lawn, rosebushes, shrubs, a weeping willow tree by our kitchen window, a cottonwood tree in the front yard, and installed a beautiful flagstone walk leading from our wrought-iron enclosed concrete front porch to the front gate. David's plants and trees continued giving us pleasure as long as we lived there — a fitting memorial to "Old David."

New Baby Frances

Mother loved to surprise people, but the best one she ever pulled was on July 28, 1929. I woke up that morning with roosters crowing just like usual, but something about the day was different. My parents were neither in their bed nor in the kitchen. Jean woke up, and after calling our mother and getting no answer, we were scared. We started creeping through the house, and when we got to the front bedroom we heard voices. I turned the doorknob and called, "Mama?"

Father quickly came out of the bedroom and stopped us and took us into the living room. He said everything was okay and that Mother was in the bedroom with a surprise for us. We went into the bedroom and found Mother in bed all covered up, with the doctor on one side of the bed and a nurse on the other side by a large oblong basket I had never seen before. Mother told us to look into the basket for a surprise. There was a baby in it. Mother said it was our little baby sister.

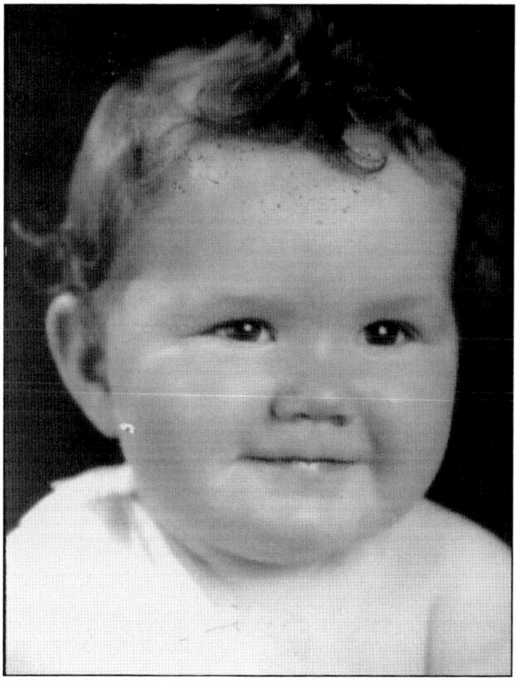

Mother surprised us on July 28, 1929, by presenting us with Frances, our new baby sister.

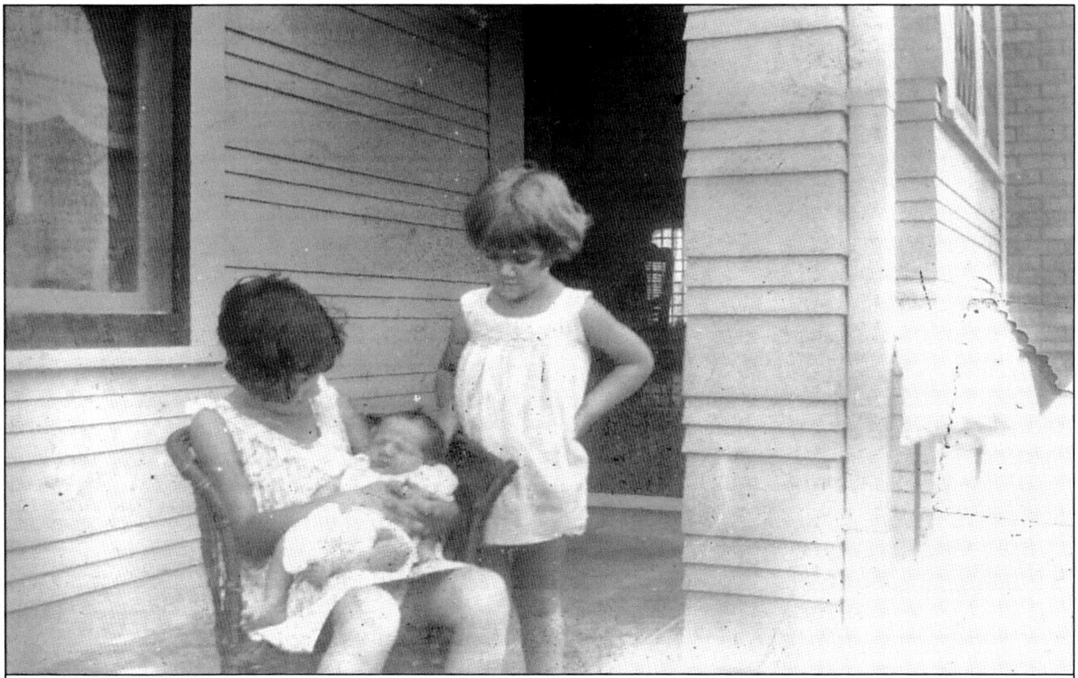

Jean and I seemed "obsessed" with looking after our new baby sister.

Mother had managed to keep everyone except Father and the doctor from knowing she was in a family way. She started out by seeing how far she could go before her family noticed. They never did, and she thought it would be fun to just wait until the baby arrived to tell them. She was overweight anyway and wore lots of gathered dresses, which helped her to conceal her condition.

She rested awhile, and then called Aunt Sissie and told her that she had something to show her. Sometime that afternoon Aunt Sissie came out to see what it was, and Mother showed her the baby. I will never forget how Aunt Sissie reacted. First it was with disbelief. She insisted that Mother hadn't had the baby and that she had gotten it from someone else. After being convinced about the birth, she started to faint and scolded Mother for not telling her about it. She said it wasn't fair for Mother to do her that way.

Aunt Sissie finally calmed down and asked the baby's name, whether it was a boy or girl, and then looked at the baby. The name, by the way, was Frances Louise. Then my parents called their respective parents and told them. They didn't believe it either.

Father more or less looked after Jean and me for the rest of the day, in between strutting around in and out of the front bedroom to check on Mother and Frances, that is. He was really "walking on air with pride," as one might say. The nurse had a time trying to keep him under control long enough for Mother and Frances to rest. She finally told him to get supper for Jean and me and leave them alone.

I can't imagine what Father might have fixed us for supper. I don't even remember eating anything as I was pretty excited myself, but I do remember what Father did later that night. First, shortly after dark, he saw to it that Jean and I had our baths and got ready for bed. Then, after the nurse told him to leave her patients alone for the night, he took Jean and me into the living room to entertain us, as we were all too excited to sleep yet.

Even though Father could play the piano very well, I had never heard him play but one piece of music. It was the "Twelfth Street Rag," and that night he put Jean and me beside him at the piano and played it like he had never played it before, over and over, with feeling. I loved every minute of it. Jean and I slept well all night.

About a half-mile from our house, there was a small grocery store where we shopped several times a week. The owner, Mr. Sueltenfuss, knew how obsessed I was with Frances and teased me about her every time we visited his store. He went on and on about how pretty our baby was, always telling me to keep an eye on her or he would steal her. I believed his threats and became paranoid about watching over her.

Mother didn't think anything about this until September came and it was time I started school. Mother took me to Morrill Ward School and enrolled me in the first grade. When she and my sisters started and leave me there, I suddenly remembered Mr. Sueltenfuss and cried out, "I can't stay here and leave Frances. Mr. Sueltenfuss will steal her." Mother assured me he was only kidding, but I did not stop crying. Becoming hysterical, I held onto her and she could see that I was absolutely panic-stricken. As I was only six at the time, and it wasn't mandatory that I start to school until I was seven, she decided right then and there to take me home and let me help her look after Frances for that year.

It didn't hurt me a bit to stay out of school, either. The next September, when I was seven, I started to school at San Jose School in the first grade. After the first semester, the teacher called Mother in and told her that I already appeared to know everything she was going to cover in the first grade and asked permission to advance me to the second grade. When Mother asked me what I wanted to do, I said, "I guess I'll go on to the second grade."

When Frances was almost grown, she sent for her birth certificate and, when it arrived, she found she had been using the wrong name all her life. The doctor had put Frances Howard on the birth certificate, instead of Frances Louise as our parents had decided. Frances ran to Mother and told her the birth certificate was wrong. After looking it over, Mother remembered that Frances Howard was one of several names she and Father had considered and talked about with the doctor before finally deciding on Frances Louise. Howard was Mother's father's name. Frances liked the name so she decided to leave it that way and be Frances Howard Rife from then on.

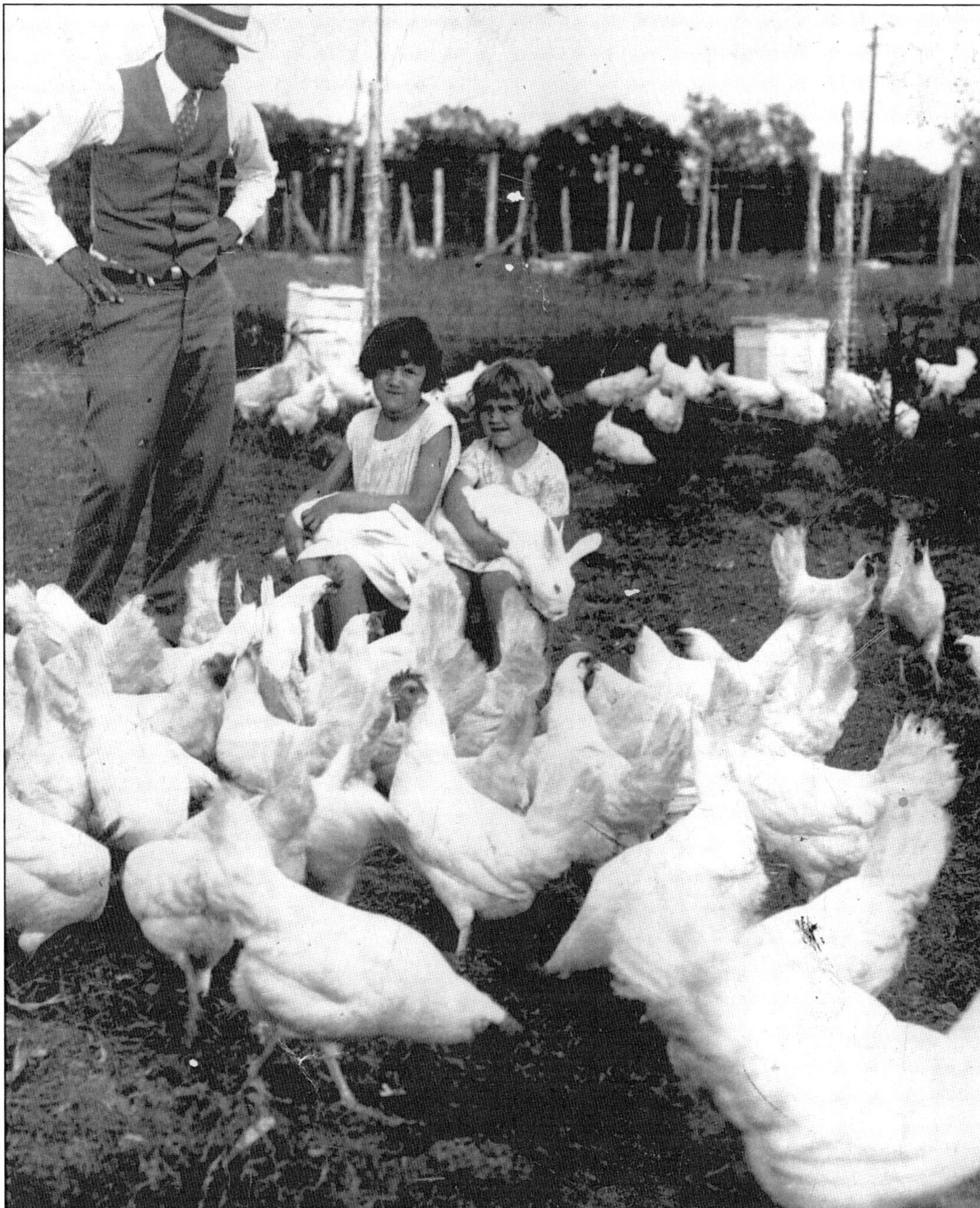

Father, dressed in business attire, was equally at home in his "domestic zoo."

Chapter Six

Childhood in a Domestic Zoo

From the time we moved in 1928 to Mayfield Park, there were a lot of things going on there that were new to me. For as long as I could remember, Father's dream had been to own a three or four hundred-acre farm with crops in the field, livestock in the pasture, fresh vegetables and poultry for food, and a horse to ride every day. The first step toward realizing his dream had been to move us to Mayfield Park and pursue various moneymaking ventures that would bring him closer to its fulfillment.

Father seemed to have a natural aptitude for animal husbandry, so when he was advised that rabbits, which multiplied like mice, were the rage at that time both for food and fur, he went for it. In addition to the pleasure of raising them, Father expected to make a huge profit from this venture.

While we were still living in the garage apartment waiting for the house to be finished, Father had rabbit hutches erected and stocked them with beautiful reddish-orange rabbits until he had the space of about a city lot filled with them. He thought these animals would reap him a fortune.

It was fun to walk up and down the rows of rabbit hutches and watch them eating or just wriggling their noses at me. It wasn't long before the rabbits began having babies, which were so little and odd looking when they were born. I gradually began to notice that the baby rabbits were disappearing. Father kept a close vigil on them for a few days and found the mother rabbits eating their young shortly after giving birth. This upset Father quite a bit and when he sought professional advice, he was told that if mother rabbits started eating their young they rarely ever stopped. This syndrome usually affected the whole bunch. Well, Father started eliminating the "syndromed" mothers and eventually there weren't many rabbits left. We sold some of them and wound up eating the rest. Eating them was easy because rabbit meat is delicious.

In celebration of our moving from the city to our rural home, one of Father's business associates gave us a peacock and two peahens. They were our pride and joy and quite a conversation piece with all our visitors. They were a special thrill to me as I had never seen peafowl anyplace before except in the San Antonio Zoo and at the Quadrangle at Ft. Sam Houston.

During the day the peacock spread his magnificent tail feathers in the air and strutted around the yard. From time to time, day or night, he suddenly let out a horrible loud screeching sound: the "peacock scream." The peacocks and peahens insisted on roosting directly across the highway from our home in the top of some mesquite trees. After a few weeks the peahens began disappearing. Mother was concerned, so she sent Father across the street to the mesquite pasture to look for them. After searching the pasture a while, Father came back with the sad news that he had found evidence that something, probably a coyote, had attacked the peahens while they were sitting on their nests on the ground and killed them. The peacock, however, had no reason to nest or roost on the ground so the coyote didn't get him. We called him "Fowlie" and thought the world of him. When he shed some of his tail feathers, we collected them, glued them on velvet backgrounds in beautiful fan designs, and framed them behind glass. Some of the feather pictures were given to family members as gifts. We also had a large bunch of the feathers standing in a vase.

Eventually Mother acquired some guineas. The peacock took a shine to one of the guinea hens and they mated. The guinea sat on her eggs under Mother's watchful care and hatched several "guinea fowls." Mother donated them to the San Antonio Zoo, who seemed very glad to get them. For many years, we saw them whenever we visited the zoo. Fowlie stayed with us ten or twelve years, giving us beautiful feathers until he finally died. Thirty-some-odd-years later, Mother still had some of his feathers in a vase.

Father's next moneymaking venture was beekeeping. He worked with the bees successfully (if not profitably) until he was about 85 years old. He never made much money from them, but he had a natural aptitude for handling them. He enjoyed working with the hives and honey, so he kept them anyway. At first he had six or eight beehives installed close to our small fruit orchard. He eventually added eight or ten more hives.

One day Father came home with some equipment to wear when working with the bees. He had a large hat with a net hanging on the bottom of it, large gloves with elasticized cuffs, and last, he had a box-like thing with a small bellows on it which produced a lot of smoke when he pumped it with one hand. He looked quite comical as he headed off to work with the bees wearing all that equipment and puffing out smoke with one hand. He told us to stay pretty far back as we might get stung but, invariably, curiosity got the best of me and I hid fairly close, peeping around a tree or something, and watched.

Once in a while Father rushed into the house shouting "SWARM," donned his beekeeping garb, grabbed his smoker, and then ran back out to a tree and placed an empty beehive under it. Next he got pans and beat on them and directed smoke at the bees. I moved as close as I dared and saw that the swarming bees had completely covered a large branch of a nearby tree, making a loud buzzing, droning noise. Finally, Father said he had coaxed the queen bee into the hive and all the other bees had immediately followed her. Then he put a lid on it and set it with the other hives. Everyone got excited when the bees swarmed, but I have never understood how Father managed to get them into the hive.

The day finally came when Father announced, "It's time to rob the bees!" The first thing he did was take out several boxes of honey frames and Mother's large washtubs, and place them here and there among the hives. Then he donned his beekeeping equipment, picked up the smoker, and started robbing the bees. First he took the lid off of a beehive and pumped some smoke into it. Then he reached into the hive and lifted out a honey-filled frame, placed it in a washtub, and replaced it with an empty frame. Father did this at all the hives, and while he was doing it I could see the bees walking around on his hat and clothes, but the smoke calmed the bees, slowing them down so that they rarely ever stung him. It took quite a while to rob all the hives.

Now the fun was about to begin for me. Father had a honey extractor in the storeroom. It was a large 30 or 40-gallon drum that was mounted through the middle on a spindle with wire compartments all around the inside of it. The honey-filled frames were dropped into these wire compartments and a lid was put on the drum. There was a handle or crank on the outside of the drum like on an ice-cream freezer which you cranked to make the entire drum spin around and around pretty fast. Father let me turn the crank for awhile, then he took over and spun it even faster. The centrifugal force caused by spinning the drum at a high speed forced the honey out of the frames. Mother filled several sterilized jars with the golden honey. Then she put a label on the jars and the honey was ready to sell.

This operation continued until all the honey had been extracted from the frames and packed in jars. It left all of us completely exhausted, but I must say I never tired of taking part in "bee-robbing" in all the times Father did it.

Each bee-robbing excursion left us with jars and jars of honey, which sold quickly until the middle of 1930. Then the stock market crash of November 1929 caused the market to dry up and we were floating in honey no one could afford to buy. Another one of Father's moneymaking ventures had gone awry. He sold or gave away all but three or four hives, which he kept for his pleasure. They also assured us of having all the honey we wanted to eat with Mother's homemade biscuits, waffles, pancakes, and hot rolls.

As soon as we moved into our new home and vacated the garage apartment, Father decided he could make a fortune selling baby chicks by converting the apartment into a hatchery. He installed some incubators and started hatching hundreds of eggs. I followed him around constantly and wanted to see how everything worked. The incubators had tray upon tray filled with eggs and each day the trays were pulled out and the eggs were turned over. A certain amount of moisture was added each day and the incubators were warmed by electricity. This was to take the place of a setting hen, who turned the eggs she was sitting on daily with her feet and kept them enveloped in warm air from her body and feathers.

In 21 days I found baby chicks cracking through eggs. The chicks were either boxed and shipped immediately to a buyer, or transferred from the incubator to a brooder house. I loved to go the brooder house and watch the baby chicks. They were so pretty, all covered with their ivory-colored downlike feathers. Most of them were white leghorns, destined to become heavy layers. On rare occasions I saw turkeys pecking through large cream colored, brown-specked turkey eggs. Now, baby turkeys were really something else. They were about twice as large as baby chickens and either had black and white specks or were all white. They were awkward looking, but very interesting to watch. They didn't know how to eat or drink when first hatched, and I watched as Father and the hired man pushed the heads of first one turkey chick and then another into the water trough and then the feed trough, until the turkey chicks started doing it themselves. The turkey chicks were watched carefully for several days to see that they got started right.

Then one day disaster struck. One of the incubators in the hatchery caught fire. Luckily Father found it right away, and by the time the fire engine arrived he already had things pretty much under control. The damage was repaired and the hatchery resumed operation, but in a year or two he said it was too time consuming and sold the incubators. Hence another moneymaking scheme went down the drain.

After Father closed the hatchery and stopped handling baby chicks, he found that he had an empty brooder house. He converted it into a pigeon house and stocked it with a large number of pigeons. He had a contract with a hotel to furnish it with squabs, which were an expensive delicacy. Father should have made lots of money on the squabs, but because of the Depression, the demand for such an expensive delicacy dwindled to nil in less than two years and he found they were costing him more money than they were worth.

The laying hens were really the only project at Mayfield Park that was quite profitable. I supposed that was why he called it "The Green Meadows Poultry Farm." He had three large chicken houses (each one in its own large fenced-in yard) designed to accommodate over three hundred hens each. They were lined with nests on one wall and had a series of roosts hanging from the ceiling for the chickens to sleep on. The doors were kept open during the daytime and the chickens came and went at will.

From time to time Father decided his hens needed something green to eat because the egg yolks started turning a pale yellow. So he loaded the oat sprouters that were in the storeroom with oats and water and waited about a week. Then he had trays of sprouted oats to feed them everyday, as long as he kept the sprouters in operation. Each oat sprouter consisted of a metal rack with tracks that held seven removable oat trays, plus a holey tray on top for water. The seven removable trays in each sprouter were loaded with oats. Water was added to the top tray daily and it gradually worked its way down through all the trays of oats to the bottom trays. When the top trays of oats had sprouted and reached a height of about five inches (usually after seven days), it was time to start taking trays of oat sprouts to the chicken yards. The operation of the oat sprouters fascinated me. The whole thing seemed like magic to me. It was fun to watch the chicken hens go after the trays of sprouted green oats. Within a day or two after eating the oats, their egg yolks had returned to that beautiful healthy looking golden orange color.

Father had contracts with the St. Anthony Hotel and several large restaurants in San Antonio to furnish them with fresh eggs daily. He bought a pick-up truck for the hired man to deliver them with. Gathering the eggs, boxing them, and making deliveries, along with caring for the chickens kept the hired man pretty busy.

The egg business went on after the 1929 stock market crash, longer than his other rural ventures. But within a year it started slowing down also and he began selling off the hens a few at a time. About once a month, the hired man loaded cages of hens in the pickup truck and sold them to Polunsky's on North Broadway, where they were sold to housewives to cook for Sunday dinner.

The downscaling of the egg business went on for several years. He kept enough hens around to lay all the eggs we wanted to eat and cook with plus eight or ten dozen a day extra to sell to cover the cost of chicken feed. He never failed to have an endless supply of hens and fryers for us to eat.

While this was going on Father turned his attention to the one thing he wanted most: livestock. He rented about 20 acres of land down the road from us a ways and bought a cow. She was taken back and forth from the cow barn to the pasture daily. At night I enjoyed watching Father milk the cow. The hired man milked her in the morning. I wanted to learn to milk, but I was only about seven years old and he wouldn't let me.

He eventually converted one of the hen houses into a feed house and milking area. Then he purchased two more cows and started going from dairy to dairy looking for baby calves. He said each cow could raise at least three calves. Some of the dairies actually gave him a calf to get rid of it.

I couldn't possibly remember the number of times Father put all of us in the car and drove to a dairy, sometimes 30 or 40 miles away, and left us sitting in the car to wait while he tried to find a calf. When he got one, he tied it up in two or three tow sacks so its head was sticking out and put it in the car trunk, propped it open a little, and took us back home. This was the beginning of a pattern Father followed for the rest of his active life, except that after a while he used a pick-up truck instead of a car. This was one venture he didn't expect to get rich on, but he did expect a small profit when the calves were big enough to sell. It was more a matter of just enjoying handling, feeding, and watching the calves grow.

After accumulating three cows, Father decided to start going to the cottonseed mill (or cotton gin) on the south side of San Antonio to buy cottonseed hulls and cottonseed meal for them to eat.

A visit to the cottonseed mill was very exciting. Father usually took us with him and while they were getting his order ready, we were allowed to go into the large silo-like room that had a mountain of cottonseed hulls. We started trying to climb up the mound of hulls and although our legs sunk in up to the knees, we kept going until we reached the top. We sat there a minute or two and let the hulls blow on us, then we gave a shove and started scooting down the mound pretty fast on the fairly mushy heap of cottonseed hulls. In the sitting position we didn't sink into them. We did this over and over until Father got ready to leave. I am sure my sisters and I got the same exhilarating thrill out of playing in those cottonseed hulls that children of today get from a roller coaster ride, and our fun was free.

Father mixed a small handful of cottonseed meal with a gallon of cottonseed hulls and about a half-gallon of ground corn twice a day for his milk cows to eat and they loved it. By the time I was eight and a half years old I had talked Father into teaching me how to milk a cow. He showed me that I had to give the cow a tub of feed to eat and make her feel at ease by stroking her side gently and talking to her in a soothing voice.

Next he gave me a wooden box to sit on and then he told me to put my hand around her teat and massage it a little. Then, with fingers wrapped loosely around the teat and thumb planted firmly on the bag, I was to push up and gradually squeeze my hand around the teat from forefinger to little finger, pull down, relax, and then start over. After a few pulls like this she let her milk down.

It was like magic to me to see that stream of white milk that I was bringing from the cow. I loved milking and Father paid me a penny every time I milked a cow. It was the first money I ever earned and before long I was making a penny a day. In those days that was a lot of money for an eight-and-a-half-year-old girl.

Mother did lots of things with the milk. First she strained it and put it in the refrigerator to chill. By the time the milk had sat overnight in the refrigerator, the cream had risen to the top. Then Mother skimmed it off and stored it in the refrigerator. Occasionally she whipped some of the fresh cream to serve with desserts and in our hot chocolate. Otherwise she waited until she had about four quarts and then she put the cream in a crock with a dasher, and someone sat beside it and plunged it up and down until the cream turned into butter and a thin milky substance. This was called churning. The churning action caused the butterfat to separate from a milky liquid called buttermilk. Mother removed the solid butterfat and pounded it in a wooden bowl with a wooden butter paddle until no more milk came out, added a spoonful of salt to each pound of butter, and shaped it into one-pound blocks in a wooden butter mold that came from Kallison's Country Store. After a few years, Mother got an electric churn that churned small amounts of butter very well.

Mother always let some of the skimmed milk sit at room temperature for a few days until it turned into clabber, which was chunks of white curds, and a clear liquid called whey. Father loved clabber with cornbread at suppertime. Sometimes Mother poured the clabber into a homemade cheesecloth bag, tied string around the top of it, and hung it on the clothesline overnight. All the whey drained out and cottage cheese was left.

Father finally got himself a horse and saddle and started riding almost every day. By the time I was ten years old I could saddle the horse myself, with a little help lifting up the saddle. Then Father brought a donkey home that his girls could ride without a saddle. I would get on the horse, put my sister Frances on with me, and my other sister Jean would get on the donkey, grab the bridle, and we would ride up and down the unpaved road north of our home.

We rode down the road like that one day and got off our animals to play awhile. When we decided to go back home, somehow Jean got on her donkey backwards by mistake. Suddenly, the donkey, sensing something amiss, bolted and started running toward the cow lot about two blocks away. Jean, sitting backwards, didn't have access to the bridle to hold on to, so she dug her fingers into the donkey's flanks, which had a lot of thick hair on them. The faster he ran the harder she dug her fingers into him as she tried to keep from falling off, and the donkey kept running faster.

It was a scary sight. Frances and I were on the horse following her and it looked as if she would surely fall off at any moment. When the donkey got to the cow lot he stopped suddenly and just stood there. Jean didn't fall off the donkey, but somehow during all the jostling, bouncing, and furor, she lost the long pants she was wearing; it shook them off, no doubt. The only thing hurt was her dignity. We all got a good laugh for years afterward.

While we lived at Mayfield Park, Father also brought some squirrels home just for fun and fixed a large wire cage for them. I spent a lot of time watching them. They had bushy tails and hopped, ran, and jumped around the cage very gracefully, stopping every now and then to stand up straight on their hind legs and exhibit a still pose like in a photograph. They looked around carefully and then started all over again.

They didn't stay around for more than

six or eight months, though, because the male squirrel bit Father on the hand while he was cleaning the cage. Father took the squirrel to the veterinarian and he watched it carefully to see if it had rabies. It did not have rabies, but the bite on Father's hand became badly infected almost immediately and he had to seek medical attention and was very sick for several days. The doctor said that Father was developing tetanus or blood poisoning, and told Mother how to administer hot packs and all kinds of treatments. Father finally got well. As soon as he was assured that the one that bit him wasn't rabid, he sold the squirrels.

Mother decided to raise Persian cats as a business venture. Everyone she knew was talking about them and wanted one. Mother loved cats anyway and the Persians had very long hair, and lots of it. They were unbelievably pretty. Father had a large pen built for the cats to stay in that was completely enclosed with cat-proof wire at the top and sides, and had a shelf about four feet up around the side of it. Before long, Mother had eight or ten female Persians in that pen raising kittens for her to sell.

There was one cat, which she kept in her home, that she named Chloe after a popular song from that era. Chloe had jet-black fur and green eyes. She didn't like me and the feeling was mutual. She ran out of sight whenever I came into the room.

At the same time she started keeping Chloe in the house, Mother was finishing a yo-yo bedspread made from the scraps of many different printed voile dresses, and accented with solid-colored orange voile she purchased. The yo-yo pattern was made from cutting circles of fabric about five inches in diameter, then the edge of each circle was was turned over about a fourth of an inch like a hem, and sewed all the way around by hand. After sewing this narrow hem around a circle, the thread was pulled up as tight as it would go and tied off with the hem on the inside. This was then flattened and pressed, resulting in a double circle about two inches in diameter with the gathers lying in the center on the topside and the other side flat.

Mother made enough of these circles to equal the size of a full bedspread when laid side by side. Then they were stitched together at four spots where they touched each other. It was a beautiful bedspread. She had made a pattern, or design, by putting 16 printed yo-yo circles together in a square and surrounding it with a row of orange yo-yos. She sewed the squares together diagonally so the spread would have triangular half-squares hanging off the bed all the way the around.

After Mother finished the bedspread, she put it on my bed for the day so I could enjoy looking at it. When that cat Chloe found it there, she circled the bed several times and then jumped on it. Before anyone knew what she was doing, she had used it for a bathroom.

Mother was devastated. She took the spread and other bedding and washed it. In a few days she put it back on my bed, but the same thing happened again. Mother thought Chloe had decided that the bedspread was put there for her to use as a bathroom, so she just cleaned everything up again and then stored the bedspread in a cedar chest for as long as Chloe was in our home.

Mother sold lots of kittens, but after a year or two she got tired of so many cats and sold all but two or three of her favorites, which she allowed to live in the house with Chloe.

I did not like the cat business, but I loved Mother's bantam chickens. They were so appealing to watch as they walked around in a stately manner anywhere they wanted. They were colorfully marked with various shades of brown, tan, red, black, and white, and the roosters were almost as colorful as the peacock. I

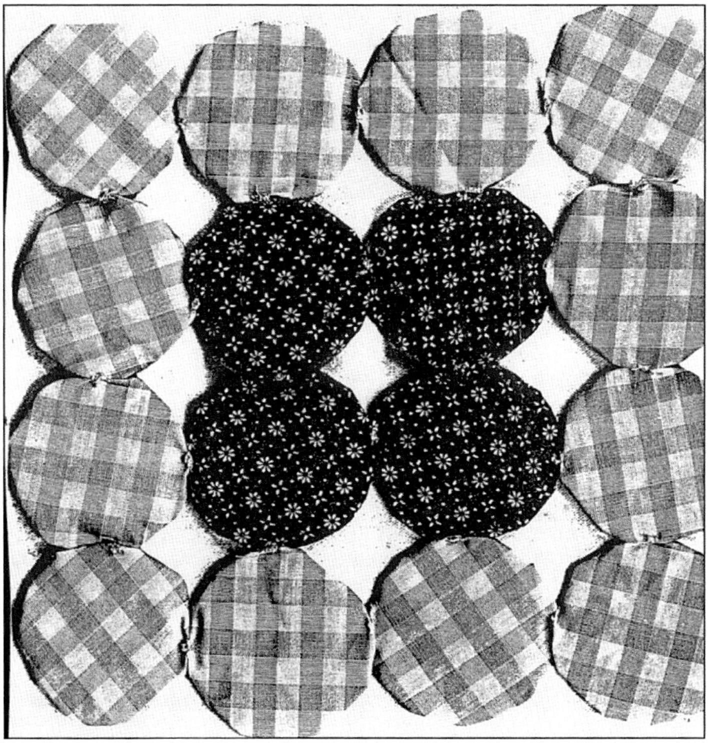

This was the design of that classic yo-yo quilt that Chloe obviously did not like.

believe Mother had them merely for the fun of it.

They were always sitting and hatching a dozen or so baby chicks. Watching the chicks follow the clucking mother hen around the yard was a sight worth seeing. Every now and then Mother sold some of the bantams to someone who came around asking for them. Mother continued to have bantam chickens around her wherever she lived, for many years.

Someone gave us a purebred German Shepherd dog for a pet. We had just seen the movie "Tarzan, the Ape Man," with Johnny Weissmuller, and we loved it so much we named our dog Tarzan. Tarzan grew up to be a large dog and lived out his years with us.

Thanks mostly to my father, between the age of five and twelve, I had gained a general knowledge of all kinds of animals and fowls: rabbits, peafowl, guineas, bees and honey making, a hatchery and baby chicks, pigeons, laying hens and selling eggs, cows and milk products, calves, goats, horses, donkeys, squirrels, Persian cats, bantam chickens, and last, but certainly not least, a German Shepherd dog. Living at Mayfield Park was like living in a zoo of domestic animals.

Father still saw every Battle of the Flowers Parade, but he did not eat breakfast in the park, go on cookouts in the woods, get to the Kendall County Fair in the fall, or rush to see the raising of the Big Top anymore. He now had many more interesting things to command his attention, because there was always some kind of animal to tend to morning and night. He never seemed to miss the things he had given up; he appeared to be much happier in his new home.

Thanks mostly to my father, as a child I gained a general knowledge of all kinds of animals. Living at Mayfield Park was sort of like living in a zoo of domestic animals.

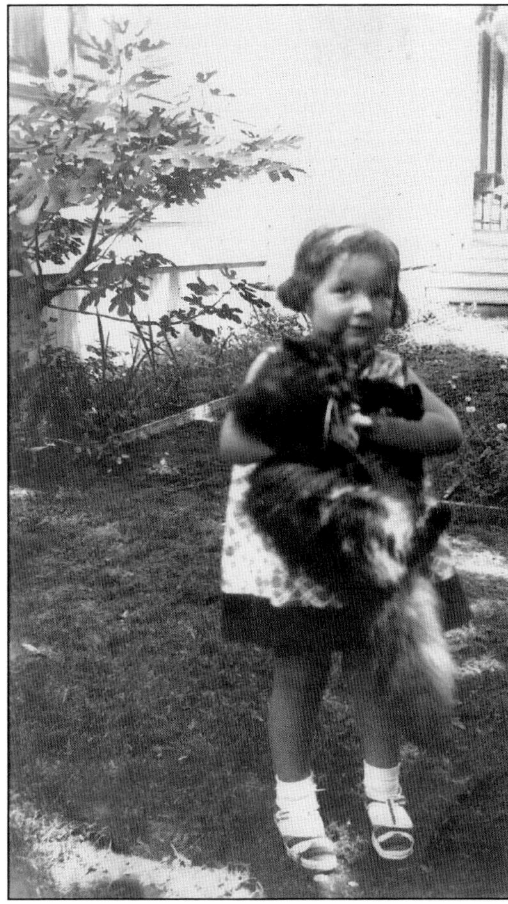

Frances is holding Chloe, that naughty cat!

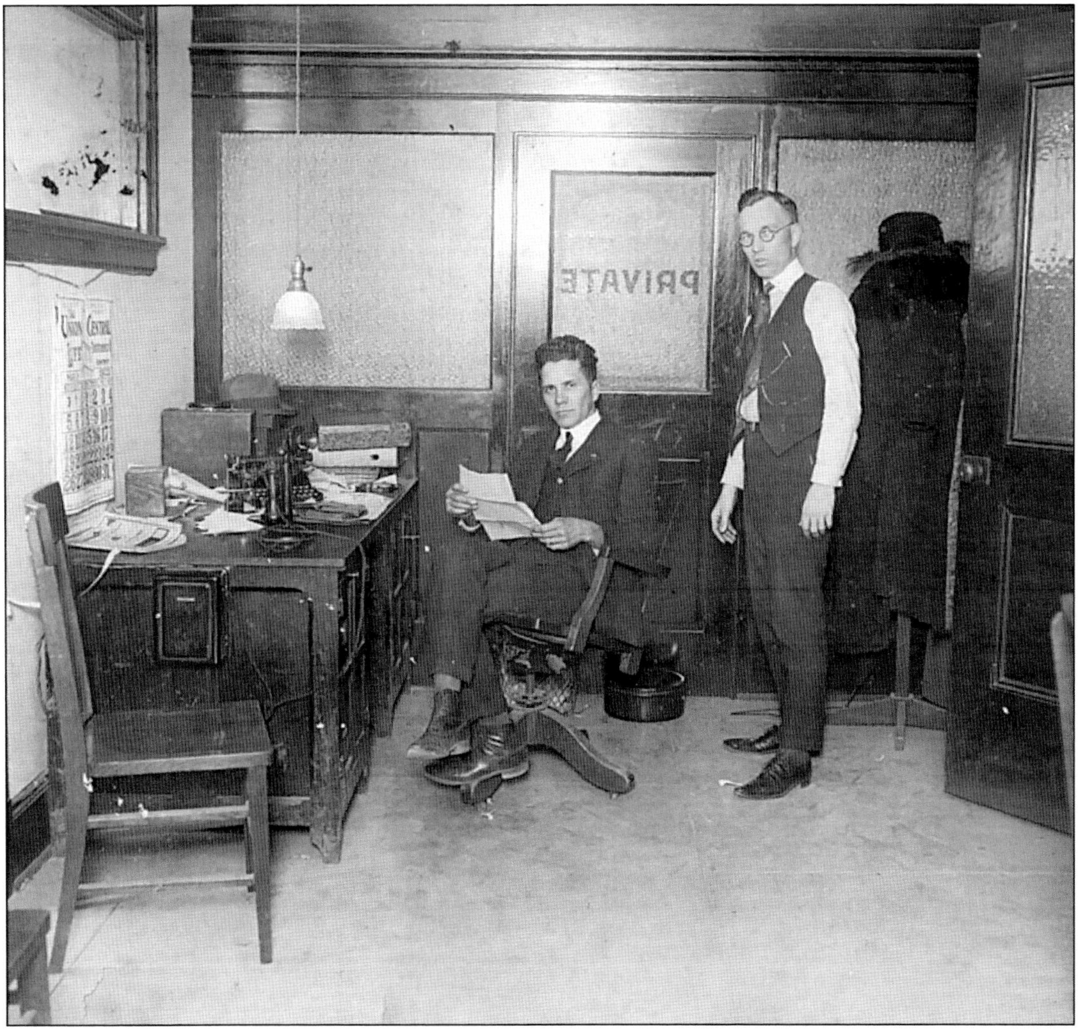

In this photo of my father, T.D. Rife, in his office in the Bedell Building, his name appears on the door and the calendar is turned to March 1922, the very month he and Mother married.

Chapter Seven

Father was a Real Estate Magnate

The same man who kept that domestic animal zoo throughout my childhood was also a real estate magnate. Yes, Father had long since proven himself to be a person of influence, expertise, and distinction as a real estate and loan broker. There was always a waiting list of licensed real estate salesmen desirous of working under him, and numerous wealthy clients consulting him about the advisability of buying and selling real estate and making real estate loans. He was also the appraiser of choice when it came to evaluating all types of real estate property.

Each morning after tending to outdoor farm chores, Father, "the farmer," transformed himself into a properly groomed businessman, in a three-piece dress suit, tie, and hat. Mother took it upon herself to choose his necktie from several dozen hanging on the tie rack. Ties were the only piece of clothing a businessman wore in that era that had any color, personality or individuality, and they certainly filled their role with all of the aforementioned qualities. They came in every imaginable color and design in bright shades and all kinds of pastels. Every man (or his wife) seemed to want at least one silk tie with a hand-painted mural on it. Hand-painted neckties were very expensive, but I do remember that Father had one with colorful flowers.

As soon as Father was dressed for the day and ready to go to the office, Mother handed him a sack lunch and he bade us good-bye as he hastily exited to the car. It was always a thrill to visit Father's office, which was located downtown in the Bedell Building, about one block north of Houston Street on North Broadway. Part of the excitement was riding in the elevator with him up to his large office suite. His suite consisted of four or five rooms with salesmen at desks talking on the telephone, asking Father questions, and generally keeping busy. He could issue orders and instructions faster than most people could think, and he started doing so as he opened the door, before he even hung up his hat, and everyone started "hopping to."

His telephone manner was completely unorthodox, certainly unprecedented, and I never saw it matched or equaled by anyone else. To begin with, he never said "Hello" or "Good-bye." When answering the phone he said, if anything, "Yes," or "T.D. Rife," or "What?" If the caller asked about a house advertised for sale, the first thing Father said was "How much cash do you have for a down payment?" If the caller didn't convince him he had sufficient cash, Father always said, without fail, "Call back when you can make the down payment." Then he hung up the phone.

There were times when a caller did have the cash down payment, that I noticed Father's next question was "Do you have school children?" If the answer was "Yes," he said "You don't want that house, the school is too far away and it isn't very good anyway." In other words, one might say Father used reverse sales tactics "to save time," and to qualify the buyer, as he put it. Buyers apparently appreciated his honest approach, as they usually continued talking, as long as Father listened, that is. They seemed to wind up trying to persuade Father to "let" them buy a house instead of him talking them "into" buying one. At any point, when Father decided the house in question was definitely not for the person calling, he hung up the phone, sometimes while the caller could still be heard talking.

I never did understand how he could treat prospective clients the way he did on the phone and have them call back, which they surely did. Many people who had purchased a home through his office came back years later to engage him to sell it. So they must have been impressed with something he did. Whenever I questioned Father on the subject of his telephone etiquette, he said it was pointless to waste his time and theirs, discussing a house on which they couldn't even make a down payment. Of course, the salesmen took most of the calls on property for sale and conducted business in a much more conventional manner.

Father never could bide with a waste of words or time. He wanted to be grinding away at something productive throughout the entire time he was working. He was usually his own boss, but the one time he worked for someone else it was as a young lad in a country post office. He stayed with it several hours before he announced something to the effect that he couldn't stand all the idle time spent waiting for customers. If he was going to "work," he was going to be "working," and then he quit.

Father had an ongoing relationship with the local newspapers: *The San Antonio Light*, *Evening News*, the *Morning Express*, and *La Prensa*. There was forevermore some kind of discourse with their classified departments over an ad being printed wrong, or not running as long as ordered, or a statement overcharging for ads. Those telephone conversations became rather "hairy" at times, until Father finally convinced the paper to take care of its mistake.

At some time during the day, each of the newspapers sent a copy boy to the office to pick up new ads for the classified section. Sometimes the salesmen wrote the ads and sometimes Father wrote them, but in any event, Father always checked each ad and approved the final wording for it. He could say more in an ad with fewer words than anyone I ever knew. For instance, a salesman might give him a 25-word ad describing a piece of property for sale, and Father, after editing, had it cut down to 12 words, without sacrificing any of the necessary particulars. That was very important as the papers charged by the word or line and the ad bills were always tremendous, especially since Father generally had 25 to 30 ads in every paper. And he always had an ad in each paper stating something like "T.D. Rife, Real Estate & Loans, Bedell Building In Business since 1920." There was also an ongoing ad soliciting listings for property to sell, as well as a blanket ad inviting buyers to call.

Each day, as soon as the paper hit the street, Father had someone bring the papers up to his office. Then the grueling process of checking the classified ads for mistakes began all over again. At the same time, Father asked the salesmen to canvas the "For Sale" ads for owners trying to sell a house, and then to contact them with the intent of listing the property to sell. The real estate business actually revolved around the classified sections of the newspapers. Father's office was a hustling, bustling, arena of work where as many as 10 to 15 people were kept continuously busy with incoming phone calls, delivery people coming and going, in addition to the many clients that were present, one after the other, throughout the day.

To my knowledge, the staff never stopped for a coffee break. There was no coffee urn in the office, or anything else pertaining to a break. Father never, ever, tasted coffee in his life and consequently didn't think it necessary for anyone else to drink it. He also didn't stop for a break except at lunchtime, and the only thing he drank at the office was water.

The salesmen never seemed to be discontented about anything, and they were always busy with something. Whenever a lull came in their regular workload, Father noticed it and instructed them to get out their Criss-Crosses and start calling persons listed in it to see if anyone was thinking about selling his home or any other real estate, and if so to list it with T.D. Rife.

The Criss-Cross was a large book listing every property in the San Antonio area by street and block number, one after the other, with the phone number beside each property. Therefore a salesman could choose a residential area and go down the block calling everyone in it and often get a listing and learn something about other persons in the area with houses for sale, also. Someone was forevermore trying to sell his own home, when it would be easier for Father's real estate firm to sell it.

When lunchtime came, Father told his secretary not to disturb him until she heard from him, and closed the door to his private office. After that he relaxed in his swivel chair and read the paper or a chapter in a library book while he ate the lunch Mother had packed for him. Next, he reclined on the comfortable couch in his office, and immediately went to sleep for approximately 30 minutes. I never saw anyone else fall asleep and wake up "on command" like he did. When he awoke, he was up and "at 'em" again as if he had never stopped. He called to his secretary and announced he was ready to take calls and conduct business, and then proceeded at full speed for the remainder of the afternoon. When things slowed down a little (usually about once a week), Father slipped out to the Strand Theater for 30 minutes or so, to watch an interlude of a western movie, and then he returned to the office.

There were many sales of property being made in the 1920s and for a year or two in the 30s. Then the Depression caused everything to come to a grinding halt for several years. The 1920s and early 1930s were a great time to be in the loan brokerage business. Banks weren't covered by FDIC insurance and when one collapsed, money on deposit or invested therein was lost by the investor. Many wealthy men found lending money on real estate and trading in real estate notes to be a good risk because if a person defaulted on repayment, the lender was left with the property to resell or liquidate in some manner instead of nothing at all.

Quite a few wealthy investors trusted Father's judgment as to which property to loan money on. There was also a steady flow of investors needing cash asking Father to sell notes at a discount which is comparable to a certificate of deposit holder of today being penalized for early withdrawal of funds when in need of cash. Father was always able to find an immediate buyer for a discounted note.

During the course of a business day, Father conversed with many of his loan clients on and off the phone. By the time he was ready to leave the office at the end of the day, he always had a list of properties to inspect and appraise and be prepared to give an opinion on by the next day. The number of properties involved helped to determine the time at which he left the office.

When ready to leave the office, Father jumped up, grabbed his hat and called to me (when I was there), "Let's go!" I followed after him (having to trot a little now and then to keep up) to the car and then we were off, so to speak. Riding home from work with Father never entailed traveling the same route twice. Each one was different from the last. His manner of driving was highly unconventional.

He would be riding along and suddenly come to a grinding halt, sometimes in the middle of the street, oblivious to the cars screeching and honking all around him, as he just sat there wherever he stopped and made a mental appraisal of a piece of property and everything in its vicinity. He took note of the age, condition of the building, the yard and the improvements, such as fence, garage, the sidewalk, the street it faced and many other things. Many times I heard him say out loud, "This property isn't worth but so much because the neighborhood is too run down, or the yard is too small, and there isn't any fence, or there is no garage, or the house hasn't been painted in years," and on and on. I always thought it odd that he rarely, if ever, entered the house to look at the interior and its state of repair before placing a value on it. He seldom wrote the appraisals down as he had an unbelievable memory and was able to recall exactly what he had seen at each address. He didn't even always write the addresses down that he was going to inspect!

It was almost frightening to ride with him during the "inspection period" of the homeward trek, as he always just stopped wherever he happened to be when he came to the place of inspection. The only thing that he ever respected on a city street was that abominable streetcar, which caused every vehicle to stop anytime it did, period. But most of the appraisals were made in residential districts away from the streetcar tracks. In spite of his erratic driving practices, he never ever received a ticket or had an accident.

During those property inspections I became acquainted with all kinds of real estate in San Antonio. I saw all the railroad stations (Katy, Missouri Pacific, Southern Pacific, I&GN), all the cemeteries, the entire west side filled with small houses, and the north side with its mansions, and at that time I knew the general value of most of them.

Once a week Father stopped at the Bexar County Public Library to check out three or four books. I remember how overjoyed he was with the new library building on Market Street and all the books it contained. He said the new library was the biggest he had ever seen.

While checking out property west of downtown, Father frequently made a stop at the Market Plaza to buy fresh fruits and vegetables. I always trailed after him and watched as he sampled

DAY MORNING, JUNE 21, 1927 C 11

Young Ranchman Finds San Antonio To Be City of Golden Opportunity

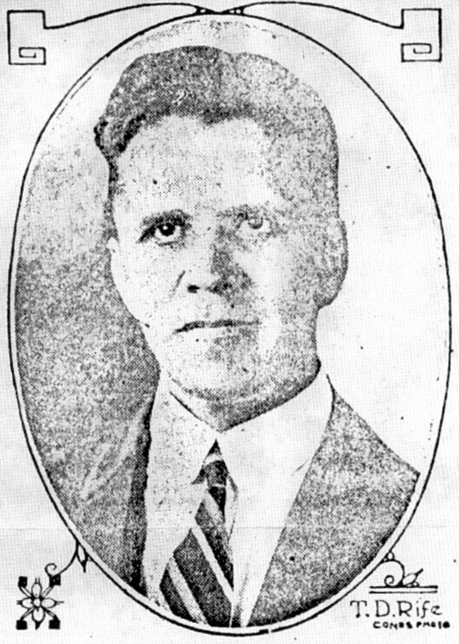

T. D. Rife heads growing Mortgage Loan business with satisfied clientele

STARTING in the real estate business in San Antonio in 1920 and six months later entering the mortgage loan field, T. D. Rife, progressive young San Antonio business man, has built up one of the most conservative and at the same time most prosperous businesses in the city, until today transactions handled by him annually total nearly $1,000,000.

Mr. Rife specializes on negotiating loans in sums ranging from $500 to $100,000 on residence and business property, vocant lots and farms. Practically all of the loans are made with private capital furnished by individuals in San Antonio and other Texas cities and in other states. In many instances the individual for whom he makes the loan never sees the property, relying entirely on their knowledge of his business ability and sagacity.

Besides his mortgage loan business, Mr. Rife buys and sells real estate. He also has an insurance department in connection with his business, handling all kinds of insurance.

The wonderful and steady growth of his business is best illustrated by statistics. The first year he was in business he negotiated only two or three loans a month, while now he closes from one to three loans per day. Last year he closed more than 300 loans, totalling almost a million dollars. The first three months this year he arranged loans totaling nearly $300,000 on San Antonio property and farms.

Loans arranged by Mr. Rife cover subdivisions,

Mr. Rife tells an interesting story of his reason for settling in San Antonio.

"I first came to San Antonio in January, 1919, after my discharge from the army," he said. "I had tried my hand at the cotton business and ranching. When I came to San Antonio I saw far greater opportunities on its paved streets than I could find in the saddle among the rocks and brush, so I decided that this

This clipping from a June 1927 newspaper shows that Father was indeed a prominent businessman.

the fruit, conversing with the vendors in Spanish as he made his way down the ramp. He then bought several bags of whatever was in season, all of which was consumed by the next week.

There were times when the last stop on the pathway home was a local dairy to pick up a newborn calf. That was not as much fun as it was an education on how dairies were operated at that time. All the cows were milked by hand twice daily, sometimes 30 or 40 at one dairy, in a couple of hours. It was a hard business. Then the milk was poured into 10-gallon milk cans, constructed especially for milk, and packed into the back of a pick-up truck and hauled and sold to a local creamery to be bottled and prepared for consumers.

One might compare a ride home from the office with Father with a thrill ride at a carnival — a thrill a minute, never a dull moment, and never the same route twice. Though it seems that I have painted a picture of my father as being a stern, strict, taskmaster with rigid rules he expected us to follow, and good habits he wanted to pass on. But, before leaving the subject of my Father, it behooves me to state that he also had a droll sense of humor and enjoyed doing things with his family around him. As I look back at the situation, I can see that the man who kept the domestic animal zoo and the one who ran the real estate office were in any instance really one and the same, the only difference being that they were attired differently.

Chapter Eight

Mother's Magic

While growing up, I spent a lot of time during the day with Mother in the kitchen watching her prepare some delicious foods, which were an integral part of her menus. There were magical things she did with eggs. It was a mystifying experience to observe Mother while she made the mayonnaise she served with meals and used in salads and sandwiches. I stood by the table and watched her break an egg, separate the yolk into a bowl, and put the white into a dish to use for something else later.

Then she took her rotary eggbeater (electric mixers were not in vogue for home use yet), and beat the egg yolk with a pinch of salt for about a minute. Next, she continued to beat it while adding salad oil in drops at first, and then gradually increasing the amount until one cup had been added. A little more beating found it just right. Last, she added lemon juice, beat it a little bit longer, and then put it in the refrigerator to chill.

The mystifying experience came with watching the egg yolk and salad oil gradually more than double in size, turn a beautiful creamy white color, get thick enough to spread, and finally become mayonnaise. I just couldn't understand how that little golden orange-colored egg yolk and that scant cup of clear salad oil could turn into a thick creamy white mayonnaise. Mother's homemade mayonnaise was delicious.

Mother wouldn't eat eggs unless they were disguised in cooked foods so she couldn't recognize them, except deviled eggs. Her aversion to eggs was a by-product of WW I. During the war there were long periods of time when the only eggs available in the grocery stores were what she called "cold-storage eggs." Mother said the "cold-storage eggs" were excess eggs, hoarded by producers during heavy laying periods, that were stored in commercial refrigeration to sell on the consumer market during molting season at an exorbitant price; all the fresh eggs during those poor laying (or molting) seasons were sent to the army. Some of the "cold-storage eggs" she tried to eat during one of those molting seasons tasted so bad that she never ate another egg again unless it was deviled with lots of mustard or cooked in something to disguise it.

Mother made homemade ice cream in an ice-cream freezer you cranked. First, she separated several eggs and beat the whites (with her rotary beater, again) until they were stiff. Then she set them aside while she put the basic ice-cream mixture of egg yolks, sugar, and milk in a pan and cooked it, stirring constantly until it almost boiled, then the beaten egg whites were folded in and it was cooked a few seconds more. The flavoring was added and as soon as it cooled it was ready for the ice-cream freezer.

The ice-cream freezer, which made about a gallon of ice cream at one time, consisted of a round wooden container with a metal can that fit inside. As soon as the ice-cream custard was cool, it was poured into the metal can and the dasher and lid were put in place. Father had brought home some ice to use in the freezer, which he had wrapped in a heavy quilt and set aside in a washtub until needed. He alternated layers of ice with layers of ice-cream salt in the wooden container all the way up and around the side of the can. The salt was necessary as it kept the water, which formed as the ice melted, from freezing. Mother said the ice cream wouldn't freeze until the water and ice around the freezer reached a temperature below freezing, and that salty water had to be a lot colder than 32 degrees for it to freeze. I wonder how anyone ever figured that one out. Every now and then I become aware of the fact that my generation isn't the first one to figure things out.

Once the custard was in the freezer and packed with ice and salt, it was time for someone like me to turn the crank making the dasher go round and round. I sat by the ice cream freezer many a time and turned that crank while Father added ice and ice cream salt.

When the crank was getting hard to turn and the ice cream was almost ready to eat, Mother added about one pint of whipped cream and then I cranked it a little longer and it was ready to eat. We almost always wanted vanilla flavored ice cream. There were times, however, when Mother made various flavored ice creams, like banana, peach, or strawberry. I have tried to make homemade ice cream, but it never did taste like Mother's.

The magic and excitement I experienced while watching Mother cook during the early days of my childhood will live forever in my memory bank of treasures, and I must say that I still experience some of it while I am cooking even today.

In the early 1930s, people all around us were becoming addicted to a soft drink called Coca-Cola. It was sold in a cute little hourglass-shaped bottle like the one still used today in isolated places.

Now and then in the course of shopping, we encountered a clerk, salesperson, or cashier who was purportedly having a "coke fit" and rushing to get a coke. I've actually heard several different ladies say they couldn't live without drinking twelve to fifteen cokes a day at least, maybe even more. They were very jittery and nervous. When Mother suggested they stop drinking at least so many cokes, they always replied that they had tried, but couldn't go without them.

From time to time, out of curiosity, I wanted to drink a coke and Mother always said, "No, it isn't good for you." She did, however, allow us to drink orange crush, root beer, and cream soda (once in a while) made by the Nehi Bottling Company on North St. Mary's Street. Mother's favorite soft drink was root beer. When she discovered that one could make root beer at home, she investigated the process and decided that she would try to make some. In a day or so Mother had all of the necessary ingredients, about four dozen reusable bottles, and a bottle capper assembled together in the kitchen. Then she got out the instructions and made the root beer. One at a time, she put a funnel in the bottles and filled them. Last she used the bottle capper to seal them. We thought we liked the root beer and for several years we consumed at least one "making" of root beer each summer.

One of those summers, six or eight bottles of that root beer got stored by mistake in the attic over the garage apartment. It was an unusually hot summer and one afternoon when it was about a hundred degrees, we suddenly heard an explosion from the general direction of the garage. While we were on the way to investigate the noise, we heard another explosion. The attic over the apartment opened into the garage and when we went in we looked up and saw the bottles of root beer exploding, one right after the other. Mother saw to it that root beer wasn't stored in such a hot place again.

Time spent with Mother was not only filled with magic, but also very rewarding, educational, and never boring.

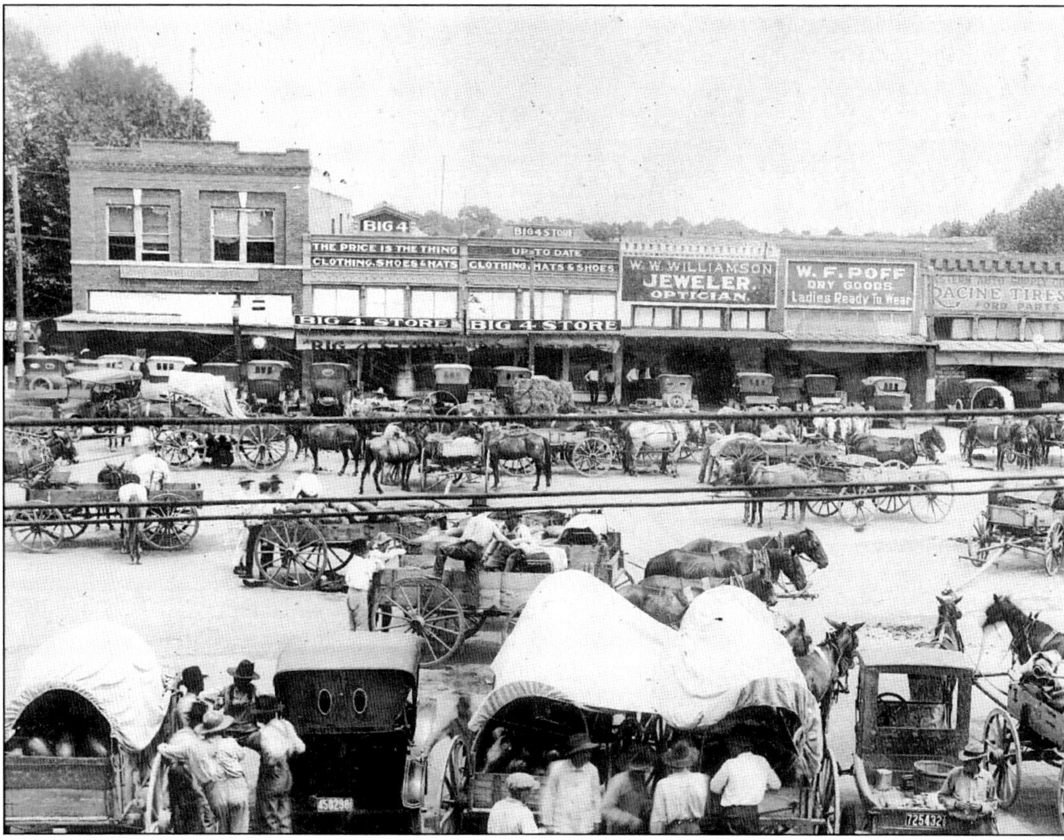

Mother grew up in Sulphur Springs. This is her hometown around the turn of the century.

Chapter Nine

Mother's Secret Ambition: Canning

Up until that point, life with Mother had been something like living in a restaurant, a bakery, a dress factory, a flower garden, a creamery, an ice cream factory, a handwork shop, a soft-drink bottling plant, a jelly and preserve kitchen, a laundry, a cat farm, and last, but not least, a master psychologist's office. You'd think that was all there was to be had from one small lady, but she was only getting started and all those things, except the cat farm, were to continue from then on with a few additions from time to time.

The next thing Mother added to her repertoire was the fulfillment of one of her long-time secret ambitions: home-canning. This endeavor began sometime after President Franklin D. Roosevelt took office in 1933. Among hundreds of other things, his New Deal called for information on pressure canning to be sent to home demonstration agents all over the United States to instruct people on how to can home-grown products in their own kitchens for consumption long after the growing seasons ended. By canning produce items purchased in the bulk at a lower price, and in both instances wind up with jars of food cheaper than those purchased in the grocery store.

In our economically depressed country where there was an overproduction of everything, this was supposed to enable people to have more food to eat. The theory was that farmers, especially, would be assured of something to eat year round, and that foods in season that would ordinarily spoil before they could all be consumed might be canned to eat later.

Mother rushed excitedly to the home demonstration meeting to learn more about home canning. Unlike most of the other women at the meeting, Mother's interest wasn't triggered with the desire to save money, but rather to fulfill her burning desire to can jars of various fruits and vegetables in her own home as she had seen for years at the Kendall County Fair.

The home demonstration agent stood up in front of the room and gave a talk about how the process worked. At the end of the discussion the county agent told everyone to come back the next week when she would actually can something in front of them. Then she gave out pamphlets to each lady present and adjourned the meeting.

I don't remember ever seeing Mother that exhilarated about anything before. She rushed us home and talked on and on to Father about canning and showed him the literature. All during the next week she looked over the canning instructions at every opportunity. Finally the week was over and we were ready to go to the canning demonstration.

As soon as all the ladies arrived, the agent proceeded to demonstrate the canning of snap green beans. She had about a peck of green beans already washed and snapped and she first put them in water and brought them to a boil in a large vessel. She then scalded six or eight-pint jars, lids and rims and left them in the boiling hot water until ready to fill. Next, she put an aluminum rack which came with it in the bottom of the large pressure cooker, added about four inches of water, set the cover on it loosely, and then placed the cooker on the stove to get steaming hot.

When the beans had boiled for about five minutes, she took a pint jar out of the steaming hot water, placed a canning funnel in it and with a large holey dipper she dipped the beans out and filled the jar, then she added 1/2 teaspoon salt, boiling water close to the top of the jar, stuck a spoon handle down into the beans two or three times to work out any air bubbles, wiped off the top of the jar, put a lid on it, and then screwed a rim on fairly tight.

Next, the cover was removed from the jar and placed in the steaming hot cooker. Then the cover was returned to the cooker until another jar was ready. This procedure was repeated with each jar until all of them were filled or the cooker was full. It held about eight or nine pint jars at one time.

Last, she put the cover back on the cooker, tightened it, made sure the petcock was open to let steam out, and turned the fire under the cooker to a desired heat. We talked and she answered questions while the cooker hissed out steam for about five or ten minutes through the petcock.

Then she closed it and we all stood around watching the needle on the pressure gauge on the top of the cooker slowly rise. When it reached ten pounds, she adjusted the burner heat to where it held that pressure.

When the 40 minutes were up, the fire was turned off and our hostess served us refreshments. By the time we finished our refreshments, the pressure had gone down in the cooker and it was ready to be opened. The agent then unscrewed the petcock to let any additional pressure out and next she unlocked and removed the lid from the pressure cooker, waited about 10 minutes more, and then took the jars of beans out with large metal tongs that had a rubber coating on the ends of them to keep them from slipping off the jars. She put them on a table to cool.

The agent told us to listen for a snapping sound that each lid would make when it sealed. Sure enough, in a short while we started hearing a loud "snap," then another "snap," and another, until all of the pints had sealed. She told us to check each lid by pressing the middle of it to see if it had sealed. If the lid was bowed-in and didn't click up and down when pressed, the jar was sealed.

We all paraded around the beans and checked the lids. They had all popped or snapped inward, and none clicked up and down when pressed and even though supposedly sealed, the agent stressed the fact that they should be kept out for observation and checked again in 24 hours, to be sure the seal had held. Then the rims could be removed and the jars of beans stored until time for use.

There they were, canned green beans, so pretty, all ready to store in the pantry until it was time to eat them. The agent reminded the ladies to be sure to boil home-canned vegetables for 15 minutes before eating them. Mother went home so excited I didn't think she could fix supper. I don't even remember eating anything that night, as I was excited too. Mother had been completely convinced that a pressure cooker was safe to use in her home and she wanted one. She rarely ever asked for anything, but that night she told Father she wanted one and almost had to have it.

Father looked over all the literature, listened to her description of the whole demonstration, and then decided that she was right, they should have a pressure cooker to can in. They agreed to go shopping for a cooker the following Saturday. We stopped at Toudouze's, Kallison's Country Store, Sears Roebuck, and then at Joske's, looking at various cookers. I remember that Mother had to decide between a National pressure cooker at Joske's and a Kook Kwick pressure canner made by Sears. Mother decided on the latter.

We bought the pressure cooker, two-dozen quart jars, two-dozen pint jars, and six or eight dozen lids and rims. We rushed home and Mother laid her new treasures out on the dining table and I walked around and examined and admired the shiny new cooker, its lid, rack and two large round pans about two inches tall made to fit in the cooker, and a few more things. For instance, she had some tongs to lift jars with, a dipper filled with holes and a wide-mouth funnel that fit in the mouth of the jars. I put some of the new crystal-clear glass jars with the word "Mason" embossed in the glass on the table and practiced lifting them with the tongs.

That afternoon, Mother went through the same procedure the home demonstration agent did when canning those green beans, and after the pressure gauge reached ten pounds, she experimented with adjusting the heat and holding the pressure there.

Mother was chomping-at-the-bit to can something and there was nothing to can anywhere around. It was Saturday afternoon and Father said he couldn't get her anything to can before Monday. Well, Mother looked through the instruction book that came with the cooker and lo-and-behold she discovered she could cook a large ham in the cooker in about 50 minutes. So we charged off to the grocery store and purchased a large ham.

Mother followed the instruction book and cooked the ham. Then she cut the outer-skin off and decorated it with brown sugar, cloves and pineapple and baked it in the oven for about 30 minutes. At suppertime that night we were enjoying fringe benefits from the pressure cooker Mother purchased to can in, before she had ever canned anything. The ham was delicious and Mother was temporarily satisfied. It looked like the ham would hold her in abeyance until Monday came and she got her hands on something to can.

Mother spent Sunday reading the instruction book that came with the cooker and a brochure she received with the mason jars she had purchased. I remember she read out loud to me a lot of things she was planning to do. For one thing, the brochure she received with the jars had recipes for making chow-chow, relishes and pickles. She declared right then and there that she was going to make pickles and relishes some day.

On Father's way home from work Monday, he went to the west side of San Antonio to the Market Plaza somewhere around Produce Row to get something to can. He bought six extra-large pineapples and came home.

Tuesday morning shortly after breakfast we started to can the pineapples. First they were washed in water and placed in the dish drainer to drip. Then Mother ran a large butcher knife and two or three paring knives through the knife sharpener. She then took the butcher knife and proceeded to cut one pineapple into slices about 3/4 inches wide. Then she took a paring knife and showed me how to cut the peeling off the slice, and dig out the black eyes which were about 3/8 inches deep, round, and scattered here and there about every inch or so on the outer surface of the pineapples just under the peeling. Mother then cut the remainder of the pineapple into chunks as she had decided against canning it in whole slices. At my insistence, Mother then agreed to let me follow suit and help get the pineapples ready.

When we had three pineapples cut into chunks, Mother decided she would grind up the other three as she wanted some crushed pineapple and, of course, she just wanted to see what it would be like when she canned it that way.

Well, I was beginning to think the pineapple business was quite a job and was ready for a change of pace that was hopefully a lot easier. Was it easier? Wrong, the pineapples she crushed were prepared at first just like the first three had been prepared and then Mother got her heavy cast-iron meat grinder out and put a medium plate in it and clamped it on her wooden kitchen stool and I started feeding the pineapple chunks into it and Mother turned the grinder. She put a large pan under the grinder to catch the ground-up pineapple, and then she had to rush to get another vessel to put directly under the grinder's clamp, as pineapple juice was running down the grinder to the floor as the pineapple was crushed through the grinder.

What a mess! There were sticky pans and kitchen utensils everywhere, two dish pans filled with pineapple peels and debris, bits of pineapple and juice all-around, on the kitchen table, the chairs, stool, floor, and eventually all over me. But Mother was undaunted, still going strong, while I was beginning to have serious doubts about the merits of home canning. The pineapple would certainly have to be to be very, very good to warrant all that furor.

When we finished preparing the pineapples, we had two large pots full and Mother could see there was enough pineapple to fill more jars than the pressure cooker would hold at one time, so she put the crushed pineapple aside to process later. Then she put the large pot of pineapple chunks on the stove in a medium syrup to boil about five minutes. She stirred it off and on and then used her dipper to put the pineapple in hot sterilized pint-jars (there were eight pints of chunks), filled them with syrup, stuck a spoon handle into the jars several times to work out air bubbles, wiped the jar top, added lids and rims and put them in her hot cooker, put on the cover, and followed the home demonstration agent's instructions to get the cooker up to five pounds pressure and held it there for 25 minutes.

Then Mother opened the petcock and proceeded to remove the cover from the cooker as directed. She then used her tongs and lifted the jars of pineapple out and set them on a table padded with newspapers to cool. It wasn't long after taking the first eight jars out of the cooker before we heard "snap, snap, snap," as each jar sealed. It was fun to stand around and listen for the "snap" and once or twice I actually saw the lid move inward when it "snapped."

As I stood there and looked at our pineapple, and saw the expression of joy and self-satisfaction on Mother's face, I decided this canning business might be worth the trouble after all, and trouble it had been, believe me. If the home demonstration agent had demonstrated the preparation and canning of pineapple instead of already-snapped green beans, "home-canning" wouldn't have been so appealing.

The next day Mother announced that she was going to the Market Plaza herself early in the morning to find something else to can. The following week we left for the Market Plaza directly after breakfast and Father followed us in his car on the way to his office. He didn't want Mother haggling with the various sellers alone.

Going to the Market Plaza was always an exciting adventure to me. An entire city lot was constructed with large elevated concrete ramps just tall enough to be level with the truck beds when the trucks were backed up to them. There were little concrete steps for the sellers to use to get up to the ramp at the back-ends of their trucks.

We walked up the concrete steps on one end of a ramp and started inspecting all kinds of fruits and vegetables that were for sale. There was truck after truck on each side of the ramp. They all had their tailgates removed and the sellers were standing on the ramp in back of their trucks trying to sell their wares. There were bushel and half-bushel baskets of the produce on the ramp ready for a buyer to purchase and carry away. They usually threw in the basket free. Father said most of them were buying for a small grocery store, a hotel or a restaurant or some other business house, and therefore purchased large quantities. The produce was only sold in the bulk, not by the pound, or piece.

The sellers greeted us, sometimes offering us a sample or taste of the items they were selling. Father haggled over the price, which generally got a little lower as we went along. We went down at least two ramps that day before Mother found a bushel of peaches she wanted to can. Father got the price down somewhat and bought the peaches.

Mother once again went into a state of exhilaration over the anticipation of fulfilling another one of her ambitions, canning peaches. First she scalded them in boiling water for a few minutes. Then she transferred them to cold water for a short time and finally she put them on cookie sheets to peel. There were peaches everywhere. By the time she had about one-third of them scalded and cooled, she decided to stop and peel them and get them ready to can. Well, I could see right away we were in for another mess; peach juice was running down my arms as I sat there doing my peeling and pitting and the peach peels were really piling up and we already had a large pot-full of peaches in medium syrup on the stove ready to boil. As Mother could only process six-quart jars of peaches at one time, she stopped peeling and went through the routine of filling six quarts and then processed them in the cooker for ten minutes at five pounds pressure. We went through this procedure three times and wound up with 18 quarts of beautiful peaches ready for the pantry shelf. In spite of all the uncomfortable mess, fruit-basket turnover condition of the kitchen, the time involved and the exhaustive energy exerted, I always found myself unable to stay away from the scene of activity and eventually wound up feeling very elated and proud of what we had accomplished.

Getting back to the peach business, it was enough to make a stouthearted person say "no more." One bushel of peaches is a lot of scalding, cooling, peeling, pitting, boiling, jarring and processing to do. Then there were the endless kitchen utensils to clean up and several containers of peelings and pits to dispose of. Of course, the entire kitchen had to be cleaned, as there was peach residue all over. Did that stop us? No, it just seemed to make us more determined to go on and to even look forward to whatever we might can next as a great adventure. After all, it couldn't get much more involved, or could it?

The next time we went to the Market Plaza we came home with one bushel of tomatoes and the procedure for canning them was almost the same as for peaches. We did this three times, for 18 quarts of tomatoes. The mess didn't seem to be any worse, maybe not as great, or was I just getting used to it? The pineapple, peaches, and tomatoes each took the greater part of a day to process. Mother had to find another place to store jars of food, as the pantry was full.

Mother and I had initiated our family in the home-canning business with pineapples, peaches, tomatoes, and corn, although any resemblance between our canning of those things and the agent's demonstration of canning snap green beans was purely coincidental. The only similarities at all were the filling of the jars and the operation of the pressure cooker. In later years, we found that green beans were by far the easiest thing to can.

Well, during the early 1930s Mother had certainly achieved one of her highest ambitions, home-canning in a pressure cooker. During the next two or three years of our tenure at Mayfield Park, she continued canning and cooking using the pressure cooker. But the things she did first that I struggled through with her, are the ones that stand out most in my mind. I might say further that I probably wouldn't remember all the details of those initial "cannings" if I hadn't stayed with it and helped her throughout all the ensuing years that I lived at home and even after that from time to time.

Chapter Ten
Making Tamales

The year Mother bought her cooker, the first cold spell blew in around the middle of November, and she immediately made elaborate plans to accomplish another of her ambitions—making tamales. Mother had gained a general knowledge of making tamales from discussing it with ladies who had made them. Her information wasn't too specific, but she came to the conclusion that she at least needed fresh pork, masa, corn shucks, and chili powder. Father said his Mother had always made tamales from the hogshead when his Father butchered a hog, so he was able to help Mother outline a procedure for making the tamales.

Once their plans were formed they proceeded to procure the necessary items. Father went to a store on the west side of San Antonio (I believe it was on Ruiz Street) and bought some masa and a bundle of shucks. Mother made arrangements with a butcher to pick up a large hogshead on a certain day. Then she invited Aunt Sissie and Mrs. Huffor to spend the day and take part in the tamale-fest. Mrs. Huffor said she was familiar with making tamales and couldn't wait for the day to come.

Tamale-fest day finally arrived; right after breakfast Mother rushed to the butcher shop for the hogshead and when she returned home she processed it in the pressure cooker with some water for about one hour at 15 pounds pressure.

We were all very excited, chattering, laughing and bustling around the kitchen and breakfast nook, all agog over our tamale-fest. The first thing Mother and her crew did was examine the dried corn shucks and remove any corn silks or other foreign matter. Then they put the shucks in hot water to stand for about an hour. Then the shucks were trimmed to be approximately the same size.

Next Mother put the cooked hogshead on a large cookie sheet and set it in the middle of the breakfast-nook table. We all sat around the table and picked meat off the hogshead until there was nothing but the huge bony skull left. Most of the meat fell apart when we took it off and we chopped up that which didn't. Next

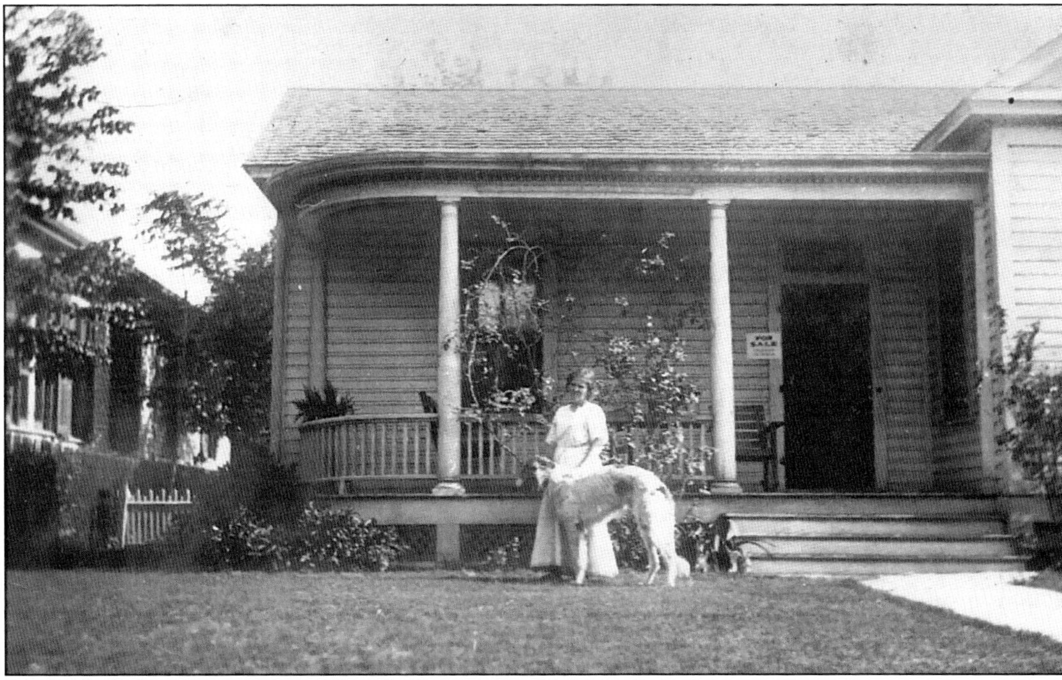

Mrs. Huffor, who took part in the tamale-making, was Mother's best friend. She was like a mother to me.

Mother put all the meat in a large pot and added chili powder and other seasonings, some of the broth the hogshead was cooked in, and put it on the stove to simmer for a few minutes. Then she added some flour to thicken it a little and turned off the heat.

Now to the masa. Mother put about eight cups of it in a large pot and added enough broth from the hogshead to make a thick dough, stirred in some melted fat, salt and chili powder, and continued adding broth and stirring it in until it was almost thin, but still seemed to have enough consistency to hold together.

Last Mother put another large pot with about three inches of water in it on the stove to simmer, Then she took a rack with very fine holes in it and found a way to elevate it in the bottom of the pot to keep it just above the water.

Now everything was ready by 11:30 a.m. or so to assemble the tamales: the masa, the meat, the shucks, the steam pot, and the crew to put them together. Mother handed each of us a plate and issued our instructions which went something like this:

Take a shuck from the hot water, trim it to about seven inches by four inches and lay it out flat on the plate.

Form a layer of masa about four inches by two inches by 3/8 inches in the middle of the shuck.

Spread about one tablespoon of meat mixture down the middle of the layer of masa, roll the shuck up on the masa and meat, sort of like rolling up a cigarette, and fold one end over to form a tamale.

Place the tamale folded end down on the rack in the steam pot.

We all started trying to put the tamales together. Was it as simple as it sounded? Absolutely not! The only thing simple about it was trimming the wet shucks and I wound up doing that for all three of them (Mother, Aunt Sissie, and Mrs. Huffor). I cut a shuck the right size and used it for a pattern, and didn't have any trouble keeping up at first because they had so much difficulty trying to handle that masa.

First it was too wet, then too dry, and finally after adding masa, and liquid, it seemed to be about right. I watched them trying to form it into a rectangle. They started out using a fork, then a spoon, and then a knife, all to no avail, and each of them wound up with her hands smack-dab in the middle of it trying to shape it.

There was masa squishing around here and there all over them, the table and eventually other places, too. There was either too much or too little. They were always adding or taking it away until Mother finally had hers just about right. She didn't leave it on the shuck though, instead she put it in a cup and found out exactly how much masa was needed. Then she put me to work measuring the right amount of masa onto each shuck as soon as I trimmed it.

After getting the right amount of masa on the shuck, the shaping was a lot easier and then it was time to add the meat mixture. They each scooped out a large tablespoon of it onto the masa and proceeded to spread it the length of the masa with a spoon, fork or fingers, until each of them found a way to do it comfortably. Next, it was time to learn the rolling-up procedure.

That was a tricky thing to do, rolling up that shuck without moving the filling over or spreading it towards the ends. After three or four rollings, they finally began to get the hang of it. Mother and Mrs. Huffor actually began to feel a little bit comfortable with the procedure, but no time records were broken that day. Aunt Sissie struggled through lagging behind all the time.

In spite of their slow start and awkward finish, they never did lose their exuberance for the "game," and finished with talking about how next time would be easier as they would know what to do.

As soon as they had filled and rolled about two dozen tamales, they had caught up with me and now and then one of them put her own masa on the shuck. When they were all assembled there were about twelve dozen tamales in the steam pot. Mother then weighted them down with heavy plates, put some large wet dish towels on top of them, covered the pot, and let the tamales steam on simmer for about two hours.

Finally the two hours of steaming was over and Mother unveiled our handiwork. She placed about one dozen of the tamales on a plate in the middle of the breakfast-nook table. We all grabbed eagerly for a tamale and burned our hands a little in the process of unwrapping it; we couldn't wait until they cooled to eat them. You might have guessed that the first bite was too hot to taste. After a short while we were finally able to savor the fruits of our labor. Those tamales were undoubtedly the best tasting things we had fixed yet with our pressure cooker.

From then on, tamale-making was a regular recurring event in our home. We usually made them once, and sometimes twice, each winter. Whenever we made tamales, there was always a fiesta-like atmosphere around our kitchen and everyone joined in making it a gala event for the entire family and any visitors who might be around.

Chapter Eleven

A Little Red School House

In September 1930, I started in the first grade at the San Jose School. It was part of the Harlandale Independent School District, and located on Pleasanton Road, about a mile and a half north of our home.

It was quite new, and could be described as a typical "little red brick school house." It had two classrooms on the south side and two classrooms on the north side, with rest rooms and hallways between the two sides. We had the same four teachers for most of the time I was in attendance.

The large playground was black dirt with a little grass. We had a tall slide and a round contraption attached to a pole in the middle that one could sit on and, after pushing it around to get started, go round and round and round.

There were several mesquite trees on the south side of the playground giving shade for us to play under. The older boys and girls played baseball on the nearby field.

Mrs. Bohanan taught the first grade. She was about my mother's age, brunette, rather attractive, and had a husband and at least two little children of her own. I always marveled that she could care for her home and family and teach school at the same time. I didn't see how my mother could possibly find the time to do that.

There are two things that I can thank Mrs. Bohanan for: the first involved discipline. Almost immediately I started talking to my classmates during class and Mrs. Bohanan told me to be quiet. I was quiet for a short while and then, there I was talking up a storm to my neighbor. The third time she stopped me, she made me stand in the corner facing the wall for the rest of the period.

The embarrassment and shame attached to standing in the corner was unbearable. I wanted to literally slip though the floorboards and disappear from view. It took me several weeks to forget and talk to my neighbor in class again. This time it only took once for Mrs. Bohanan to put me in the corner, but that was the last time ever, because from then on I

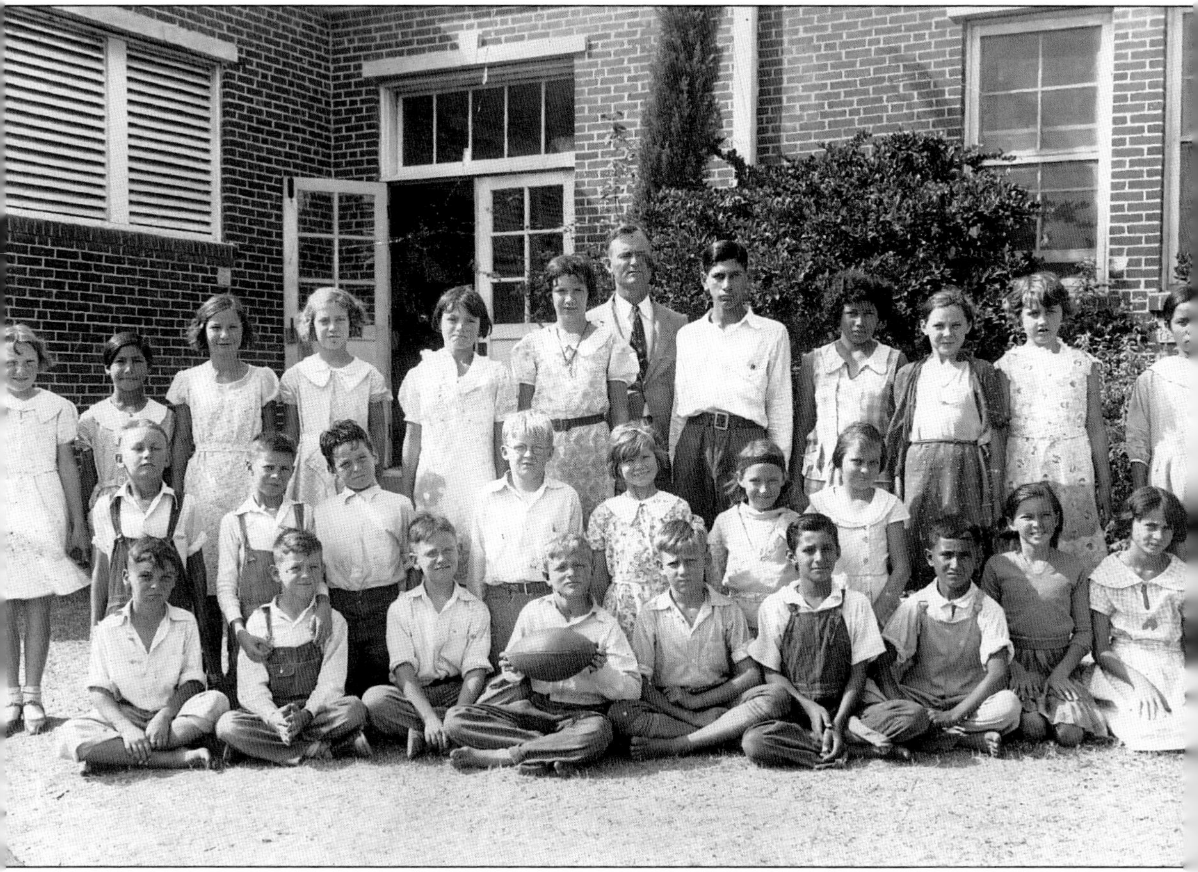

In this photo of my fifth grade class at Carroll Bell Elementary School, Mr. Bell is standing on the back row next to me.

conducted myself sufficiently to avoid a public reprimand.

The second thing Mrs. Bohanan did for me happened at the end of the first semester. She asked Mother for permission to promote me to the high second grade, as I already knew everything necessary for that level. Mother said, "I think that would be great. She started a year late and that would bring her up to date." Mrs. Bohanan said, "It's worth a try, but if she doesn't make it, she'll have to take the entire second grade over next year."

Miss Griffin taught the second grade. She was a very pretty blonde lady, who I remember as always taking us on a "nature hike" through 20 or 30 blocks of our neighborhood each fall and spring, examining leaves, flowers, insects, and other outdoor things.

Miss Griffin used to walk up and down the aisles waving a ruler as she passed desk after desk, inspecting our penmanship. We used old-fashioned penholders with removable pen points. When the pen point needed more ink, it was dipped into an inkwell. Even with a blotter in hand to blot my work now and then, I somehow managed to get ink on my fingers. By the end of the semester, however, I had learned to read easily and write passably anything I wished in longhand. I also managed somehow to receive a C average in penmanship, and have been trying to improve it ever since, but I'm sure it would never have pleased Miss Griffin. I had no trouble with the other subjects she taught, such as reading, arithmetic, spelling, etc., and at the end of the semester she passed me to the third grade.

When I was in the third grade, Miss Higdon taught both the third and fourth grades. She had brown hair and was very quiet and reserved. I wondered how she could keep up with teaching two grades at the same time in the same room. She had the third grade seated on the south side of the room and the fourth grade on the north side and we all seemed to learn very well.

Miss Bowen taught me in the fourth grade, and then Mr. E. Carroll Bell taught the fifth grade and was also our principal. An excellent teacher, he was by far my favorite.

I can recall the names of quite a few of my classmates, such as Violet Salazar, Constance Rosemary Marie Rowkowski, Mildred Holden, Frances Richter, and Albert Jackson, whose. father owned the Jackson Lumber Yard located almost across the street from the school. I really enjoyed my grammar school friends.

As I look back now, I can see there were things indicative of the Depression in various ways on the school ground that I didn't find relative when a child. For instance, children sometimes brought odd things for their lunches and sometimes no lunch at all. A few regularly had a sandwich, homemade cookies and fruit, but it was more common for a lunch to consist of only one sandwich containing one or two slices of bread with nothing but peanut butter and jelly or a dry slice of bologna between them. Mayonnaise and condiments were not taken for granted as they are today. Once in a while someone only had bread. It was not unusual to see a child shelling a hard-boiled egg to eat for lunch, and nothing else.

I was one of the lucky ones, as Mother managed to fix me a lunch of at least one sandwich. She also included a piece of fruit and most of the time two or three homemade cookies. She saved all the bread wrappers to wrap the sandwiches in. On rare occasions some of my classmates actually brought sandwiches wrapped in newspapers.

I never saw students starving or acting hungry. If they were, their pride kept them from letting anyone know about it. As I remember it, pride was the master of many feelings in those days, and took precedence over the pangs of hunger. Clothing was another matter. You could see just by looking if classmates were dressed adequately. Some had very few changes of outer garments. Shoes were always wearing out and many times I could see cardboard through the holes in the soles of someone's shoes if the wearer held his feet up accidentally. There were always several children who did not have coats or sweaters to wear on very cold days and pride took over again as they always insisted they forgot the garments, never letting on they were cold, and they didn't even own such a garment.

There were no school buses or any public transportation in Mayfield Park at that time and since most of the students lived within three miles of the school, they usually walked. Now and then parents brought their children to school in a car. I lived only about one mile from school; Mother usually drove me to and from school during the first two years, after that she considered me mature enough to walk by myself.

Being without shoes and warm clothing usually caused several students to be absent due to illness, on extremely cold days in the wintertime, as it was just too cold to walk that distance without proper garments. I don't remember any of us ever teasing a classmate because he or she didn't have this or that, or something didn't look or fit right. We had respect for each other in spite of our youth.

I have many treasured memories of the San Jose School, but my favorite of all is of Mr. Bell and the "general assembly" he held once a week. It lasted over an hour with the entire school attending. I loved those general assemblies; in fact I think everyone did.

To begin, one of the teachers played the piano to accompany us while we sang. Then Mr. Bell stood up and guided us through the Pledge of Allegiance, salute to the flag, and the singing of "The Star Spangled Banner." After that, Mr. Bell, with a baton in hand marking time to the music, led us as we enthusiastically sang one song after another from *The Golden Book of Favorite Songs*. (Copyright 1915, 1923, by Hall & McCreary Co, Chicago, Illinois).

We regularly sang patriotic songs, folk songs, religious hymns, holiday tunes, and several songs reminiscent of the various wars. I was fond of almost all of the two hundred songs in that book, but my favorites were "Home Sweet Home" and "Believe Me If All Those Endearing Young Charms."

The enthusiasm Mr. Bell exhibited while leading those general assemblies was contagious. We were all immediately singing out in loud voices filled with a sense of togetherness. In fact, the first time I saw Lawrence Welk (many years later, of course) cheerfully leading his orchestra on television, it reminded me of Mr. Bell and his lively, spirited leadership in those general assemblies. He was an all-around marvelous person and teacher who had a manner about him that instilled his students with a sense of individual importance and self-worth. Furthermore, he had a sense of humor that made him seem human to them. Mr. Bell exuded patriotism, Americanism and everything needed to insure good citizenship. The boys and girls I went to school with at San Jose School were for the most part very well-behaved, cooperative students. I thought Mr. Bell had something to do with that. I also thought years later, when I saw young American men and women anxious to fight and work for their country during WW II, that there must have been a lot of teachers like Mr. Bell in America. I feel quite sure he had a positive influence in the shaping of the character of the many young people he reached through his leadership as a teacher and principal. Twenty some-odd years later I found that the Harlandale

Independent School District evidently thought quite highly of Mr. Bell also, as they renamed the San Jose School the "Carroll Bell Elementary School" in his honor.

Chapter Twelve
San Antonio Parks and Missions

I actually felt that San Antonio, Texas, was indeed, my town. Not only was I born there, I have spent my entire life in and around that colorful city, which I love so much. I always refer to it as the "Alamo City" and am proud to have the Texas Shrine in my hometown. Many of the things I enjoyed about San Antonio are unique to that city alone. I remember quite a few of them very well from seeing them while joy riding on the way home from Grandfather Templeton's office. My favorite places to joyride were the many parks in the San Antonio area.

The first one that came to mind was San Pedro Park, which was about two miles north of downtown, between North Flores Street and San Pedro Avenue. It had a swimming pool and bathhouses with a large expanse of green lawns, shade trees, and picnic tables. On several occasions in the summertime, we stopped to watch the bathers swim and dive for awhile.

Next, Woodlawn Lake was practically surrounded by Josephine Tobin Drive, and was located four or five miles north of downtown. It appeared to be at the head of the Alazan Creek.

Woodlawn Lake was very pretty and quite large. In fact, it appeared to me to cover an area the size of four or five entire city blocks. There were white, gull-like water birds on it from time to time and now and then a small rowboat could be seen in the middle of the lake with a fisherman in it casting out his line, and later reeling in a fish or two. A small recreation building and boat dock were located at the north end of the lake. And a beautiful green lawn, which probably covered several acres of land, surrounded them. Even without the water birds and fisherman, Woodlawn Lake was always very picturesque to ride around because of the cattails and water lilies which grew in and around its edge.

A public swimming pool with bathhouses was located in Woodlawn Park on the southeast corner of the lake. A large recreation building in which community gatherings and other events were held was situated near the pool.

Then there was Roosevelt Park on Roosevelt Avenue, which was unique in many ways. It was only a mile or two from downtown. Brackenridge High School (once the largest one on the south side) was a block or two north of it on Roosevelt Avenue. It has long since been razed and rebuilt. There was once a branch of the Bexar County Library across the street on the east side of Roosevelt Avenue. Furthermore, the park actually fronted the west side of Roosevelt Avenue (a very busy city street) for a length of possibly one or two city blocks.

The main part of the park was accessible from Roosevelt Avenue by way of a paved road on the north side of the lawn area. Directly beyond the lawn, on the left side of the park road going west, there was a large public swimming pool with bathhouses, all of which were plainly visible to anyone driving by on Roosevelt Avenue. In summer months, swimming classes were held in the morning and the pool was always full of swimmers the rest of the day. With all its green grass, trees, and pool of water, Roosevelt Park felt like an oasis in the midst of the strife and hub-bub of the city traffic.

Beyond the pool, there were lots of tall trees and several different picnic areas with tables and benches. A very rustic, country-type paved road (the one that began on Roosevelt Avenue) wound through the picnic area and came out on the west side of the area on a small bridge, which crossed the San Antonio River. Roosevelt Park was and still is a peaceful place to visit.

Comanche Park was a good distance (probably four or five miles) east from downtown on East Rigsby Avenue. There was a stream of water running through it that I think was called the Salado Creek. The park was quite large, covering possibly 40 or 50 acres. There were lots of trees and a number of different picnic areas and types of facilities. I remember it had an extra large pavilion in it for private parties and large gatherings. I have special memories of office parties and Sunday school gatherings I attended there. I think the policemen held a barbecue in Comanche Park each year (in that era) as a fund drive event. The park was well equipped to handle gatherings numbering several hundred people, such as office parties, family reunions, and wedding receptions. A drive through Comanche Park just before suppertime on a summer's afternoon was very shady, peaceful, and woodsy.

Olmos Park probably included at least 40 acres, and had lots of tall shade trees, green grass, and picnic facilities. It was located in a very low place, four or five miles northeast of downtown. It only took an inch or two of heavy rain to cause the Olmos Creek to swell and run rampant through the park, temporarily flooding the roads, causing them to become impassable until the water ran off.

Adults of that era fully appreciated the importance of the Olmos Dam, because at least once during the early 1900s, heavy rains had caused the San Antonio River to flood, spilling into and inundating every basement in every building in the downtown business district with water. It also flooded many of the street floors of the stores. The damage was tremendous. Thus engineers proposed constructing the Olmos Dam to control flood waters and the city contracted them to build it sometime around 1920. It has served very well as a flood deterrent ever since. Businesses in the downtown area have not suffered to any great extent from flood damage since the dam was erected.

The dam also acts as an instrument of flood control for the surrounding area, and helps to keep the San Antonio River under control for many miles to the south during heavy rains.

Concepcion Park was different from the others in that it was located practically in the riverbed of the San Antonio River, just off Mission Road, on Theo Street, several miles south of downtown, making it about a mile southwest of Roosevelt Park. There were numerous native pecan trees throughout the park grounds, which probably consisted of about 30 acres, give or take a little. We occasionally drove on to Concepcion Park after leaving Roosevelt Park. One of the things I remember passing on the way was a large seminary called St. Anthony's. Many times we saw the young men walking around on the grounds, all dressed exactly the same with their hair clipped alike carrying prayer books.

My favorite parks, in every respect, were Brackenridge Park, Koehler Park, and the San Antonio Zoo, which altogether comprised close to 350 acres of land. They were located about three miles northeast of downtown between North St. Mary's St. and Broadway. As far as I was concerned they were one and the same park, which we always called "Brackenridge Park," or "The Zoo" as there was no distinction, to a child at least, as to where one stopped and another started. The gentlemen for whom those parks were named (Col. Brackenridge and Mr. Koehler) either donated or willed the land to the City of San Antonio to be used forever as a free public park where people could enjoy a bit of nature in the midst of a city. It was further stipulated that the park grounds would be free to the public and that no fee for their use would ever be charged by the city.

The park area was many times larger than any other park in San Antonio. There was a large public swimming pool with bathhouses, and three or four different main picnic areas, each with its own tables, benches, and outdoor cooking facilities. Hundreds of giant trees graced the picnic areas, which sprawled over about 30 or 40 acres of land with the San Antonio River winding throughout. The park also featured a roadway and bridle path through acres of natural forest-like brush and trees. It was also the home of the San Antonio Zoo, the largest exotic animal zoo in South Texas, maybe all of Texas at that time.

We generally entered the park from the west side by way of North St. Mary's Street, passing the riding stables on the way. Horses were kept there for people to rent and ride on the horse trail (bridle path) that wound on through the park several miles beyond the picnic area. The stables also rented bicycles for visitors to ride in the park.

The road through the picnic areas wandered around past the zoo, through first one picnic area and then another, coming finally to a place where the highway dropped down sharply to a water bridge crossing the San Antonio River, which usually had at least two or three inches of water flowing across it. There were several occasions when the water wasn't high enough to flow over the bridge, due to a drought.

The view from above as we approached the crossing revealed an inviting scene with the promise of a quick thrill for those riding over the bridge, especially a child. The water flowed over the road from one side to the other, between what appeared to be square solid blocks of flat rock. They were spaced approximately one foot apart on either side of the bridge so as to keep autos from running off the side and allow pedestrians to have a good sense of balance, a dry place to walk when crossing the river.

It was always fun and quite a thrill to ride across the flowing river. The water could be heard splashing and spraying out from under either side of the car as we rolled along. I couldn't resist the desire to stick my head out the car window and watch the "water show." Many times I dangled an arm out also, hoping it would get wet. Someone walking across the rocks on either side of the bridge while a car was crossing the river was in danger of getting splashed.

During the early 1940s my girlfriend Alberta and I rented bicycles at the St.

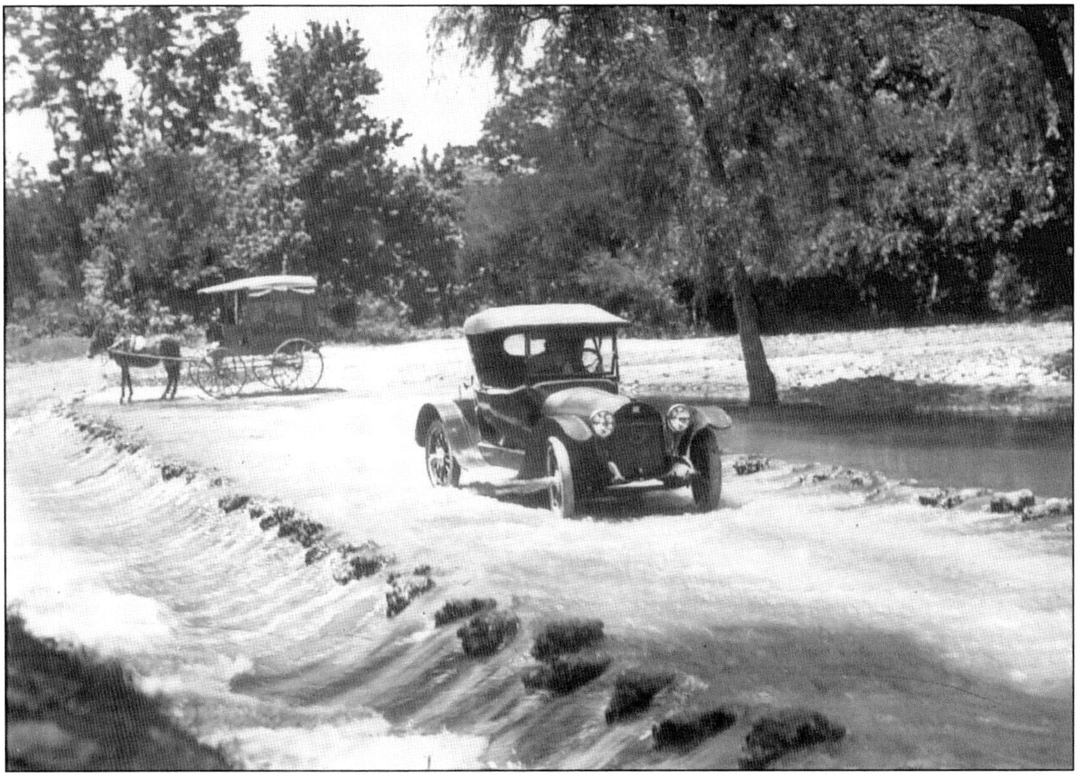

An automobile and a delivery wagon are pictured on a low-water crossing over the San Antonio River in Brackenridge Park. This crossing is still there today, and it's still a thrill to cross it! (Photo courtesy of the UT Institute of Texan Cultures.)

Mary's St. entrance of the park and rode all over the zoo and picnic areas. Then with some apprehension, we decided to go for a thrill and ride the bicycles across the water bridge. About halfway across, Alberta's bicycle slipped out from under her and she wound up sitting in the river with water flowing all-around her. The day was very hot and sunny, so she didn't stay wet very long. I was fortunate enough to cycle to the other side without incident. It was quite an experience.

When we left the picnic area on a joy ride, we would ride through the rest of the park on what appeared to be (even though it was paved) a rambling country lane which went through a densely wooded area, offering a glimpse of the bridle path with riders now and then. It was a ride through probably as many as several hundred acres of peaceful, picturesque, forest-like land, all the way across the balance of the park, coming out on Broadway, and back to the reality of the dense civilization and traffic of the city. The two gentlemen who gave that land to the City of San Antonio for parks would have been very happy with the way their gift had been handled and with the pleasure and relaxation the parks were giving to so many people.

Sometime during the 1930s, a large rock snake pit, about 16 feet in diameter and maybe ten feet deep, was built next to the Brackenridge Park grounds at the corner of Broadway and the Park Road.

A chain-link fence and a rock wall several feet high were constructed around it and it was stocked with up to as many as one hundred rattlesnakes at one time.

People paid a small admission fee for the privilege of walking around the enclosure and watching the trainers work in the pit with the poisonous rattlesnakes. Many of the spectators actually got a thrill out of the fact that the trainers were in great danger of being bitten. One of them was bitten on several different occasions by a rattlesnake.

Individuals from miles around were known to make a business of capturing rattlesnakes and selling them to the Rattlesnake Garden. A steady supply of rattlesnakes was needed to replace those being butchered on the spot, fried, and sold to customers to eat. I remember seeing people walk around eating a snake sandwich talking about how good it was, and how it tasted just like fried chicken. I wanted no part of that. I believe the Rattlesnake Garden has been gone from there for many, many years.

The San Antonio Zoo is always fun to visit in retrospect. I remember that during the 1920s, we actually rode through the part of the zoo where the animals were kept. But my clearest recollection of the zoo is from visits made there with my parents, Aunt Sissie, and with school groups. In any event, I loved to see the animals and the birds.

In the animal section there were monkeys, lions, tigers, leopards, zebras, bears, hyenas, wild dogs, coyotes, baboons, foxes, llamas, giraffes, exotic hogs, rhinoceroses, hippopotamuses, elephants for children to ride, and many more animals.

At the area where the bears were kept, there were bags of peanuts for sale which visitors could toss to the animals. The bears rarely missed catching a peanut in mid-air.

I spent a lot of time looking at all of the animals, and each one seemed to have its own way of entertaining me. For instance, the zebras would suddenly kick high with their back legs, for no apparent reason. The lions and tigers lumbered around their cages when they weren't sleeping. The monkeys picked bugs off each other, the baboons made loud squeaking noises, the hyenas screamed and the donkeys brayed. When we came to the elephants, it was time to stop for awhile and watch as one child after another was taken for a ride on its rocking, wobbly back. It didn't look to be at all comfortable. The rhinos were very large and mean looking, but the hippos were fun to watch. They had their own quarters with a bathing pool, and I looked forward to seeing them move around in the pool and spew out streams of water. The leopards were jet black and moved in a slow graceful manner, or were perfectly still. The area with the foxes, coyotes, hogs and wild dogs always smelled terrible. One of the prettiest and most fascinating animals was the giraffe. I spent a lot of time watching them.

The zoo also had an entire section of birds such as flamingos, ostriches, guineas, peafowl, exotic chickens, parrots, cranes, storks (which were supposed to bring babies in that era), and an endless array of small birds of every color and species imaginable. Most of my experience with the birds was with Aunt Sissie, who frequented the zoo regularly to see Mr. Stark (the zoo director) about her birds and ask him where to find a new bird to add to the bird collection in her backyard bird cage. He helped her find quite a few birds and if she had one she could not keep for some reason, she gave it to the zoo.

Near the birds, there were trained seals, or sea lions, kept in very nice quarters including their own swimming pool. At certain times during the day, the trainer brought out the seals and together they put on a free show. Among other things, the seals waddled across boards, dived in the water, flapped their fins, and caught the fish the trainers threw them after each trick.

Sometime during my childhood, I heard about the huge Monkey Island being constructed in the zoo, which, when completed, became inhabited by a large number of monkeys that sat around all day grooming one another and chasing each other around the island. Many spectators at the zoo spent quite a lot of time standing around watching and laughing at them.

The zoo kept adding more interesting animals for visitors to view, such as hundreds of beautiful tropical and exotic fish, and dozens of different varieties of poisonous snakes, including snakes almost as big around as a human and way too many feet long. The fish and the snakes each had their own temperature-controlled buildings, which were very pleasant to just stroll through in the summertime. I saw many different species of fish and snakes I had never seen or heard of before, but none as appalling as the giant snake.

After many years of admitting visitors free of charge, zoo officials decided it would be necessary to charge a small admission fee in order to continue to properly care for and feed the animals, because the cost of everything was getting higher all the time. Somehow the "powers that be" managed to sidestep the "no charge" stipulation made by the donors of the land, and from that time on the fee (which started at 25 cents per person) has been steadily rising to keep up with inflation. Entry to the park grounds is still free of charge.

There were two more points of interest in association with Brackenridge Park and the Zoo: the Sunken Gardens and the Japanese Tea Garden. They are located about two blocks west of the zoo, with an entrance on the St. Mary's St. side of the park, and on the north side of the Park Road.

There was no charge to enter the Sunken Gardens. They were also accessible outside of the park from a street on the open edge of a cliff, which constituted their north wall. Whenever we parked our car on that cliff, day or night, we got a clear view of the downtown business district of San Antonio. The view of the downtown area at night, with its lights all lit up, was very pretty. Next, we walked to the edge of the cliff and looked straight down about 30 or 40 feet onto the Sunken Gardens.

Viewed from above, it was easy to appreciate the artistry and the landscaping feat accomplished in creating them. There they were, a mixture of numerous pools and streams of water, sprinkled with green and white water lilies and other plants, accented with a maze of walkways and steps making their way over, around, and through the fish ponds and streams. Any part of the view that wasn't covered with water or walkways was landscaped with beautiful plants and flowers. The entire garden area must have taken up close to half an acre of space. The view from above was breathtaking.

The stairway leading down to the gardens was made of wide steps carved in the side of the cliff in a zigzag fashion. The bottom of the stairway was a manmade paradise of flowerbeds, sidewalks, mini-bridges, streams of water, and fishponds. My, those gardens were beautiful. Seeing the goldfish alone in the fishponds was well worth the walk down the cliff. They were brilliant colors of orange, black, and white.

The entire sunken garden area could also be enjoyed at night, because every wall, walkway, fishpond, and flowerbed was lit up. The sunken garden area was a charming place, especially when the water lilies and flowers were in full aromatic bloom.

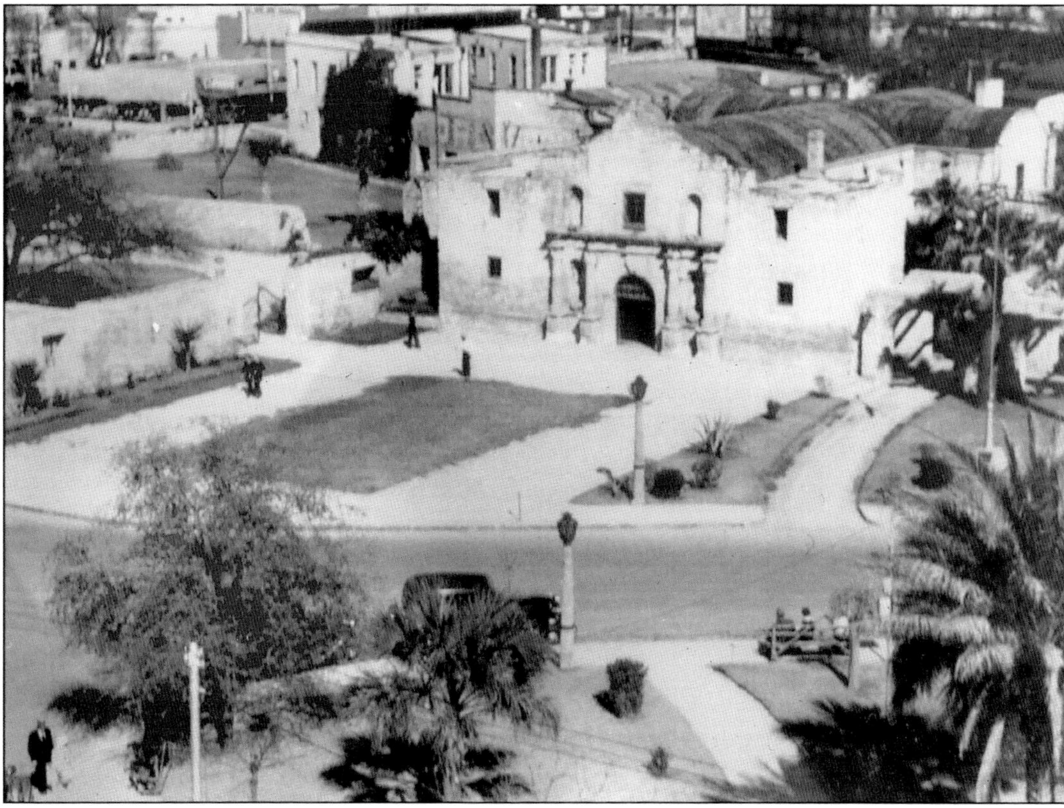

I always think of the Alamo as being a Texas shrine. This picture was taken in the 1930s, and it is exactly like I remember it when I was a child. (Photo courtesy of the UT Institute of Texan Cultures.)

San Antonio Missions

Ten of the missions built in Texas have managed to survive the test of time and are still standing today. Five are located in San Antonio: the Alamo, Mission Concepcion, Mission San Jose, Mission San Juan Capistrano, and Mission Espada.

I first became acquainted with those missions and started learning about them during afternoon rides with my grandparents. Then later, in school, we were taken on guided tours through them on several occasions. Touring the missions was considered "the thing to do" at that time (1930s). From a historical standpoint, every school child was supposed to see the missions that had been built so long ago. Their being Catholic had nothing to do with it. I wonder if school groups are still going on guided tours through the missions.

One thing I noticed that the missions all have in common is that, starting with the Alamo and going south, they are scattered along the banks of the San Antonio River.

The first mission, going from north to south, is the Alamo, which is located on Alamo Plaza, about one-half mile east of the San Antonio River. I never think of the Alamo as anything but a Texas Shrine, but it was indeed originally erected shortly after 1700 as a mission with the name of Mission San Antonio De Valero. Later it was converted into a fort and henceforth became known as the Alamo.

I have been through the Alamo and its grounds many times in years past. The historic documents and pictures on the walls are very impressive. The front of the Alamo is recognized throughout the United States as a symbol of the Texas Shrine, where so many men died for Texas's independence. It is also one of the most visited tourist attractions in the United States. The Alamo is open daily for visitors to tour free of charge, although many of the visitors make a donation that is used for the upkeep.

After the Alamo, Mission Concepcion is the next one I remember seeing as a child. It is a little over two miles south of the Alamo, just west of Roosevelt Avenue, fronting Steves Avenue. The mission is almost due west of and adjacent to Concepcion Park and about one-half mile east of the San Antonio River. Mission Concepcion has twin-bell towers, one of them being on each side of its frontispiece. The building was very large and pretty, as were the well-kept grounds. Sometimes we rode by Mission Concepcion on the way to or from Concepcion Park.

Now and then we drove past the San Jose Mission en route to the Mission Cemetery. It is about four miles south of the Alamo at the junction of Mission Road and Roosevelt Avenue, fronting Roosevelt, and about one-half mile west of the San Antonio River. San Jose Mission is very unique among the missions. Sometimes, it is even referred to as the Queen of Missions.

One window on the south side of the mission was finished with ornamental metal grillwork. It was so pretty we called it the Rose Window. Also, on the south side, near that window, I remember seeing several decorative carvings on the outside stone wall. The courtyard-like grounds were covered with grass, a few shrubs and a mesquite tree or two. It was a very peaceful and appropriate setting for such an important mission.

The chapel was quite large. After leaving it, I walked through the remainder of the building structure which included many archways, hallways and rooms, upstairs and downstairs, and then found a stairwell leading up to the tall, stately bell tower that crowned the front corner of the place. After that I went on toward the back of the mission and out to the backyard. That's where I saw the remains of the granary and storage areas for supplies and other things. The mission also had a long-since idle, water-powered gristmill for making flour. It was a very complete compound. Yes, San Jose Mission was by far the most impressive of the lot. I don't know what it is like today. I haven't been inside the grounds since the late 1940s, but I frequently pass it on the way to and from San Antonio, and it still looks very impressive from the highway.

Mission San Juan Capistrano is about six and one-half miles south of the Alamo, on Ashley Road and Villamain Avenue, on the east side of the San Antonio River. It has a triangular shaped triple-bell tower, directly over the chapel door, with a bell on the top, and the other two evenly spaced on either side beneath it, forming the triangle. The mission building sprawls out on one side of the frontispiece and includes a chapel and several large rooms. The remains of a courtyard were conspicuous here and there on the green lawn that covered the outer perimeter of the mission.

Mission Espada is just south of Southeast Loop 410 on Espada Road, making it a little over a mile due south from Mission San Juan Capistrano, and seven and a half miles south of the Alamo. It is on the west side of the San Antonio River and has the same type of triangular-shaped bell tower over its chapel door as Mission San Juan Capistrano.

I am glad our forefathers had the presence of mind to maintain and preserve those missions. It is good to see structures from our past spelling out a historical account of times long gone. I have been told that one can still go on guided tours through the missions when they are not in use for special occasions. Several different events are held at the San Jose Mission more or less on a regular basis that tell the history of all the missions.

Whenever I went on a tour of the missions, it always included the Spanish Governor's Palace, located in downtown San Antonio due west of the City Hall. When I visited, it was in excellent condition in spite of the fact that it was possibly over two hundred years old.

The Governor's Palace was a fascinating place to visit. It was a large, square, stucco-like white structure, with several of its rooms opening onto a large courtyard on the west side of the building. The courtyard was laid out with flowerbeds and had several walkways winding around among them. It was my impression that the large trees in the courtyard were mesquite or oaks. Inside the Palace one could see chairs, beds, tables, linens and other things of the same period of that when the governor lived there. The furnishings were sparse, but very authentic looking.

I always looked forward to and enjoyed a tour of the missions, even if now it is only in memory.

Other Points of Interest in San Antonio

Beyond a doubt, the parks were my favorite places to remember, but by no means were they the only ones. There are quite a few military installations in and around San Antonio, which I visited many times throughout the years, first with my grandparents, and then with my parents, and later with friends. I watched most of them grow from almost nothing into large prestigious installations and also noticed them change the last part of their names many times to keep up with government changes.

One of the most impressive was Randolph Air Force Base. The ride to and from it was by far the pleasantest of them all. The route we used was north of downtown on the Austin Highway. The trip was, for the most part, out in the country. When we entered the airfield, the first thing in view was a large oval-shaped brick building (I think it was brick) with a long rectangular extension of offices jutting off one side or the other. A tower with windows all-around it from which someone directed incoming and outgoing airplanes projected high up in the air over the oval building. There were landing strips in front of the building. On several occasions, we were privileged to watch an airplane either take off or land. The size of the planes was awesome to me as a child, but by today's standards, were only the size of toys. Even if we didn't see an airplane, the rural country-like ride to Randolph Field was, in itself, worth the trouble.

Randolph AFB is still a flight-training center, training experienced officers (pilots) in the use of the most modern up-to-date military aircraft.

Lackland Air Force Base was the next installation, located about ten miles southwest of San Antonio. It served as a training station for cadets who were preparing to become pilots and officers in the air force. My earliest recollection of Lackland Field was that after riding out in the country some distance, we came to a row of wooden, frame, barracks-like buildings, office buildings, hangars, and airstrips. Once or twice we saw the cadets going through some kind of exercise or drill on an athletic field.

Each time we returned, it was interesting to find that the air base had grown a little. One day, we noticed that a huge hospital was under construction on the north side of and adjoining Lackland AFB. We made trips at different intervals over a period of many months before we finally found the construction completed. It was quite an impressive building. Today it is known as Wilford Hall Hospital.

Kelly Air Force Base, was located only about seven or eight miles southwest of San Antonio. It was due east of and adjoining Lackland AFB. It started out as an airstrip, a small hanger, and a few other buildings during WW I. One of my earliest recollections of visiting Kelly AFB was to see the large airplane hangar Uncle Arthur's (Father's brother) construction company had built, sometime around 1930. It was just a huge building that seemed to go on forever, with giant doors .

Other than airstrips, a few airplanes and some small buildings, there wasn't much more to attract my attention or make an impression on me at that time at Kelly AFB. Little did I know how large and important Kelly AFB was destined to become. It is now a major supply, maintenance and repair center for all types of aircraft used by the military.

Brooks Air Force Base was only six or seven miles southeast of downtown on what is now known as Southeast Military Drive. It was named for the son of my grandfather's law partner, Judge Sidney Brooks.

When I first saw Brooks AFB, it was just hangers, airstrips, and some small buildings. Many times I have sat in a car parked on the Old Goliad Road, on the east side of the airstrip, and watched airplanes land and take off.

Each air force base has its own purpose, neither one duplicating another. Lackland AFB trains cadets to be flight officers; Randolph AFB is manned with trained flight officers and equipped with modern aircraft; Kelly AFB maintains and repairs all types of military aircraft; Wilford Hall General Hospital, USAF, furnishes medical treatment and care for air force personnel, and Brooks AFB is involved in medical research for the USAF and NASA.

All of the military installations in and around San Antonio were interesting, but my favorite was the army post and Quadrangle at Ft. Sam Houston, the one and only army base in the midst of all those air bases. It is located only a few miles northeast of downtown.

Unlike the air bases, Ft. Sam Houston had probably been around since well before the turn of the century. This you could tell at a glance from viewing the very old two-story brick and wood enlisted men's barracks while riding north on New Braunfels Avenue; their architecture definitely dated them.

My favorite part of Ft. Sam Houston was the old Quadrangle area at the entrance to the fort, on the corner of East Grayson Street and North New Braunfels Avenue. It covered an area at least as large as an entire city block, on the northwest corner of the intersection, and was semi-enclosed with a rock-like wall. As soon as I realized we were heading for the Quadrangle, my excitement and anticipation started to rise, and I looked forward with high hopes of seeing the peacocks and the deer that were lived on the grounds. It was always a thrill to see three or four peacocks strutting around with their tail feathers spread out, stalking a peahen or just prancing around. Now and then a deer could be seen foraging on the green grass lawn, or scampering to conceal itself behind a rock fence. Also, there was a large building in the quadrangle with horse stalls in it where horses were quartered. Sometimes I actually saw a soldier riding one of them.

The San Antonio General Depot was across the street from the Quadrangle, on the east side of North New Braunfels Avenue. It was the Quartermaster Supply Depot for military installations in Texas, New Mexico, Arizona, and other places on request. The depot consisted of a large two-story office building and numerous

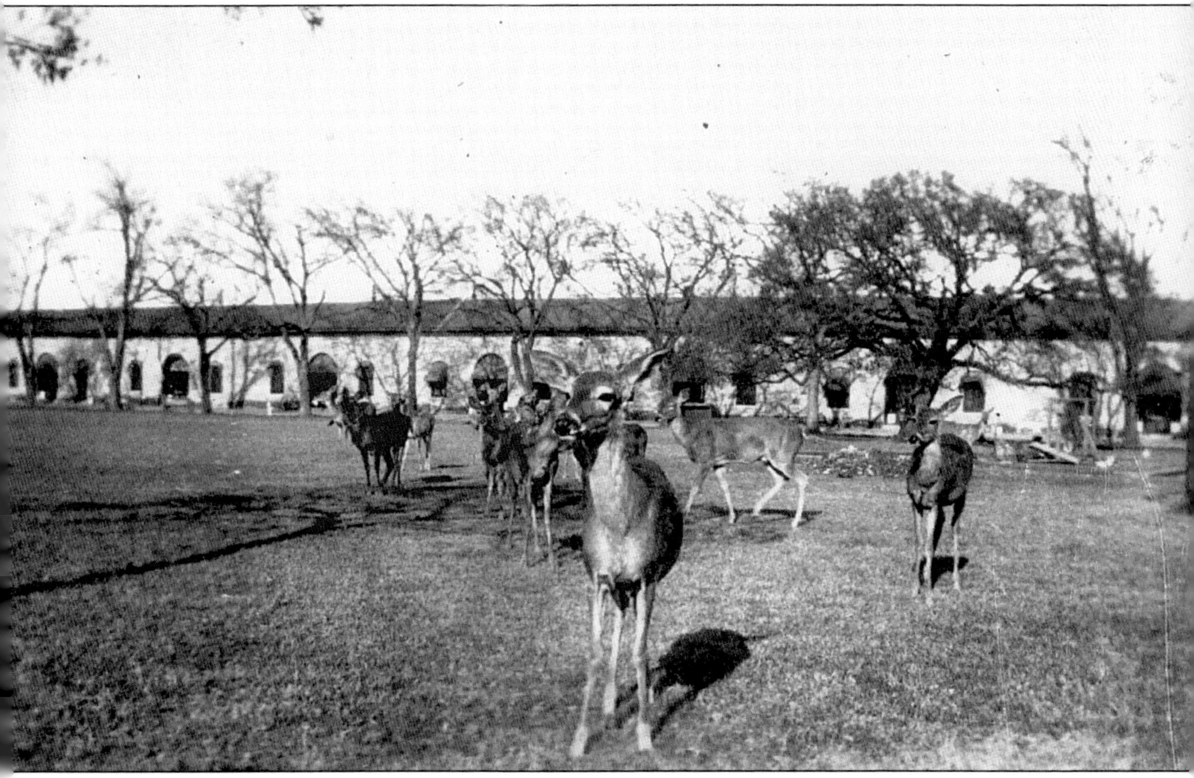

The Quadrangle at Fort Sam Houston was one of my favorite places.

giant warehouses filled with all kinds of Quartermaster supplies that really didn't mean much to me as a child.

Last, there was Camp Bullis, which seemed to be a storage place of ammunitions and the site for maneuvers for various units of the reserve corps. It was about 20 miles north of San Antonio on the corner of NW Military Highway and Wilderness Trail. I have been there several times. The drive took us way out in the country, and the grounds approaching, in and around Camp Bullis, reminded me of a large natural park. We also had the bonus of seeing wildflowers in the summer and colored leaves in the fall, during the ride.

Up until 1947, the San Antonio Arsenal located off South Flores near the Katy Depot, was the repair depot for the maintenance and storage of precision instruments related to all kinds of artillery items. Some of which were binoculars, range finders, watches, clocks, and all sorts of heavy artillery end items. The ammunition for those items was stored north of San Antonio somewhere in the vicinity of Camp Bullis.

The unpretentious arsenal building was situated in the middle of a fenced-in block and offered no interest to me other than a feeling of security that the military bases aforementioned had access to artillery and ammunition if needed. (Or so I thought as child.) The San Antonio Arsenal was closed in San Antonio in 1947 and its operations transferred to Texarkana, Texas.

All those military installations (except the San Antonio Arsenal) are still in San Antonio today and remain very active. All are many times larger, very modern and up-to-date, notwithstanding the fact that the ancient barracks at Ft. Sam Houston on New Braunfels Avenue are still standing as well as most of all of the original structures on all of the bases. The huge hangar my Uncle Arthur built long ago at Kelly Field is now used as a workplace for repairing aircraft parts.

We frequently passed schools and colleges on our rides, and Grandmother always pointed them out to me. I remember the Central Catholic High School (CCHS), Texas Military Institute (TMI), and St. Mary's Academy. Each one had a ROTC unit. Many times we passed by one of those schools when a drill team was in uniform on the athletic field going through various drills and maneuvers.

On several occasions we drove to the Peacock Military Academy for the sole purpose of our watching an exhibition of drills and maneuvers by the ROTC drill team. It was fascinating to watch the young teenage boys, all immaculately groomed and dressed alike in their perfectly fitted military uniforms. They performed precision drills, one after the other.

The other high schools I remember from childhood are Main Avenue High School, which was downtown on North Main Avenue; Brackenridge High School, about one and a half miles south from downtown on Roosevelt Avenue; and Harlandale High School, five or six miles south of downtown on South Flores Street. Sometime around 1930, my parents took me out to see the new elite high school being built on the north side of San Antonio, Jefferson High School. It really was a beautiful building, with architecture resembling that of an Arabian palace more than a school building.

As far as schools of higher learning are concerned, the first two that come to mind are Catholic: Incarnate Word College and Our Lady of the Lake University. Nuns or sisters operated them. Incarnate Word College was northeast of downtown, on the corner of Broadway and Hildebrand. The building was an impressive red brick structure about four floors tall. But Our Lady of the Lake University, on the west side of Elmendorf Lake, facing 24th Street, was the one that overwhelmed me. It was way out Commerce Street, due west of downtown San Antonio. The university buildings were quite large and architecturally designed in such a manner as to exude old-world charm. Since it was a Catholic university, we frequently caught a glimpse of nuns walking around the grounds in their long, black flowing robes and habits. Their appearance always filled me with a sense of awe.

St. Mary's University was also Catholic, located in a large complex of buildings on the northwest side of San Antonio. Trinity University was located on the northwest side of San Antonio at that time, in a very old but well-preserved building. It was quite small compared with what it has become today in its new location on the north side of San Antonio.

San Antonio Junior College, which was somewhere around South Alamo, was later moved to the San Pedro Park area and became the very large and prestigious San Antonio College (SAC) of today. It really wasn't very large at all when it was in the South Alamo area.

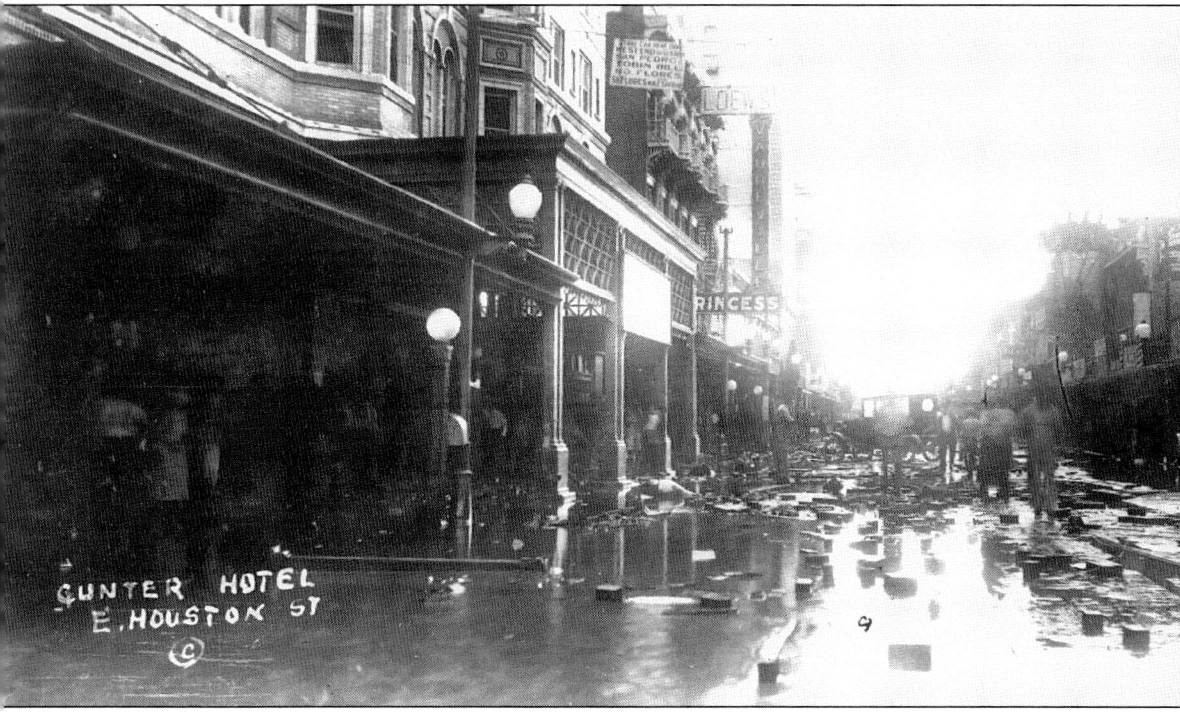

This photo, looking east on East Houston Street after the catastrophic 1921 flood, shows the devastation that resulted in downtown San Antonio. (Photo courtesy of the UT Institute of Texan Cultures.)

Chapter Thirteen

Downtown

As previously mentioned, I loved the parks, missions, military bases, schools, and residential districts in and around San Antonio, and was also familiar with most of its other desirable, as well as unsavory parts, all of which included just about everything in the vicinity of the city; but by far my favorite part of the city was downtown.

The layout of the downtown area (and other parts of town also) seemed to have been derived at as an afterthought, without any set plan, as many of the streets were crooked as a dog's hind leg, curving and weaving back and forth, with places of business constructed on either side. When I inquired of old-timers as to why the city had so many rambling, weaving streets, I was told they originally were cow-trails, made by cattle winding their way in bovine fashion (never quite in a straight line) one behind the other, on their daily trek to the San Antonio River for water. It seems that the town built up gradually over a long period of years on either side of the cow-trails, as the animals would have tried to follow their self-appointed pathway in any event.

There was never anything dull or boring about the shopping district of San Antonio at that time. The main retail area was located in and around four or five blocks on Houston St. and two blocks on Alamo Plaza. It contained at least five major department stores (Wolff & Marx, Frost Bros., The Vogue, J.C. Penney's & Joske's); six dime stores (Grandsilver's, McCrory's, Grant's, Kress', Neisner's, and Woolworth's); two expensive shoe stores (Zimmerman's & The Guarantee); six or eight inexpensive shoe stores (Irving's, Carl's, Chandler's, Burt's, Baker's & Allen's); probably 10 or 12 inexpensive ready-to-wear clothing stores (Peyton's, Grayson's, Lord's, Mode-O-Day, Franklin's, Mangle's, Arvin's, The Fashion, & Ewing's, Three Sisters, Lerner's & Jean's); a number of men's shirt and tie shops and two or three men's clothiers (Pincus Co., National Shirt Shop, Fomby's and Stein's); several leather goods and luggage stores (San Antonio Trunk Co., & Fentiman's Trunk Co.); numerous small novelty and gift shops and two or three pawn shops whose names escape me; six or seven drugstores (three Sommer's, Medical Arts Drugs, Brady Building Drugs & Walgreen's); three or four stores that made candy on the premises (Mexican Pecan Candy Store, Martha Washington Candies & Russell Stover); countless cafes, restaurants, and a delicatessen; a button and lace shop; a tailor's supply house; sporting goods stores (Wright Sporting Goods, C&S Sporting Goods & Potchernick's); music stores (San Antonio Music Co. & Thos. Goggins); three office supply houses (Paul Anderson Co., Clegg Co. & Maverick Clarke); a medical supply store; some grocery stores (one was Piggly Wiggly); and the list goes on and on. In addition to these stores and shops, there were four major hotels (Gunter Hotel, St. Anthony Hotel, Bluebonnet Hotel & the Menger); ten or twelve large office buildings (the Moore Building, Maverick Building, Brady Building, Bedell Building, Texas Building, Majestic Building, Nix Hospital & Office Building, Medical Arts Building, the main U.S. Post Office & Federal Building, and two or three more whose names escape me); several banks (Bexar County National Bank, Alamo National Bank, National Bank of Commerce, Groos National Bank & Frost National Bank); and five or six theaters (the State, Texas Theater; Majestic Theater; Aztec Theater, and Palace Theater, and in the 1920s, The Strand). Just about anything a person needed or wanted could be found somewhere in the downtown area. Why, there was even the Alamo to walk around and admire when a shopper wanted a change of pace, and I mustn't forget the riverwalks, which were under construction in the late 1930s, where one could temporarily escape the hustle and bustle of the city.

There were many picturesque little idiosyncrasies about downtown San Antonio that fascinated me as a child. Some of them might have been found in other cities, but I only knew of the ones in "my town."

One of my earliest and most unique memories, is of a huge horse-drawn wooden wagon, filled with ice, lumbering its way up or down Houston Street and alleyways, with ice water from melting ice trailing behind it as it delivered ice to lunch counters, cafes, hotels and restaurants. As soon as the ice wagon stopped, the iceman grabbed a chunk of ice with his tongs and carried it into a place of business. Sometimes he used some kind of a trolley to deliver several hundred pounds of ice at once. Between stops, the horse moseyed along, clippety-clop, clippety-clop, clippety-clop, up and down the city streets and alleys, always seeming to stop automatically at the next point of delivery. Now and then the iceman could be seen standing in the moving wagon, separating blocks of ice with an ice pick, in order that he might make delivery as soon as the wagon stopped. There were times when I noticed two icemen carrying ice from the wagon at the same time.

It was for many years the only horse-drawn vehicle on the streets of San Antonio. I was told that the ice plant, being only about eight or ten blocks from the main downtown area, and having the wagon and trained horses still on hand from pre-auto days, found it easier for all concerned to deliver the ice with them rather than a motor-driven truck. For one thing, the horses "ran" themselves, whereas delivering ice in a truck would create the necessity of starting and stopping an engine over and over again; there were probably 20 or 30 deliveries in the space of a few blocks on Houston St. alone. Also, the iceman, being able to direct the horses from the sidewalk or beside the wagon,

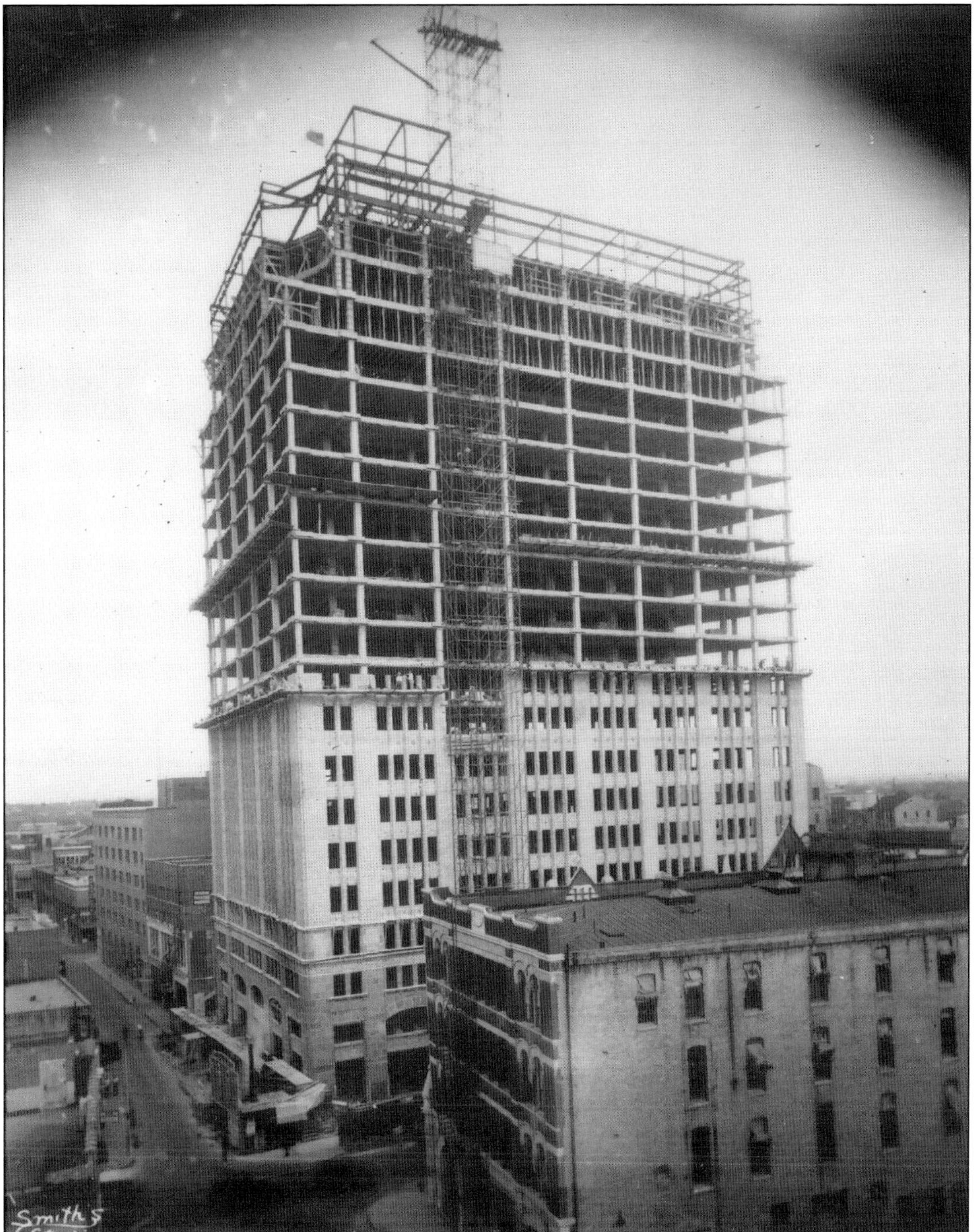

The Nix Building was under construction at the time of this photo, which was about 1930. (Photo courtesy of the UT Institute of Texan Cultures.)

didn't even have to board it between making deliveries, unless he so desired. It seems to me those horse-drawn ice wagons were used until well up into the late 1930s; they might have even been used during WW II to save on tires and gasoline for the war effort.

The next thing that comes to mind, which wasn't as unique as it was indigenous of that era and could probably be seen in cities everywhere at that time, is the "lamplighter," as I called him, making his daily rounds. The stores and shops were all closed for the day by 5:30 p.m., while it was still daylight. Many is the time I have been downtown just before dusk and watched as the lamplighter strolled down the street swinging a long stick. As he came to each place of business, he stopped, raised the stick up to the top of its entranceway to a switch, flipped it on, and lit up showcase windows filled with displays. He flipped a light switch on each business house, leaving behind him a brightly-lit array of various kinds of merchandise to tempt window-shoppers into returning the next day to purchase it. In that era, nighttime window-shopping was a popular pastime with theater-goers, as they made their way to and from the movie houses.

As the lamplighter came to the streetlight on each corner, he raised his stick up to a switch on the lamp pole and turned it on also. He walked the distance of the downtown area lighting up one side of the street and then crossed over to the other side and lit it up also as he made his way back to where he had started. Those lights remained on until sunup the next morning, when the lamplighter returned and reversed the operation, turning all the lights off.

Regular shopping trips with Mother were instrumental in acquainting me with the downtown area. Every month or so I enjoyed a shopping excursion with her that "covered the waterfront," so to speak. Actually, Mother never had any reason to make many purchases as she sewed all our dresses and most of our other clothing and she absolutely refused to buy anything she did not need. But now and then she went in search of a particular item, such as shoes for one of us, a special gift for one of my grandparents, or piece goods to sew our clothing and linens from. We took full advantage of those trips to "shop around" and look at as many things as we could along the way. In fact by 1935, "shopping around" had become a national pastime for thousands of women all over the United States. This was especially true as so many shoppers were short of funds due to the Depression and just wanted to be near, look at, touch, and even try on, pretty new things, whether they could afford to buy them or not.

A few days before Christmas, Mother decided we could go downtown on a shopping spree for the first time in almost six months. We were all immediately filled with excitement about taking an excursion through the entire retail district of downtown San Antonio. I knew it would follow the same general pattern as always.

On shopping day, Mother saw to it we ate an early lunch and were ready to leave home by 11:30 a.m., intending to return home by 5:00 p.m. The ideal place to start was at Wolff & Marx, which we considered "the beginning," it being the first and only store on the western-most block of the Houston St. shopping strip.

Wolff & Marx was a large department store with four or five floors of merchandise. It covered the entire south side of a very short block (between Main Avenue and Soledad), extending all the way back to an alley south of the store. The only thing on the north side of Houston Street in front of it was a parking lot.

My sisters and I trailed along after Mother through Wolff & Marx, looking at anything that interested us along the way. Of course, Mother enjoyed the "in-store window-shopping" also. First we looked

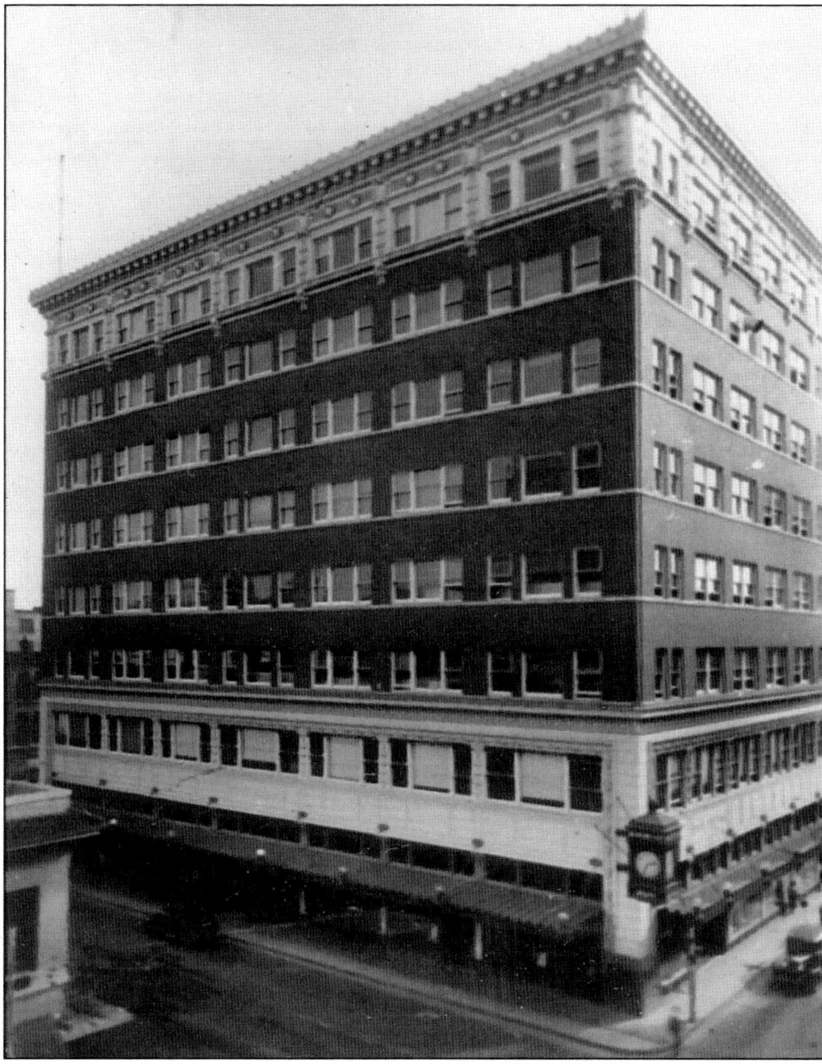

The Rand Building, home of the fantastic Wolff & Marx Department Store, was generally the first stop we made on our downtown shopping trips. (Photo courtesy of the UT Institute of Texan Cultures.)

over the cosmetics, frivolous lingerie, jewelry and shoes, and then rode the elevator to the second floor and examined another assortment of other brands of more down-to-earth lingerie and foundation garments. The next stop was the third floor and ladies ready-to-wear clothing, all of which were rather expensive name-brand items. Mother looked at the ready-made dresses to get ideas for sewing projects. After that came the fourth floor with piece goods, notions, and another large shoe department filled with all kinds of expensive shoes. The piece goods department was Mother's and my favorite place to browse through. Mother and I always spent too much time admiring the expensive bolts of fabrics priced way too high to enjoy sewing, and then Mother wound up at the remnant counter, where everything was marked down half price. Now and then she found something for some dresses. I always managed to look over the expensive shoes on the way out.

We followed that same general routine in most of the other department stores as we came to them.

If we could spare the time, the next stop was Solo Serve on Soledad St., across the alleyway southeast from the backside of Wolff & Marx. Solo Serve was our favorite shopping place. Without even realizing it, we could spend half a day there going through table after table of mill-end remnants and seconds of piece goods, which were separated price-wise into three or four categories according to their quality, length, and amount of damage on each, if any. In addition to many women who were very poor and there to save money, Mother and I found ourselves scrounging around, elbow to elbow, with lots of rich and elite ladies of San Antonio, who, like ourselves, also received a "high" from the experience. My Aunt Grace said she came to San Antonio from Dallas many times for the express purpose of going on a shopping spree in Solo Serve. She said there wasn't a store like it in Dallas or anyplace else she had been.

In addition to remnants of piece goods, Solo Serve also featured table after table of drummer's samples of sewing notions, and leftovers from clothing factories such as giant cones of thread and sacks of buttons, all of which sold for practically nothing compared to the original price. It was so much fun to rummage through and purchase sewing items for almost nothing, even though we didn't need them. In many ways, Solo Serve resembled the flea markets of today, except that it also carried full bolts of first quality fabrics and all kinds of new sewing notions, shoes and ready-to-wear clothes. If we were planning to shop the entire downtown "strip," the visit to Solo Serve had to be cut short, or even postponed until another day.

After leaving Solo Serve, we continued our trek eastward on the south side of Houston Street, passing by and window-shopping in novelty shops, pawn shops, inexpensive jewelry stores and other miscellaneous places before coming to a bridge crossing the San Antonio River. At that point we jaywalked to the north side of the street toward the Texas Theater, bypassing the National Shirt Shop on the southwest corner of Houston and St. Mary's streets.

As soon as we crossed over, we came face to face with the stairway leading down to the Pitcher Cafe. It was entirely below ground level on the west side of the Texas Theater (under a cut-rate ladies ready-to-wear shop), abutting the riverwalk. There were quite a few china and crystal pitchers on display in the showcase windows by the stairway going down to the dining area; once downstairs (we did go down once in a while) we found the walls lined with displays of the large pitcher collection owned by the cafe proprietor. After admiring the pitchers, we returned to the street and passed the entrance to the Texas Building (an office building over the Texas Theater) and then induced Mother to walk through the extra large outer lobby of the Texas Theater to look at the billboards advertising the current and coming attractions.

The Martha Washington Candy Shop was next door to the Texas Theater. Sometimes Mother went in and we bought some candy. The owners, Mr. and Mrs. Tobias, made the chocolate-coated creams upstairs over the candy store. I found out many years later that Mrs. Tobias was the aunt of former Texas Governor John B. Connolly, being his mother's sister. Mrs. Tobias was always so cheerful and happy when she greeted her customers in her starched white cotton uniform and cap. The chocolate-coated creams came with many different flavored centers, and were sold in several different sizes of boxes. The bulk chocolates were all on display in trays behind a glass showcase. On more than one occasion, I watched as Mrs. Tobias packed a box "to order" for a customer. Many is the time she sacked my order of one of each of three or four different flavored chocolate-coated creams and gave me a smile as she handed me the candy and asked me to be sure to hurry back; it mattered not that my purchase was small.

After we left the candy store, we all slowed down to look admiringly at the window displays in Hertzberg's Jewelry Store. Hertzberg's was by far the most prestigious jewelry store in San Antonio. After admiring the beautiful window displays, I always checked the time by looking up to the impressive Hertzberg clock that was mounted in a green metal circular case at the top of a ten or twelve-foot green pole on the northwest corner of Houston and St. Mary's Streets. It always showed the correct time. The clock is still there displaying the exact time, in spite of the fact that Hertzberg's Jewelry Store has long since been razed and replaced with a new bank building. The next thing I always did was to look diagonally across St. Mary's Street toward the southeast to see the marquee over the entrance to the Empire Theater and find out what movie was showing there.

On rare occasions, Mother let us go to the Goober Shop (that's what I called it) across the street from the Empire Theater on St. Mary's Street. Whenever I did get to the Goober Shop, I was in for a treat. It was unique in that there were eight or more elbow-height tables, (no chairs or stools), lined up, one right after the other, at right angles to the wall opposite a long counter where orders were placed for soft drinks and sandwiches. When I was with Mother, I drank my soda without a sandwich, but when I was older and by myself, I, like many others, brought a sandwich from home and ordered a large nickel drink to sip while standing at one of the counters eating.

The soft drinks were large and tasty, but the Goober Shop's big drawing point was the large bowl of shelled, roasted, salted, giant goober peanuts that was placed in the middle of each counter and kept full by an attendant. Everyone standing at the counters scooped out peanuts with the large spoons that were in the nut bowls and ate them from napkins on the counters. Customers were encouraged to eat all the goobers they desired FREE OF CHARGE. Needless to say, the shop was always crowded. Many times I enjoyed eating a cup of free, shelled, giant goobers with or without a homemade sandwich and was out only five cents for the soft drink. I never found goobers like those anyplace else. I would have gladly paid for them. It was unbelievable that the Goober Shop could give away all those goobers and still manage to stay in business, but that it did for many years.

Then we returned to Houston Street, crossed over to the north side, and continued our way east. The Gunter Hotel (on the northeast corner of St. Mary's and Houston Streets) was first. In years to come, it was fun to dine at the Smorgasbord in that restaurant. That was beyond a doubt the most versatile place I ever had the pleasure of dining in. For a modest price, diners were issued a plate and given the privilege of roaming around a large buffet in the center of the restaurant. Diners ate as much as they wished, and then returned for seconds as many times as desired, drinks included. There were maybe ten kinds of meat dishes and as many vegetables dishes, salads, breads, and desserts; the assortment of choices changed from time to time. It was fabulous.

Shaw's Jewelry Store was located right there under the hotel. Once again I loved to look at the expensive jewelry on display. Shaw's was destined to become very important to me because when I was a young lady, my husband-to-be purchased my engagement and wedding rings there.

Sometime during the late 1930s, Russell Stover opened a candy store near the entrance to the Gunter Hotel. It gave the Martha Washington candy store a lot of competition. I still see boxes of Russell Stover candy for sale today in drugstores and other places everywhere, but no Martha Washington candies.

Frost Bros. was considered the most elite department store in San Antonio. If high prices had anything to do with being elite, it was certainly dubbed correctly, as a person could frequently find an item carried by Frost Bros. for half the price at another not-so-ritzy store down the street a ways. But there were women who didn't want to wear anything unless it came from Frost Bros., regardless of the price; there were also those who refused to buy anything on sale. The store carried all kinds of ready-to-wear clothing, high-priced cosmetics and perfumes (some of them exclusively), shoes, bags, fine china, silverware, crystal, piece goods, and other things. Frost Bros. was renown for having shoppers come regularly from as far south as Mexico City, Mexico, for the sole purpose of purchasing "items that came from Frost's." The store was very conveniently located for tourists, being between the Gunter Hotel on the south and the St. Anthony Hotel a block north.

Once a year, Frost Bros. held a half-price remnant sale on piece goods. The sale was really just a way to mark down and move out bolts of material that had not sold as soon as expected at the regular price. I have actually been told by sales clerks that the remnants were made up by taking full and partially-full bolts of cloth, cutting them deliberately into three-, four-, and five-yard lengths, marking them half-price and then mixing them up on a large remnant table. Frost Bros. might have saved time and money in the long run by just marking the entire bolts down to half-price and cutting off the amount customers wanted, instead of forcing them to either take a little too much or not quite enough, in unnecessarily created, half-price remnants. But no, the store management wouldn't hear of offering material, on the bolt, uncut, for half price; it would hurt their prestige. When Frost Bros. held a half-price remnant sale, Mother usually attended and managed to find beautiful materials for dresses. It didn't matter if there was too much material in a remnant, as Mother could always find something to do with piece goods.

When we left Frost Bros., I rushed next door to see the window displays of fine jewelry in McNeel's exclusive family-owned jewelry store. There was always something exquisite to admire there, such as a complete sterling silver tea service, exquisitely polished to a spotless mirror finish. It always seemed to me that sterling silver of all kinds was a specialty of McNeel's.

As we proceeded toward the east on the north side of Houston St., the next thing I remember after McNeel's in that block is Carl's, an "almost elite" ladies clothing store. As far as prices were concerned, it was elite. Next, I recall Paul's Shoe Store, and maybe another shop or two before coming to Grandsilver's dime store. It always had birds, goldfish, and turtles for sale in the basement, and we frequently went down to see them. The last thing on the corner of that block was the South Texas Building, which fronted Navarro Street.

After that, we crossed over to McCrory's, on the south side of Houston Street, and enjoyed browsing through all the knick-knacks, odds and ends, and notions, paying particular attention to the sheet music department and the pianist playing the latest hit songs on a piano.

For quite a while, the high point of a trip to town was checking out the progress on the Nix Professional Building and Hospital that was under construction a short block south of Houston Street on the east side of Navarro Street. Construction was finished around 1930, with a Sommer's Drug Store on the ground floor beside the lobby. It was a beautiful building,

Frost Bros. was San Antonio's most "elite" department store. (Photo courtesy of the UT Institute of Texan Cultures.)

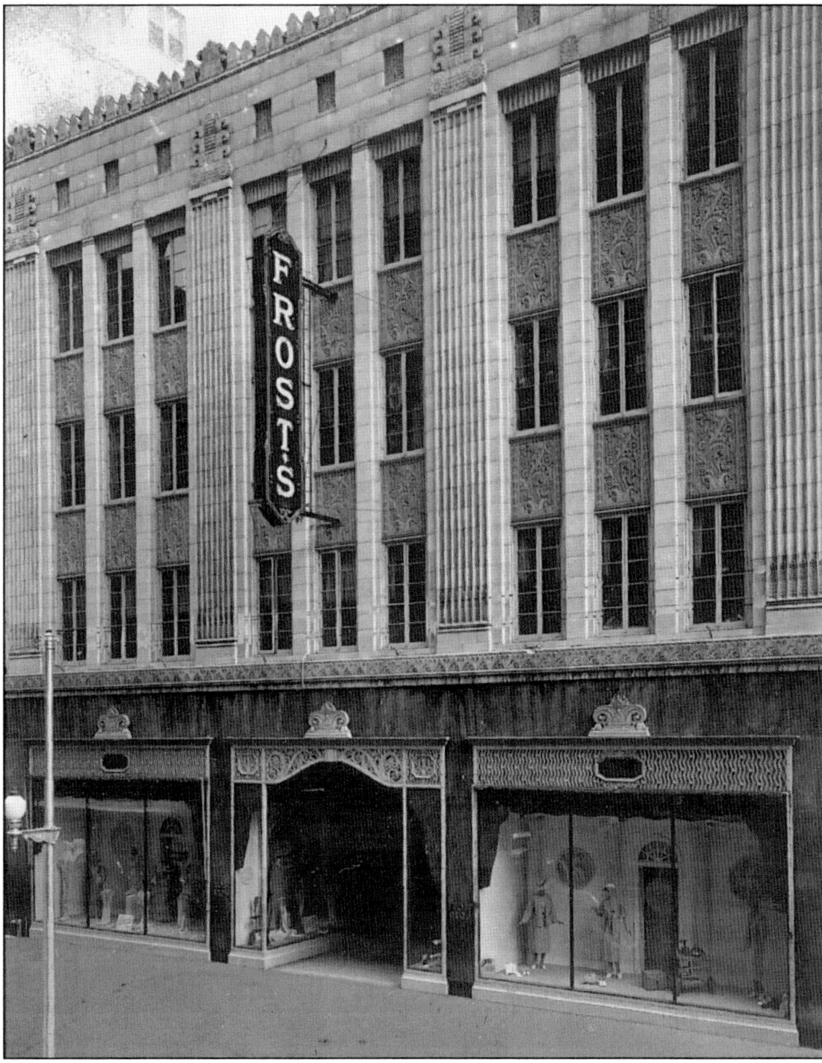

constructed of tan bricks, accented inside and out in mosaic designs made with aqua and salmon colored tiles. Everyone loved the valet service for the indoor parking garage that occupied the first three or four floors. The elevators were manned by uniformed operators who expressed persons to the requested floor with unbelievable speed. The Nix Professional Building and Hospital Complex is still there in its original architecture and decor, functioning in the same way today as then, except that it now sports central air-conditioning and the elevators, having been converted to "automatic," are now run in a very impersonal, mechanical manner; they no longer ZOOM up or down, as they did so long ago with a real live operator in control.

When we crossed over Navarro to the next block of Houston Street, it was anyone's guess as to which side of the street Mother would decide to take; sometimes she covered both. On the north side of that block there was first, The Vogue, followed by Grant's, an office building, Kress', and several small shoe stores and shops. On the south side, I remember Walgreen's Drug Store on the corner, followed by several shoe stores, less expensive dress shops, men's clothing stores, and other shops. Some of the store names I remember are Lerner's, Grayson's, and Three Sisters.

Actually the north side of that block was usually more interesting to me. The Vogue, the first store on the block, was a very large, expensive department store, but neither Mother nor I had much interest in it. It was the dime stores east of the Vogue that interested all of us. The first one was Grant's. While looking over the candy counter and all kinds of nickel and dime items, and generally having fun, the heavenly aroma of their hamburgers always overcame me and I would try to talk Mother into buying some. She almost always said we would wait and eat at home, that we didn't have time to eat in Grant's and she certainly wasn't going to allow us to walk down the street eating hamburgers. But there was a rare occasion now and then when she gave in and we feasted on the most unusual hamburgers I ever ate. It was always the same, grilled hamburger meat topped with a generous serving of Grant's own version of cabbage slaw on a toasted bun. The grated cabbage mixture wasn't exactly a slaw, having mustard, relish, and other things in it not found in coleslaw. The hamburger was delicious and it only cost 10¢ at the most, even when cabbage was out of season in the San Antonio winter garden district. The cost for the cabbage was very likely not more than a penny a head, during the six- or eight-month growing season of the Belgian Gardens (winter garden district) of irrigated farms on the south and west sides of San Antonio.

The winter gardens were a sight to behold during harvest time. Many times I have ridden through them and seen acre after acre of moss green cabbages and snow-white cauliflower either almost grown, or ready for and being harvested; at harvest time cabbage sold for only a few cents a head, and cauliflower for 10¢ a head or less in the local grocery stores. In fact, I have seen so much cabbage and cauliflower at the market plaza at times that some of it went begging, and was eventually purchased for a mere pittance by hog farmers to feed to swine, for which there was very little market either. There was too much of everything and no one had the money to buy anything. For that reason I suppose the cost for the cabbage dressing in the hamburger was much less than mayonnaise, mustard, lettuce, tomatoes, onion, and pickles would have been; thus Grant's could sell those large hamburgers for 10¢ each year round and still make a profit.

My favorite dime store, Kress's, was considered by most people to be the "king" of dime stores, especially after a large new four- or five-story building was erected to replace the very old original one. The basement in the new building had a modern cafeteria and rest rooms, in addition to a large shopping area containing numerous counters of items for sale. The store also had another cafeteria on the second or third floor, accessible by elevator, supposedly for the employees, that was also open to the public, where one could choose from many of the same food items offered for sale in the main basement cafeteria for at least one-third less. I have eaten there many times, as well as in the main cafeteria. The food was very good. The street floor of Kress's was crammed full of all kinds of nickel and dime items, including the largest dime store candy counter in San Antonio; and there was always someone demonstrating something to sell on the spot, such as a cookie press, a slicing tool, a cake decorating kit, and many more things.

While waiting to cross Presa Street, one could see the Maverick Building to the south, which is where the Fuller Brush Company had an office and sold combs and brushes to walk-in customers. The Maverick Building was an eight-story office building that I will never forget and with good reason. At the age of 19, I was working as a secretary in the San Antonio Rubber Stamp Co., which was across College Street. One summer day, it being quite warm, the doors and windows to the street between the Maverick Building and our building were open. Suddenly, the sleepy, summer droning office sounds were interrupted with a loud PLOP from the direction of the rear of the Maverick Building. Immediately thereafter, one of our employees dashed from the rear of the store through our office to the street (with his helpers running after) shouting, "I just saw a man jump out a window on the eighth floor of the Maverick Building!" So we all followed the typesetters to see what had happened. There, directly across the street, right in front of us, lay the man, lifeless, dead, at the base of the Maverick Building. Later, the elevator operator in the building told us the man rode up to the eighth floor five or six times, then down again. The last time he only rode up to the sixth floor and got off. Shortly thereafter, he heard that the man had jumped out the eighth-floor window, so he presumed the jumper had walked up the remaining two flights of stairs. We were never given any reason as to why he jumped. And that's why I'll never forget the Maverick Building.

Underneath the Maverick Building, on the southwest corner, was the little hat shop under the southwest corner of the Maverick Building, facing South Presa. I think it was the Rhealee Hat Shop. Mother didn't go to the hat shop very often, but when she did, I was in for quite a sideshow by various lady shoppers seeking "just the right hat." It was customary for a shopper to enter the store, sit down in front of a mirror, ask for a certain type and color of hat, and then proceed to try on hat after hat, brought to her by a sales clerk. All the while she would look in the mirror each time to see how it looked on her. Most of the large department stores and many small dress shops carried hats also, as hats were a social necessity for many occasions at that time. I frequently noticed the same performance going on in those hat departments, but the Rhealee Hat Shop was my favorite place for watching such a show as it was ALL hats, nothing else, and the show was totally graphic. Only on rare occasions did I see a customer actually purchase a hat. A sales person's job was very trying.

By the time we finished with the hat shop. Mother was ready to proceed eastward on Houston Street once again. The next block (between Presa and Broadway) was quite short. There were only a few shops on the south side such as Zimmerman's high-priced, family-owned shoe store, Pincus and Stein's men's clothing stores, and a few other businesses. On the north side of the street I remember J.C. Penney's and Neisner's dime store.

Mother always shopped around in J.C. Penney's, so that was our next stop. It was a complete department store, with just about everything that Wolff & Marx had, only the merchandise was less expensive. We always spent time in the piece goods department in the basement.

Penney's, and some of the other major department stores at that time, used an overhead tube for taking payments for merchandise and making change. The floor clerk made out the bill, took the money from the customer, and put them in a cone or carrier like the ones used in banks by outside tellers. Then she placed the carrier in the overhead tube, and air pressure, or something, caused it to fly across the ceiling upward through the tube to the office cashier. The cashier

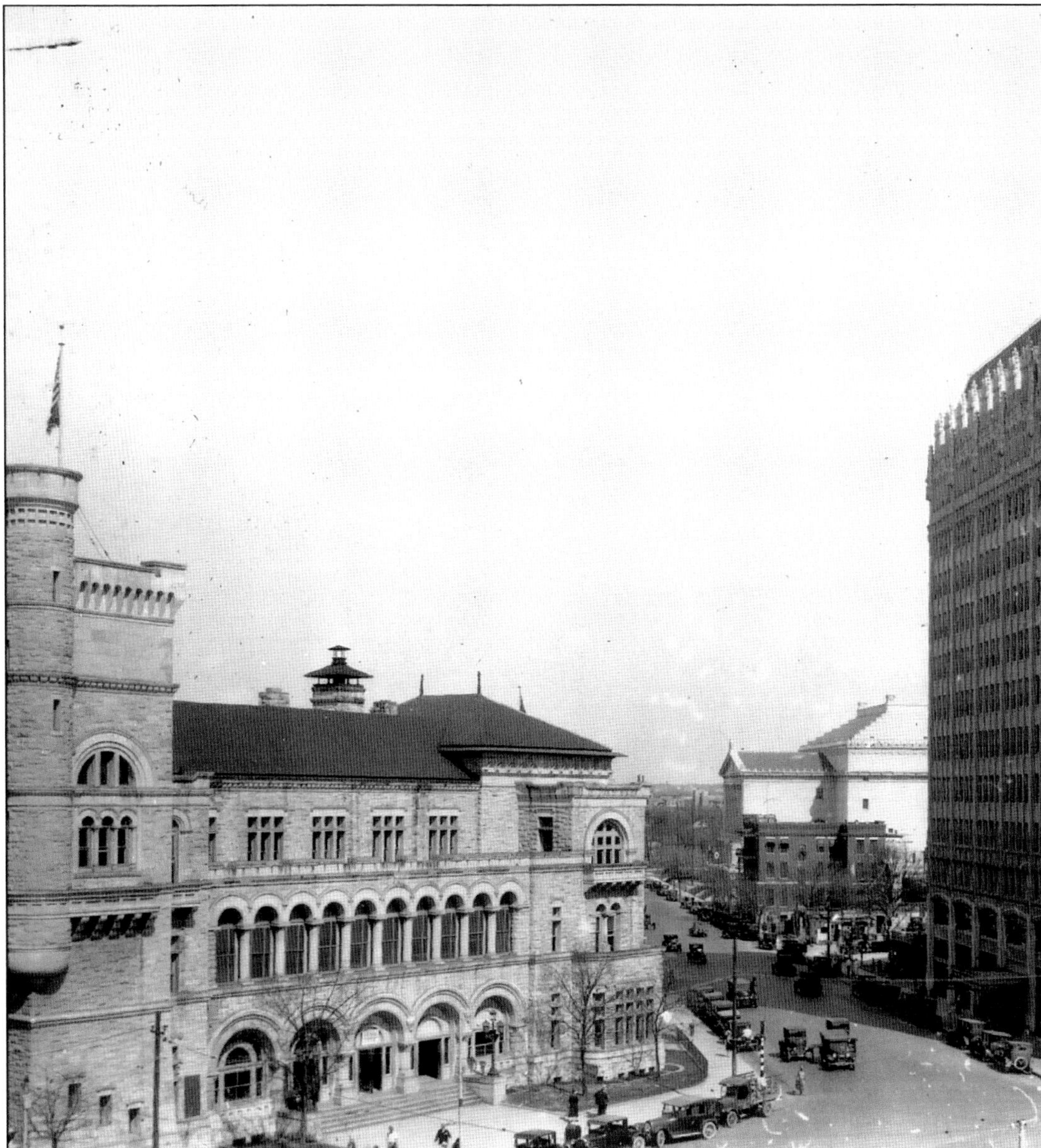

The Medical Arts Building was located at the intersection of East Houston Street and Avenue E.

made change and the carrier was "shot" back via the tube to the floor clerk who completed the transaction by counting out the change to the customer and handing him his purchase. No currency was kept on the floors with the merchandise. The noisy process took extra time and prompted a certain amount of otherwise unnecessary waiting; when I was a child I found the procedure intriguing, but when I was older, I found it tiresome to wait until it came my turn for the elevated cashier to make change.

After leaving Penney's, we went on to Neisner's dime store. In the three and one-half blocks between the Brady Building on St. Mary's St. and the Medical Arts Building, we passed six large drugstores, three of them named Sommer's. All the dime stores had soda fountains with lunch counters and short-order dining areas. They served a different plate lunch each day at noon and a variety of fresh made-to-order sandwiches. They also served several different kinds of pies, cakes, and breakfast rolls, as well as all items pertinent to a soda fountain, such as ice-cream sundaes, banana splits, ice-cream sodas, milk shakes, and malted milk shakes. The soda fountain and fast food areas seemed to be constantly busy in all of the drugstores, and I failed to mention that all the dime stores also had large busy lunch counters and soda fountains.

Any Sommer's Drug Store was my favorite place to eat an open-face roast beef sandwich. Tender slices of hot roast beef were draped across toasted white bread and covered with scoops of dark brown gravy, with mashed potatoes and butter on the side, all of which were made colorful with a garnish of lettuce leaf and tomato. The price was between 50¢ and $1. The soda fountain in Sommer's served the tastiest chocolate ice-cream sodas I have ever had anywhere. Generous splashes of chocolate syrup were mixed with a carbonated water and two or three large scoops of vanilla ice cream were added. The soda was crowned with a peak of whipped cream, sprinkled with chopped pecans, and topped off with a large, bright, red cherry. The price ranged from 15¢ to 19¢ each.

In that era it really did prove to be worthwhile to look in all the dime stores, as they didn't all carry the same items and brands. What one store didn't have, could very well be found in another. When we finished at Woolworth's, it was time to start south on Alamo Plaza. At that point we were about two blocks north of Commerce Street. The east side of Alamo Plaza contained the Alamo, Menger Hotel, Strand Theater, and Joske's. We usually stayed on the west side until we reached Joske's. In addition to the Palace Theater, it was sprinkled with numerous small shops and stores. The ones I remember are the San Antonio Trunk Co., Fox Photo Studios, Frank Bros., and last, the Guarantee Shoe Store, the best shoe store in San Antonio, carrying shoes for the entire family.

Twice a year the Guarantee Shoe Store held a large sale. People stood in line at 9:00 a.m. waiting for the store to open and only the number of customers for which there were salesmen on duty, usually about 15 or 20, were allowed in at one time. As soon as one customer left, another was ushered in. Shoppers stood in line all day waiting to get into the store and take advantage of the sale. When I was very small, Mother bought my shoes at The Guarantee. The store had an X-ray related machine that I stood under wearing the new shoes, and looked into a viewmaster-like contraption to actually see an X-ray of the bones in my feet, revealing whether or not they were crowded. If they were, it meant the shoes didn't fit and another size was tried until one looked right. It was merely a way to be certain a small child didn't get home with an ill-fitting shoe that was too small. I believe that X-ray related machine was eventually considered harmful and outlawed from use, because of excessive exposure to X-rays.

There were at least a dozen small shoe stores in San Antonio, and in addition to them, most of the department stores had at least one shoe department, some as many as four. Now and then Mother needed a new pair of walking shoes, and she visited most of them before deciding on a pair; consequently, I knew them all well.

Shopping for shoes in those days was absolutely unreal. I was familiar with all the ins and outs of the procedure in detail, having witnessed it so many times while waiting for Mother to find shoes that suited her, especially, since we almost always had to wait a considerable length of time for a salesman. In the first place, a customer never, ever, helped herself. Instead she got seated and waited for the next available salesman (almost always a man). When one finally came to the customer he first greeted her, and then he proceeded to remove her right shoe and measure the length and width of the foot. Many times he measured the left foot also. Nevertheless, customers invariably seemed to feel that they already knew what size shoe they wore and it was usually smaller than the measure indicated. Even when the salesman showed her the measurement, she insisted it was wrong. Next, she described the shoe she was looking for. Then the clerk would bring out shoes for the customer to try on.

There was absolutely no self-service at that time anywhere. A lady never removed a shoe from, or put one on, her own foot, not even her own shoes. Customers weren't allowed in the stock room, so they had to take the clerk's word for what the store did or didn't have on hand. This meant the shoe clerk continued to bring out, right or wrong, pair after pair of shoes. Many times, I watched a customer try on 20 or 30 different pairs of shoes only to ask that her shoes be put back on her feet as there was nothing she liked that day. And when someone did purchase a pair of shoes, there seemed to be an unwritten rule of some sort that she had to try on at last 12 pairs first, even if she knew from the start she was going to buy the first pair she tried. I reiterate: the whole shoe-shopping process was unreal. Anytime someone bought a pair of shoes, they were then led directly to the hosiery counter, which was usually managed by the cashier, who was always female, young, and pretty. The "stocking lady," as I called her, then proceeded to demonstrate and try to sell hosiery by putting the stockings on her perfectly manicured hand, stretching them around and bragging about the shades available. A person buying shoes couldn't get out of a shoe store without being accosted by the "charming stocking lady." Nevertheless, she made very few sales of the overpriced cotton, rayon, and sometimes-silk hose, which were all she had to offer until nylons arrived shortly after 1940.

Usually, the last store we visited was Joske's. Sometime in the 1930s Joske's purchased the remainder of the extra large block that encompassed it and built the largest department store in downtown San Antonio. A Catholic church in that block with land about the size of a city lot refused to sell, so Joske's purchased everything but it and built a store several stories high, that completely surrounded three sides of the church.

The new store was air-conditioned, which was very nice. Up until sometime in the 1930s, none of the department stores were air-conditioned. They all had large windows that opened and ceiling fans throughout. Most of the street-floor windows were up high over the showcases, and necessarily rather small. Many of the upper floors had eight- or ten-feet-tall windows that swung in or out vertically, which made those floors much cooler.

The Guarantee Shoe Store's x-ray shoe fitter was thought to be a real marvel! (Photo courtesy of the UT Institute of Texan Cultures.)

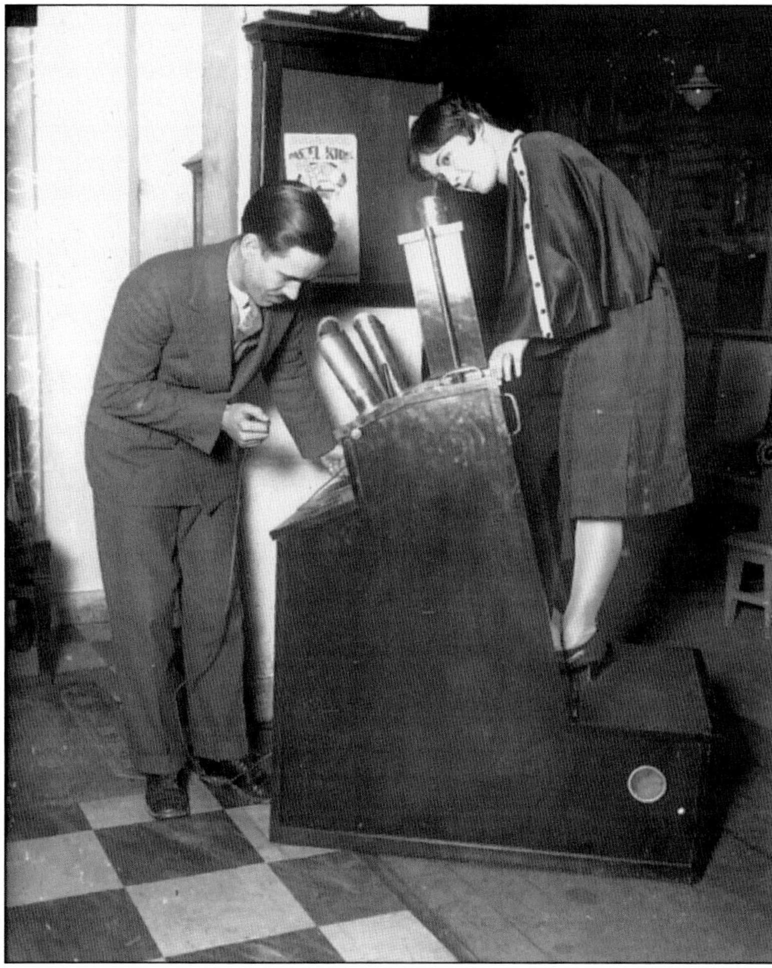

Joske's was a shopper's paradise. It had an escalator (the first one in San Antonio) to ride up and down to three or four floors of merchandise. There were three or four different ladies' shoe, lingerie, and ready-to-wear departments and several different departments carrying a complete line of men's, infants, and children's clothes. In fact, it contained at least two or three complete stores with different levels of quality and price of merchandise, starting with the bargain basement that had everything imaginable in it for men, women, and children, and all kinds of household items. The street floor was packed with almost as many different things, including an elite candy counter selling the most desired boxed candies as well as fine chocolates in the bulk, and a complete book department.

The store had an economy cafeteria on one floor and an elite restaurant on another. I didn't believe a person could ask for any name brand household and kitchen item or electrical appliance that Joske's didn't have. It also carried sterling silver, fine crystal and china, and many more things. There was even a Joske's furniture store across the street south of the main store.

There were at last four ladies shoe departments in Joske's and Mother frequently shopped in several of them. Two of them were located next to ladies ready-to-wear, lingerie, and foundation garments. Many times I was distracted from the shoe buying ritual by another kind of scenario being acted out in a ready-to-wear department. It didn't take me long to see that a lady thought nothing at all of trying on dozens of dresses, girdles, bras, and lingerie that a sales clerk had located and brought to her, while she relaxed in the dressing room between fittings. Then, more times than not, after as long as one or even two hours, the customer suddenly jumped up, put her own clothing back on, announced there was nothing that suited her that day, and left, only to go on to another store and repeat the same charade.

The 1930s was an era when the customer was not only always right, she could also try the clerk and store manager to the point of complete exasperation and not buy anything, and still be told as she left, "I am sorry we didn't have anything for you today. Please come back soon. I hope next time we find something that pleases you." The clerk, at the same time, knew full-well that the customer probably never intended to buy anything in the first place as she didn't have any money. But times were hard, and on the outside chance that the customer did have a few dollars to spend, salespersons never stopped grasping at straws, hoping always that the next shopper would be the one with funds and that those who weren't would indeed come to their store when and if they ever did have money to spare.

There were other times after the riverwalks were built that we went down the steps at an entrance and walked along one side of the river for a block or two. I watched, off and on, the construction of all the riverwalks and crossovers and the stairways leading down to the river. When I was young, I enjoyed many strolls on those river walkways. I was downtown recently and rode through that Houston Street, Alamo Plaza strip that was so alive with shops and things when I was a girl. Lots of the buildings are still standing, but most of them look vacant. The only businesses I saw that were still in operation were Walgreen's Drug Store, the Sommer's Drug Store in the Nix Building (without soda fountains and lunch counter), and Woolworth's dime store. All the other large department stores, theaters, drugstores, jewelry shops, and shoe stores are gone, although not forgotten, by me at least.

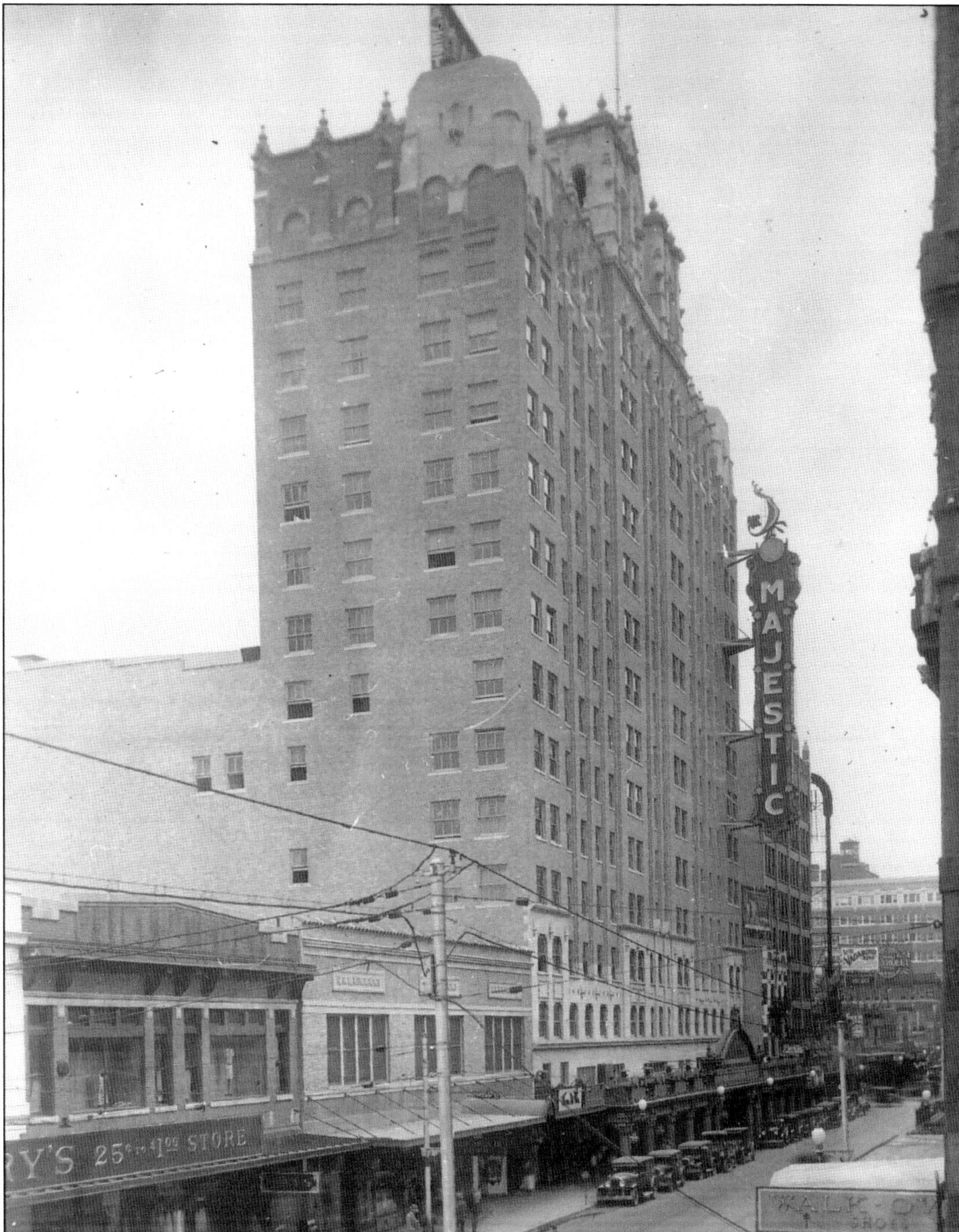

Although the other theaters were magnificent, the Majestic was beyond a doubt the most magnificent of all. (Photo courtesy of the UT Institute of Texan Cultures.)

Chapter Fourteen

Going to the Movies

My earliest memory of movies is going to see silent films. We went into the theater, got seated, and then watched as various scenarios were silently and dramatically acted out in black and white on the screen.

There was always someone (sometimes Aunt Sissie) playing a piano, which was located in front of the stage, usually on the left side of the theater. The pianist tried to mimic and enhance with music what was being acted out on the screen.

There were words printed on the bottom of the jerky, moving pictures, depicting what was being said and what was happening in the plot. Mother read those lines to me. There were other mothers all over the theater here and there reading them to their children. It didn't matter if someone talked softly during a silent film, as there was no sound to be interrupted.

Charlie Chaplin was my favorite comic actor in silent films. I don't think we ever missed one of his movies. But beyond a doubt, the one, single most outstanding straight actor I ever saw in a silent movie was Lon Chaney Sr. He was a natural contortionist who could do almost anything with his limbs.

I remember distinctly one movie in which he portrayed a man who had no arms, and consequently no hands. That in itself was a very preposterous thing for a small child to view. But when he proceeded to enter a cafe wearing a black hat and a long flowing, black cape, and displayed his expertise of living without arms and hands by casually lifting and using a foot to remove them, it was absolutely mind-boggling.

But the best was yet to come. He seated himself at a table and ordered coffee and things to eat. When he was served he raised his feet to the table (after removing them from his shoes), and deftly proceeded to use his toes to manipulate a spoon to add cream and sugar to, and stir his coffee. Next, he sat back in the chair comfortably and used his toes to lift the cup to his mouth and drink the coffee. It was quite a feat in itself, but that wasn't all. He went on to use his feet and toes to handle the silverware as he fed himself just as easily and nonchalantly as someone with hands might have handled the situation.

I couldn't believe my eyes as he went through the entire movie using his feet and toes to do first one thing and then another that was ordinarily done with the hands and fingers. It was scary and unreal to me.

State Theater

Through the years I came to know almost all the movie houses in San Antonio very well, having attended all of them frequently. The first one that comes to mind is the State Theater, where we saw so many silent films. On the other hand, it might have been known by another name in the 1920s. At any rate, it was located on the west side of Main Avenue, in the block directly north of Houston St., and was considered one of the nicest theaters in San Antonio in the 1920s.

The most outstanding film I ever saw at the State Theater was *The Jazz Singer*, starring Al Jolson. It was the first motion picture made with sound. We went to see *The Jazz Singer* in the afternoon when it was first run in San Antonio.

Shortly after Father purchased our tickets, the box office was closed as all the seats had been sold for the remainder of that day's showings. We got in the line and wove back and forth, first outside on the sidewalk, and then inside in the huge theater lobby (which I remember being larger and very different in 1927 than it was in years to come), until more than two hours had passed and we were next to be seated and close enough to hear Al Jolson singing now and then while we waited.

Finally, we actually managed to enter the main theater, sit down and listen and watch as Al Jolson sang and acted out song after song, such as "Mammy," "Toot, Toot, Tootsie Good-bye," "Blue Skies," and others. It was fabulous. The thing that I remember most, aside from standing in that line for so long, was his kneeling beside a hospital bed and singing Sonny Boy to his little boy who lay dying. Al Jolson had always been one of my favorite singers, and now that I had watched him perform, I wanted to see him again and again.

The State Theater is no longer standing. The building was razed many years ago to make room for progress.

After the advent of talkies (or sound), movies got better and better and lasted longer and longer. There seemed to be no cost spared in making spectacular musicals, dramas, and adventure stories. However, for many years, movies were almost all filmed in black and white.

The Strand

I remember a very small, "almost not there" theater that was situated on the east side of Alamo Plaza, between the Menger Hotel and Joske's, on the northwest corner of the block Joske's was located in. Joske's eventually bought the building the theater was in, had it razed and constructed a new Joske's store that covered almost that entire block.

Going to The Strand with Father was really a peculiar experience. I would be visiting in his office and he would suddenly jump up, grab his hat and say, "Come on. Let's go see the western movie." Of course, I cheerfully followed after him, as we were going to see a movie. Father proceeded to the theater in a pace (normal for him), almost equal to a trot, and I had to run a little now and then to keep up with him. When we reached the box office, he bought tickets and then found a seat next to the aisle. I slipped in beside him with high hopes of being entertained.

But after several such trips, I learned that all I would ever get out of going to a movie in The Strand was watching cowboys creep across the prairie from cactus to brush, or a bush, back to cactus, or clumps of rocks, stopping once in a while to aim and fire a gun at someone or something not shown on the screen. Now and then a few words were uttered that meant absolutely nothing to me.

All this was done without any background music whatsoever. The only sounds I ever heard were gunshots, an occasional bit of dialogue, clopping noises, and other sound effects when appropriate. Once in a while a cowboy suddenly jumped up on a horse that appeared as if from nowhere, and clopped off loudly across the prairie in a cloud of dust.

There were several occasions when I was privileged to see one of the cowhands do something besides wander around from prop to prop and that was to watch him arrange a cluster of rocks in a sort of circle, gather up twigs and small pieces of wood and start a fire. Next he went to the "inevitable stream," that was forevermore conveniently nearby in such instances, and filled a pot and/or a can with water. After placing the container of water on the fire, he took some coffee and food items from his saddlebag and squatted before the fire to prepare a meal.

Once I saw a cowpoke stick a freshly dressed rabbit on a stick and hold it over the fire to cook. All of this was done without any other sound save a word now and then, the crackling of the fire and occasional cooking and walking noises. Anytime we saw a cowboy cooking over an open fire, Father always said the same thing: "That's the way I cooked my meals when I was a boy punching cattle on the open range in west Texas." And those are the only words Father ever uttered to me during a sojourn in one of those cowboy movies, until he was ready to leave.

After watching the movie for about 30 minutes, Father suddenly sprang up, grabbed his hat and called out to me "Let's go," and we returned to his office. Father never saw the entire movie when I was with him. Little wonder that I doubted if he knew what was going on either, but he seemed to be completely content just to watch cowboys make their way across the prairie. Perhaps those days he spent on the range while a youth had something to do with his fixation over seeing bits and pieces of those boring cowboy movies at that particular small theater, that might have been called the Strand, next door to Joske's.

Harlandale Theater

After we moved to Mayfield Park in 1928, the Harlandale Theater, which was only about two miles from our home, was the one my entire family went to about once a week, usually on a Friday or Saturday night. The theater was an attractive new Spanish style, white stucco building, with a red slate roof. There were no special architectural features about the lobby or the inside of the theater but the seats were very comfortable and it had everything required to show a movie, and that was all we needed.

It featured second showings of really great movies that had already been run in a downtown theater several months earlier. The Harlandale Theater changed its bill of fare at least twice a week and charged much less for admission tickets than the downtown theaters did for the same movies when they were billed as first run shows.

Some of the movies we saw there (that were my favorites) were all of the Shirley Temple movies, "Tarzan of the Apes," "King Kong," and many dramas and musicals.

Mother was partial to anything starring Shirley Temple, while Father's favorite actor was Will Rogers. We saw everything Will Rogers starred in at least once and sometimes two or three times, first at a downtown theater when first run, and then at the Harlandale Theater second time around. Our favorite Will Rogers movie was "Life Begins at Forty." Father also tuned in Will Rogers on the radio every time he had the opportunity and read the Will Rogers column in the newspaper.

Will Rogers first gained notoriety for his performance on the stage. He made one humorous quip about American life after another, which he accompanied with various rope tricks. I think one of his oft-quoted quips went something like this, "Everybody talks about the weather, but nobody ever does anything about it." When Will Rogers was killed in an airplane crash in Alaska in 1935 (along with celebrated aviator Wylie Post) not only Father, but also all of America went into shock and mourning for days.

Texas Theater

My parents took us to the Texas Theater when they wanted to see something they didn't think would ever be shown at the Harlandale Theater. It was located on the north side of Houston St. (facing south), just west of St. Mary's Street, between Hertzberg's Jewelry Store and the San Antonio River. There was an office building directly over the theater. The Texas Theater and office building above it were razed, except for the facade (front wall), about 15 years ago to accommodate a new bank building, which incorporated the facade into the architecture of the new building in an effort to preserve an historical architectural structure. The entire west wall of the Texas Theater (above the exit doors) was covered with a picturesque mural portraying a street scene in a small Latin American town.

We saw "The Sign of the Cross" at the Texas Theater sometime in the early 1930s when I was about ten years old.

Aztec Theater

The Aztec Theater is located on the northeast corner of the intersection of Commerce and St. Mary's streets, with its entrance on the east side of St. Mary's Street, facing west. There was a nice restaurant downstairs under the theater. The theater lobby was average in size but the inside of the theater was exceptionally nice, especially the plush seats.

Many great first-run movies have been enjoyed there throughout the years. We must have seen several Eddie Cantor movies there because when they come to mind I always think of the Aztec Theater. I remember "Whoopee," "Kid Millions," "The Kid From Spain," and "Roman Scandals."

The Aztec Theater building is still there, but I don't believe movies are shown in it today. I also don't know if the restaurant under it is still in operation. I waited in line for and enjoyed many good meals in that restaurant in the 1940s. And later in the 1960s and 1970s, when it was a Mexican Restaurant, it was one of my favorites.

Empire Theater

The Empire Theater was located on the southeast corner of St. Mary's and Houston streets, with the entrance on the east side of St. Mary's Street, facing west. It was a small theater without any spectacular physical attraction. We saw many movies (mostly B) in the Empire Theater. I remember when we first started going to it, there was always an attendant in the ladies' restroom seeing that everything was in order and keeping the restroom clean.

The only thing outstanding I remember seeing at the Empire Theater in the 1930s wasn't even a movie. My cousin Mary Jean went with my sister and me to see Roy Rogers and his horse Trigger perform on the stage there, shortly after 1935. They were an extra-added attraction, after the movie, although I don't remember anything about the movie.

Seeing a real live western star in person was such a thrill. Roy Rogers came out on the stage leading Trigger and asked him to count, dance, do rope tricks, and lots of other things. Then after Roy sang some songs, he left the stage with Trigger following, right up the aisle through the audience (close enough for me to touch them, if I

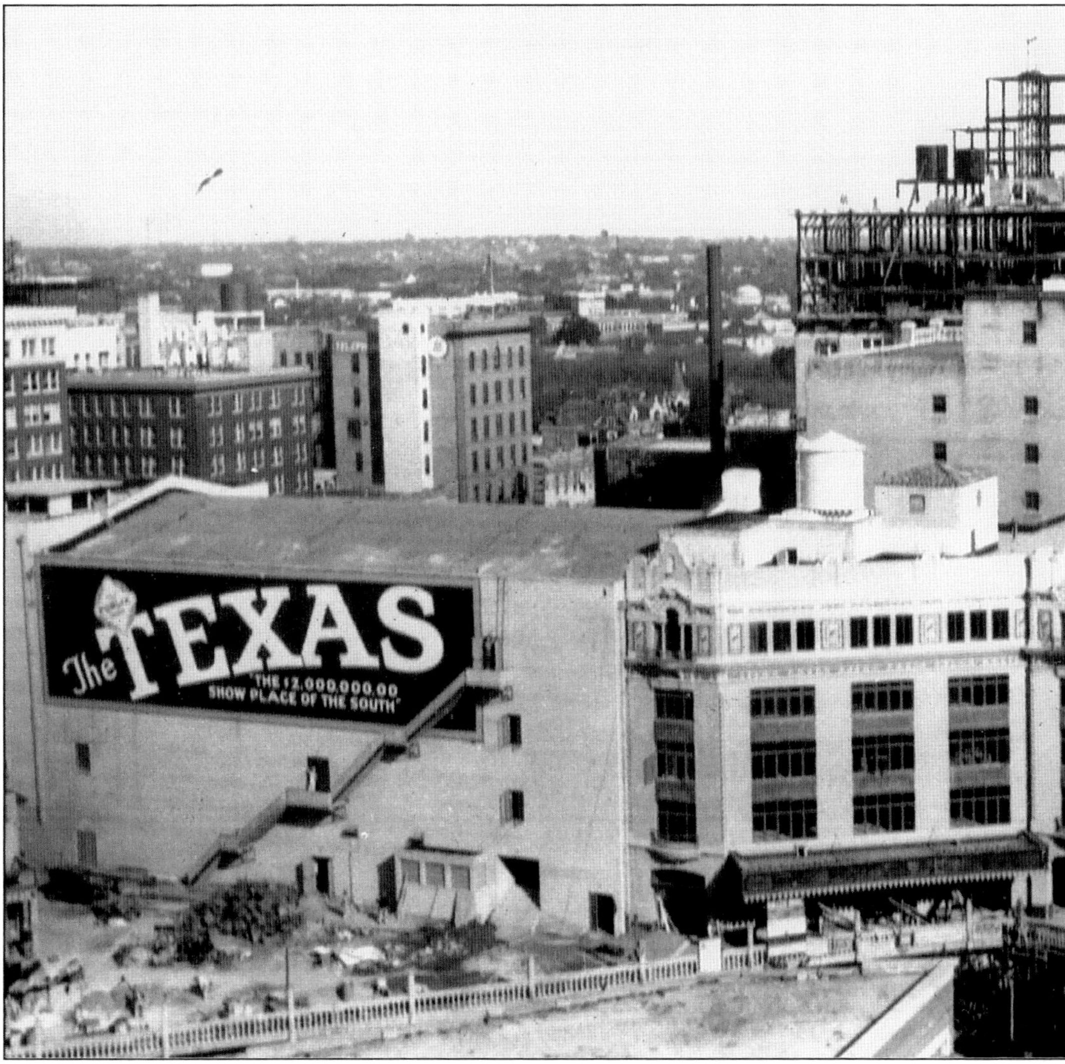

The Texas Theater was one of my favorites. In the background, construction of an addition on the Gunter Hotel can easily be seen. (Photo courtesy of the UT Institute of Texan Cultures.)

dared), and then out the front door into a horse trailer, and away they rode. Roy Rogers was just beginning to gain fame as a singing cowboy and from then on I wanted to see every movie he made.

The Empire Theater building is still standing, vacant. I don't believe there has been a movie shown there in over 15 years.

Majestic Theater

The Majestic Theater, which was by far my favorite theater of all, was located in the exact middle of town on the south side of Houston Street.

The Majestic Theater was a work of art from the entrance all the way to the third balcony. It was considered "the showplace" of that era in San Antonio.

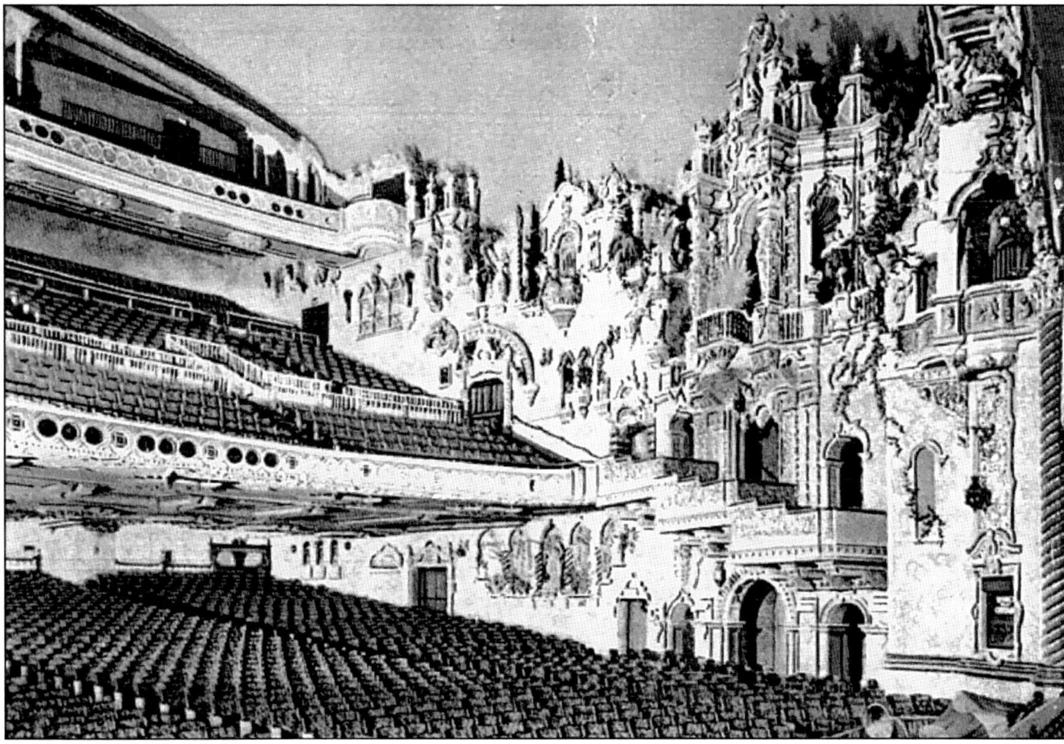

The Majestic Theater was our favorite.

I haven't been to it in 40 years, so I will have to trust my memory for the description that follows.

During the short walk from the box office to the lobby entrance, patrons faced a wall with a built-in fish tank, which sported quite a few brightly colored fish of varying sizes. They were beautiful and easy to see through the side of the tank. It was so pretty, and having a fish tank in a wall was something new to me. After a turn to the right and a stop at the ticket-taking counter, patrons found themselves in the downstairs lobby, which was very ornately decorated.

The most impressive and ornate part of the Majestic Theater, however, was the upstairs lobby, which was luxuriously decorated and furnished in a beautiful decor that was carried out throughout the theater. I remember wandering around that lobby before and after shows, admiring the red carpeted staircase with mirrored wall leading up to a landing at the base of three or four entrances to the stairways leading up to the middle of the first balcony. On the right side of the walkway was an ornately finished railing made of a fine, dark wood. The railing encompassed the edge of the walkway. I could walk alongside it, lean down, and see the middle of the first-floor lobby. On the opposite side of the walkway to the left, there was an alcove in between each stairway leading up to the balcony seats. Each alcove contained a large sofa and one or two chairs of an antique design.

My favorite thing of all in that lobby was the artistically lit fish pond nestled at the base of a cascading waterfall, which originated on the wall at the far end of the walkway railing. Some of the goldfish were huge, and the whole thing was just plain pretty.

The Majestic Theater had at least three balconies, each with its own beautifully decorated lobby and restrooms. There was an attendant in the first balcony ladies room at night to keep it clean and stocked with supplies and help patrons when needed.

I remember the elevator that took people up and down when they didn't care to climb stairs or were unable to do so. Sometimes people like me rode in the elevator just for fun. Unformed ushers with flashlights escorted patrons to their seats.

The loge area protruded from the wall, fairly close to and on either side of the stage at a level about halfway between the main floor seating area and the first balcony. There were at least three separate loge sections on each side of the theater, each one with six or eight seats. I wandered around in that section once, but preferred sitting in the middle of the theater in the first balcony.

When I first looked up toward the extra-high ceiling, I actually thought I was looking outdoors as it feigned the appearance of a nighttime sky filled with twinkling stars, and the stars seemed to be moving. The Majestic Theater was a beautiful place in every way.

On the west side of the theater, there was a very large, new Sommer's Drug Store with an ultra-modern soda fountain and lunch counter. In addition to the counter at the soda fountain, it had 15 or 20 large, upholstered booths where one could sit and eat. The eating area was always busy, with frequent periods of having to wait for a seat.

A Mexican pecan candy store was located on the east side of the Majestic Theater. It made the candy in a kitchen upstairs over the retail shop. I went upstairs to pick out candy on several occasions. It was by far the most delicious Mexican pecan candy I ever ate. There were pralines, pecan logs, sugared pecans, and divinity balls covered in pecans or chocolate, just to name a few. All of the candy was sold in bulk or in one or two-pound boxes containing a mixture of the candies.

The Mexican pecan candy store also made taffy, sweet delicious vanilla and strawberry taffy, not the kind that mother made that was amber-colored. The taffy was cooked to the pulling stage upstairs and then transported to the display case in the front of the store to be pulled by an electric taffy-pulling machine. Almost anytime I passed by that candy store I could see the machine pulling away.

Chapter Fifteen

Junior High Days and Diseases of the Time

During the last week of December 1934, my parents bought me a bicycle with the plan that I would ride it to school. Learning to ride that bicycle was a memorable experience in itself. I rolled it out into the rarely traveled street in front of our home, straddled it, and tried to balance myself long enough to start pedaling, which was harder than it sounds. Every time, before I could pedal even one stroke, the bike and I both started to topple over.

Mother, seeing my plight, took pity on me and came out to help. She finally wound up trotting alongside the bike holding it up until I had managed two or three pedal strokes. After going through that procedure over and over again for three or four days, I gradually got the hang of it and all of a sudden found that I could ride off all by myself, which was exciting. Then I felt brave enough to pedal the distance to the Sueltenfuss store. Since the venture was a success, I announced I was ready to ride the bicycle to school.

The second semester started sometime around the tenth of January. Mother took me to the Harlandale Junior High School the first day so I could enroll. We were told when we arrived that for the low sixth grade at midterm, I would have to go to school at Huff Avenue Elementary School, six or eight blocks farther down the street from the junior high school. So I enrolled at the Huff Avenue School. Most of the time from then on, I rode the bicycle to school, which was a distance of over two miles.

Going to school at Huff Avenue wasn't anything at all like going to the San Jose School. In the first place, there wasn't a single solitary student there whom I knew. The boys and girls I had been attending school with up to that time had all enrolled last September in the low sixth grade at the Harlandale Junior High School, and were still there in the high sixth.

Next, I was almost a head taller than any of the girls and several inches taller than most of the boys. The only boy who was taller than me ended up being a constant source of aggravation to me from the very first day.

Being that much taller than the girls seemed to put me on another seemingly inaccessible plateau that they considered too remote to approach. In fact, all of the students acted as though they couldn't care less if I was there or not. I decided I could certainly survive without them also, except in the classroom, and I did. Making good grades was no problem. I always made mostly A's with a B now and then, and I don't remember having to study very much, if at all.

There was one thing about the Huff Avenue School that I really enjoyed and that was being in the Glee Club. I loved singing three or four part group harmony. I was delegated to sing with the alto group.

Our teacher's name was Mr. Jones. I remember what he looked like and the enthusiasm with which he directed our singing group. The one song that I enjoyed singing most was "Love is Just Around the Corner." We mastered it in three-part harmony and sang it in general assembly and for the PTA.

Finally it was May and time for school to be out for the summer. It was a wonderful feeling. No more school at Huff Avenue. Mother had been assured that come September I would attend Harlandale Junior High School for the high sixth grade.

When September came, I rode my bicycle to Harlandale Junior High and enrolled in the high sixth grade. Things hadn't changed much, as I was still several inches taller than my classmates, who immediately started referring to me as "the telephone pole." There was still evidence of the Depression all-around me, manifested in the way the students dressed, what they ate for lunch, and other ways. If anything, the effects of the Depression seemed to be getting worse all the time.

There are two things about that school semester that I remember. First, one of the subjects I took was a class in speech, or drama, in which I memorized Lincoln's Gettysburg Address and then recited it for my classmates on the stage in the high school auditorium. That wasn't hard to do at all. I learned and recited other things also, but they escape my mind at the moment.

The other thing I remember is polio. Poliomyelitis was the medical term for polio but the paralysis aspect and the fact that it frequently attacked the young were reasons for it being dubbed infantile paralysis. I always referred to it as just plain polio. It was something we all lived in fear of catching.

I had been seeing and hearing about polio on newscasts in movie theaters for several years. I even knew that President Roosevelt (in spite of the fact that he carefully concealed it in public appearances) had been crippled by polio and was destined to live out his life in a wheelchair.

There was nothing new about polio, its having been around since before the turn of the century, but having a president who had been crippled by it helped to bring it to the forefront and draw the entire nation's attention to it. In 1935 the polio scare was running rampant throughout the country causing almost as much fear as the AIDS epidemic is today.

Polio was highly contagious, and unlike AIDS, could be transmitted to others by casual contact during a short communicable stage of the disease. That made everyone near a person with polio a possible victim. Therefore, it was necessary to sterilize everything the patient came in contact with in order to protect medical personnel, family members, and anyone else around him. There are recorded instances of an entire family of five or six members having the disease at the same time.

Polio didn't affect everyone the same way. I was told that it attacked various points in the central nervous system and therefore could affect almost any part of the body. Some polio victims were sick for awhile and then recovered, with little or no side effects. Whereas other victims (actually about one in every hundred) had lasting infirmities from the disease.

Newsreels in movie houses showed pictures of people in iron lungs who could not breathe without them because polio had paralyzed their lungs. The reports stated that they would never be able to live without breathing assistance.

Also, polio sometimes paralyzed other body members, such as the legs. Young people who contracted it were often plagued by its appearing to stunt the growth of the affected body part, because the diseased nerves had caused paralysis making the muscles shrivel and atrophy. Hence, there were persons walking around with braces on one or both legs, looking deformed because their atrophied legs were not only paralyzed, but also small in comparison to their fully-grown bodies. Most of them carried walking canes to help balance themselves, even with the braces on. There were instances when victims who couldn't walk at all were confined to wheelchairs.

The polio fear was at its height when I started attending school at the Harlandale Junior High School, and it didn't allay my fears any to meet face to face with several students who had been through polio and were wearing braces and carrying walking canes. Every time I saw one of them either in a wheelchair, or struggling around the school ground with those heavy leg braces, I felt ashamed that I was brooding about being so much taller than my classmates. Compared to the problems those polio victims had facing them in life, my being too tall was no big deal at all. I never actually knew anyone while he or she was in the communicable stage of polio and no one in my family had it.

Sometime in the late 1930s, President Franklin D. Roosevelt was instrumental in establishing a national foundation for Polio research. The foundation held a fund drive, dubbed the March of Dimes, throughout the month of January each year to obtain money to fund research for a cure, and/or a vaccine to prevent polio.

Several different things were done during the January March of Dimes each year. For instance, cardboards with 10 or more slots on them to slip dimes into were distributed everywhere for donors (especially children) to fill with dimes and mail to the foundation.

A dime in the 1930s was a lot of money. It could buy any one of the following: two cups of coffee, one sandwich, a piece of pie, two double-dip ice-cream cones, two loaves of bread, or a ticket to a matinee at some of the theaters. And that is only to name a few things. Nevertheless, children frequently found enough dimes to fill one of those cards during January. If they didn't get the card filled, it was returned anyway, even if there was only one dime on it.

In addition to that, large glass jars labeled "March of Dimes" were placed near the cash registers in most places of business (especially restaurants, pharmacies, and stores) asking for donations of change to be dropped in. Every business house wanted to see its jar filled with coins.

Then each year, around the 30th of January (President Roosevelt's birthday), a different lady from each neighborhood volunteered to march through her area, ring doorbells, and ask for a donation to the March of Dimes.

All of those things really worked, as it always seemed to me that everyone contributed at least a dime. The proceeds went to scientific research, which paid off gloriously when a vaccine was finally developed in the mid-1950s and put into use, henceforth preventing polio.

Due to continuous donations of anything from a dime from the smallest child to thousands of dollars from the wealthiest man for over two decades, polio is more or less nonexistent today, at least in the United States.

Smallpox was another much-dreaded, sometimes-fatal disease of that era, and the first one to my knowledge for which a vaccine was administered universally. Mother and Father had both known people who had had smallpox which left large, deep pitted marks on their faces and probably their bodies as well. The memory of my parents' depiction of those smallpox survivors is rather grim. When I was quite young I actually saw a man with those disfiguring pockmarks on his face. A person had to actually see those scars to realize how grotesque they were.

I was vaccinated for small pox when I was about six years old. Even though most of the mothers I knew were anxious for their children to receive the smallpox vaccinations, they were afraid they might leave large pockmarks on their arms. Imagine being upset about one pockmark on the forearm, when the child could have been pocked all over the body and face if he or she had the disease itself.

Some of the mothers had a special apparatus constructed by the doctor for the child to wear over the vaccination site until it healed, usually about two weeks. It consisted of a little glass cup inverted over the vaccination that was held in place with tape and bandages.

There always seemed to be at least one little girl walking around bragging that she had a glass cover on her vaccination to protect it and keep it from causing a large scar. It was supposed that if the sight of the vaccination was kept completely dry and not touched at all until it healed, it would leave a much smaller scar, but it is doubtful that the glass cover did any good at all.

My vaccination only left a small scar, which reminds me of another thing. Several times throughout the years, the health department sent a nurse out to the school to examine our vaccination scars. If she found one that wasn't definitely discernible, indicating to her that the vaccination had not taken sufficiently to suit her, she sent the child back to a doctor for another vaccination. Once or twice a classmate was ordered to be re-vaccinated. The last time I was examined I barely missed being sent back for revaccination because my scar was so dim.

There was always a mother protesting in vain against the required smallpox vaccination because she feared it would give her child the disease, rather than prevent it. In fact, as I look back on the whole thing, it seems that everyone was just a little bit apprehensive, one way or another, about being injected with the smallpox vaccine. Such a procedure was more or less unknown and not understood at that time.

The smallpox vaccination was required by law, as part of a worldwide vaccination program that began in the first part of the twentieth century in an effort to eradicate smallpox, which had previously reached epidemic proportions. I read someplace recently that the vaccination program was so successful that the World Health Organization declared the world free of smallpox sometime around 1980 and ordered cessation of vaccinations for everyone except laboratory workers directly involved with the smallpox virus.

There were several other communicable diseases that had to be dealt with one way or another in the 1930s. They were diphtheria, whooping cough, measles, and mumps. There were no vaccines with which to inoculate persons against any of those diseases at that time, so the best way to deal with the situation was to try to stay away from persons while they were in the communicable stage.

Diphtheria was a very debilitating, sometimes fatal, disease that had been known to reach epidemic proportions. One of my cousins suffered through diphtheria. No one else in my family had it.

Whooping cough was highly contagious and quite serious, especially in very young children, taking several weeks to completely run its course. I had whooping cough when I was about four and one-half years old and remember that I nearly choked to death during the coughing spasms.

Measles was also highly contagious, causing a very high fever and a painful rash. Back then, people believed that future medical problems were caused by measles. For instance, I went to school with a girl whose vision was extremely impaired, one boy with a heart murmur, and another boy with rheumatic fever; all of whom claimed their physical problems were caused by measles. My sisters and I all three had measles without any untoward side effects, that I know of.

Mumps was unbelievably uncomfortable and sort of a peculiar disease. My sisters and I all had mumps. I had it when I was about 13 years old. It started with the gland under my right ear and the gland under the left side of my chin, swelling to several times their natural size and remaining swollen and extremely painful for about a week. Then I returned to school for one day. The next morning, the glands under the opposite ear and the opposite side of my chin were swollen and I went through the whole miserable thing again for another week. The doctor sent me a large, white, milk-glass jar filled with an axle-grease like paste that smelled horrible, to rub on the swelling, supposedly to make it feel better. But it didn't seem to do anything but dirty up the pillowcase and distract me from the pain that continued to be excruciating.

Mumps also caused me to be extremely weak. In fact, during the first week of illness I got out of bed, started walking across the room and fainted dead away for the first time in my life. It was very frightening. My sisters, who were both a lot younger than I when they had mumps, were not nearly as weak and ill as I was. It was common knowledge that if mumps occurred in a mature male, it could cause sterility. I also knew a woman who said that mumps had caused her to be sterile.

Today there is a vaccine available for use in immunization against all of these diseases, and the public schools in Texas require that every child present certification of vaccination for specific diseases before he or she can be enrolled. That's quite different from the way I grew up. Without vaccines we more or less took it for granted that we would have most of those diseases in childhood. It wasn't uncommon for a mother (after deciding her child was healthy enough and at the right age to best endure it) to deliberately expose her child to measles, chickenpox, mumps, and sometimes even whooping cough, so he or she would contract the disease and get it over with. The mother always said the child would contract the disease anyway and it was best if he or she was under ten years of age when it occurred. After a person had had one of those communicable diseases, he was generally immune to it for life.

In thinking back to the 1930s and communicable diseases, one more comes to my mind that I don't believe any children knew about at that time: syphilis, a sexually transmitted disease which is still prevalent today. There was no cure for syphilis in the 1930s, but today it can be cured with penicillin if it is diagnosed in the early stages and treatment is started immediately. Before the discovery of penicillin around 1950, there was no suitable treatment and certainly no cure for syphilis.

The stages of development were varied, as syphilis was capable of invading almost any part of the body.

Many of its victims in whom the disease was latent, were unaware for years, (some never) that they were contaminated with syphilis and could transmit it. Perhaps that's why it was required that persons in Texas have a Wassermann blood test to show that they did not have syphilis before they could obtain a marriage license. My husband and I both had to have those blood tests in 1947 in order to get our marriage license.

To my knowledge, I never knew anyone who had syphilis, so all of my observations of the disease are secondhand, gleaned from things I have read in books and seen on the screen. In fact, I myself never heard of syphilis until I was over 20 years old and working at the San Antonio General Depot, Ft. Sam Houston, Texas. While riding on the army post one day with some co-workers (ladies twice my age), we passed a large hospital barracks marked ISOLATION way out on a large lot, sort of by itself, and saw men in hospital pajamas wandering around on an outside verandah. The women I was with made remarks about how sad it was that those men had syphilis, were contagious, had to be isolated, and would never be cured. I asked what syphilis was. They then, after expressing disbelief that I had never heard of it, enlightened me on the subject. I was grateful I had never heard of syphilis before then.

Remembering polio and other communicable diseases we lived with in the 1930s, makes me realize the vast accomplishments made by medical science since that time, strengthening my belief that medical research will eventually find a cure for, or vaccine to prevent, the main disease that is plaguing us today—AIDS. It will just take a lot of time, dedication, patience, money, and faith.

Chapter Sixteen

The Great Depression Brings Hard Times

We called it the "Great Depression," but the only thing great about it was the enormity of the misery it exuded on the average American. In spite of the fact that I was only a little over six and one-half years old when it was ushered in by the stock market crash of October 29, 1929. I can still remember very clearly many incidents resulting from it. The newsreels shown in movie theaters during the weeks following the crash related tragic stories about extremely wealthy gentlemen who, having lost an entire fortune in one day, committed suicide either by jumping out of a skyscraper window, using a pistol, driving off a cliff, or some other means.

Within the next year or two the newsreels began to show hundreds of people in various cities waiting in lines at numerous charitable and civic organizations for a free meal or free food. Many of the churches collected food to give to unemployed members until they found jobs. It seems there were thousands of hungry out of work people everywhere in the United States trying to get food for themselves and their families.

Then the news stories started telling about men who were unable to find work of any kind, just walking away and deserting their wives and children because they couldn't bear to watch them starve. The womenfolk had to learn to fend for themselves, and they usually did.

This created a network of men traveling around the country by hitchhiking, walking, or stealing rides on railroad boxcars. They tried to find a day's work here and there in exchange for meals, and now and then one of them even managed to make a little money to send back to his family.

Almost every large town or city had a "hobo jungle" just outside the city limits near the railroad tracks, which was a make-shift outdoor campsite that those wandering men stayed in. Periodically the local police or sheriff broke the camp up and the men just moved it on to another site.

The closest I ever came to knowing anyone in that situation was the men who rang Grandmother Templeton's doorbell asking for handouts. Every time we visited her there were as many as six or eight such requests. Alex answered the doorbell and, according to Grandmother's instructions, gave each one the price of a meal, probably about 50¢. We never had a man ring the doorbell for a handout at our home in Mayfield Park, I suppose we were too far out in the country for them.

All of these things filled me with sadness and confusion and made an indelible impression on me which I have not forgotten even to this day.

I also remember hearing the grown-ups talk about banks beginning to fail all around the United States. More and more often, it was becoming necessary for them to foreclose on homes because the borrowers no longer had employment and could not make payments on their bank loans.

Many of those bank failures occurred when a bank found its assets had been reduced from cash to a large inventory of repossessed real estate. Since it was virtually impossible to dispose of land at any price in that economically depressed era, the bank found itself unable to honor withdrawal requests from its depositors.

In that day and age there was no such thing as Federal Deposit Insurance Corporation (FDIC). Therefore, when a bank reached the point of insolvency it was closed and individuals with money deposited in that institution simply lost their money.

Thus, a panic wave started to spread among people with money deposited in any bank. As this panic built to a frenzied peak, it began to cause depositors in otherwise sound financial institutions, to rush to their banks and demand their money, for fear they would fail before such funds could be withdrawn.

This action (commonly referred to as a "run on the bank") caused many of those otherwise-sound banks to fail as they could not honor such large cash demands at once, the common practice being to loan deposited money out for interest.

I remember that shortly after taking office, President Roosevelt closed all the banks in the United States for a short period of time in order to stop those bank "runs" before they all collapsed. This closing action, even though temporary, caused a virtual panic among just about everyone. Something was done to stabilize the situation immediately, and then the FDIC was created to protect depositors against future bank failures (up to a certain amount) and everyone rested easier but with skepticism as to whether it would really work.

At the time, I didn't know of anyone in my immediate family losing any money due to a bank failure, but many years later my husband told me that his grandmother lost $700 in a savings account when the San Antonio bank that the money was in failed. That $700 doesn't sound like very much money today, but it was quite a lot in the early 1930s.

Then later, the United States went off the gold standard and all citizens were ordered to turn in any gold coins in their possession in exchange for other monetary equivalences. That caused a lot of grumbling as many people didn't want to part with their gold pieces and they even doubted that the paper money it was exchanged for was worth anything.

I remember hearing from newsreels and my parents that the Depression had been caused by an overproduction of everything from foodstuffs to housing facilities. For example, most of the farmers had raised bumper crops of everything, and when they took their corn, grain, livestock, vegetables, and other farm products to market, they found it flooded with other farmers bearing the same merchandise, which brought the price down to zero almost overnight. For instance, it was totally a "buyer's market" as everyone with a product to sell kept asking less and less in an attempt to attract a buyer until all of the buyers had been satisfied, leaving farmers everywhere with items for which there was no market. They eventually didn't even take their wares to town to sell, but left them in the fields to rot.

Shortly after taking office, President Roosevelt started a program wherein the government arranged to destroy thousands of farm animals and other farm commodities in an effort to deplete the overage and re-establish a normal supply and demand and eventually stabilize the prices.

I remember coming face to face with part of that "program" in action one day when we were returning home from purchasing fruit at the Market Plaza. While riding across a bridge, we saw and heard a large herd of cattle running down the small almost dry creek bed beneath it. Father said those cattle were in the process of being destroyed, as were thousands of other cattle throughout the United States, in an effort to stabilize the supply and demand and price of cattle. Mother and Father just sat there beside the creek for a few minutes with sadness in their faces as they thought about it, but they said something had to be done and they hoped that was the right thing. Father said an overproduction of livestock and farm commodities should never happen again and it never did, as President Roosevelt established in 1933 an Administration of Agriculture to set quotas on, and support the price of, many things grown and produced by farmers.

I couldn't exactly understand all those things at that time, but I knew the adults were discussing them and were extremely worried about them. Mother tried very hard to shield us from the disaster and as far as our everyday home life was concerned, she made it seem that things were continuing in a perfectly normal manner.

When I think about the Depression period from a personal standpoint, my mind wanders first back to my school days. I find it interesting to note that my entire public school attendance (starting in September 1930 and ending in May 1940) was spent after the onset of and during the Depression. It may have been an extremely economically depressed era in the United States, but I remember my school days as a time of carefree happiness which I look back on with great fondness.

Nevertheless, the Depression eventually brought about a traumatic change in our lives. Actually, it took about six years of that Great Depression "trickling down" on Mayfield Park to culminate in an enormous "deluge" which completely engulfed us, causing Father to seek "higher ground."

As far as things in our home were concerned, it seemed to me that Mother had been born with a natural desire to save everything and be frugal in all matters pertaining to money. In fact, pinching pennies seemed to be a hobby with her, and hunting bargains, which included getting as much as possible out of anything purchased, was her favorite pastime. Therefore, the Depression caused very little change in her daily life.

However, as I look back now, I realize that she did a lot of things in order to stretch foodstuffs and make inexpensive meats more palatableast. One of our favorites was salmon croquettes. Salmon was very inexpensive (about 10¢ for a large can) and, cheap or not, I loved it. She drained, boned, and skinned the salmon, mixed it with one egg, some of the drained liquid, and three slices of wheat bread crumbled into bits, salt and pepper and one-half of a minced onion which had been sautéed in a little butter with a stick of chopped celery, shaped that mixture into patties and fried them in hot shortening until golden brown. They were especially delicious served with a little tomato ketchup.

In the 1930s, giant sardines packed in tomato sauce were surprisingly savory eaten cold directly from the giant cans they came in. Mother and Jean loved to eat baby sardines from small tins. They were unbelievably cheap, strongly flavored, and I didn't care for them at all.

Hamburger meat, also very economical, played an important role in her meat dishes. She frequently made meat patties, meatballs, chili, hash (with potatoes and onions), and of course fried hamburger patties, served in hamburger buns with mustard and homemade mayonnaise, relish, tomatoes, and lettuce.

There were even occasions when Mother suddenly said she was going to give us "a treat" and served fried bologna with pinto beans.

Then there were the giant, foot-long frankfurters she served from time to time; they were delicious. In the wintertime, she reverted to pork spareribs (also inexpensive) baked with canned or fresh sauerkraut. I loved that dish and even though I always had an allergic reaction from the pork, I ate it anyway, every time. Another economical treat that we enjoyed often in the wintertime was Mother's homemade vegetable soup, made with lots of fresh vegetables and a large soup bone, or marrow bone, as she called it, that even had some meat on it.

Mother still served large steaks, hams, roasts, and chicken, but not nearly as often as in the past. I, for one, was completely satisfied with her "economical meats." They gave us much more variety and were all very tasty.

In spite of the fact that a loaf of bakery bread was only 5¢, Mother served a lot of homemade bread, as it was still more economical. I suppose that is because she always had an abundance of milk, eggs, and butter in her kitchen to prepare them with, much of which would have gone to waste if not used for that purpose. She made biscuits, cornbread, muffins, rolls, and yeast breads. I thought those homemade breads were better than bakery breads any day.

Many times I watched Mother sift two cups of flour with four teaspoons of baking powder, add one teaspoon of salt into a mixing bowl, add three or four tablespoons of shortening or lard, blend it until it was the consistency of coarse cornmeal, make a hole in the middle, add 3/4 cup sweet milk, and then stir those ingredients together with a fork until "damp" and blended. Next she rounded the dough up and kneaded it four or five times on a floured table top, patted it out to about 1/2 inch thick and cut it into biscuits with a round cookie cutter dipped into flour.

She cooked them in a one-inch deep biscuit pan, being sure they touched each other, until they were light brown on top. When broken open, they were snow-white and feather-light and as I remember it, they were always best when made with fresh hog lard.

On many occasions when we didn't have a dessert with our evening meal, Mother took six or eight biscuits leftover from breakfast, broke them up somewhat and stirred them into a cast-iron skillet with about one cup of boiling hot Brer Rabbit molasses and 1/2 cup butter and continued stirring them around over the heat until they were completely coated and very, very sticky. We called them "sticky biscuits." I always ate them until the syrup and butter made me feel a little sick, or they were all gone.

In the wintertime she frequently stewed a chicken and then dropped strips of biscuit dough into the liquid around the chicken and let that simmer, and then we all enjoyed "chicken and dumplings." This was almost a "free meal" as there was always a molting hen in the laying house walking around just waiting to be eaten.

Mother had two cookie recipes she made quite often: Corn-Flake Macaroons and Cousin Leal's Molasses Cookies, which I list below.

CORN-FLAKE MACAROONS

2 eggs whites
1 cup shredded coconut
1 cup granulated sugar
2 cups corn flakes
1/2 teaspoon vanilla
1/2 cup pecans (if available)

Beat egg whites until stiff with hand beater, and then add sugar gradually while continuing to beat. With spoon fold in remaining ingredients. Drop by teaspoonful onto greased or oiled cookie sheet.
Bake in moderately hot oven of 400 degrees until delicately browned. Makes about 36 macaroons.

(We rarely ever had the pecans.) Those macaroons were crunchy and had a distinct coconut flavor. In the early twenties, before the Depression, I remember that Mother made them with much more coconut and left the corn flakes and nuts out. But the coconut was much more expensive than the corn flakes, hence the change during the Depression.

COUSIN LEAL'S MOLASSES COOKIES

1 cup shortening
1/2 teaspoon cloves
1 cup granulated sugar
1/4 teaspoon nutmeg
1 cup molasses
1 teaspoon salt
4 teaspoons soda
2 to 6 cups flour
2 teaspoons ginger
1 cup buttermilk or clabber

Cream shortening and sugar, add molasses, sift two cups flour with dry ingredients and add alternately to first mixture with buttermilk.
Add enough more flour to make a soft dough. Roll out on floured board, cut into fancy shapes, sprinkle sugar on top and bake five to eight minutes in a rather quick oven (375 degrees).

Those cookies were thick and soft, the kind that taste so good between meals. Sometimes she left the sugar off the top and iced them with powdered sugar icing after they were baked. They tasted almost exactly like gingerbread, due to all that ginger, but even a child found it almost impossible to eat more than one cookie without feeling overly full. They kept quite well for a week or more and seemed to get even more flavorful after the first day or two.

Maybe those things combined were the reasons why Mother wanted to bake them so often, in spite of the fact that they were a lot of trouble to make, what with all that rolling out, cutting, and the mess involved. Or was it simply that she and Father both really liked the cookie's rich gingerbread flavor? Many years later, when I questioned Mother about that all she would say was, "I don't remember where the recipe came from and I don't remember having a Cousin Leal," so I'll never know.

Of course, Mother did make other cookies from time to time. The ones I remember were peanut butter cookies and Mrs. Huffor's oatmeal cookies. Tollhouse cookies hadn't been invented yet, nor had chocolate chips.

Here is Mrs. Huffor's oatmeal cookie recipe, which was my favorite.

MRS. HUFFOR'S OATMEAL COOKIES

1 cup shortening or butter
2 cups flour
1 1/2 cup granulated sugar
1/2 teaspoon soda
2 eggs
1 teaspoon cinnamon
2 cups oatmeal
1/4 cup sour milk or buttermilk
1 cup chopped pecans

(You can add nutmeg, coconut, and/or peanut butter to this recipe; or leave all extra-added attractions out and flavor with vanilla extract only)

Mix shortening and sugar; add eggs and mix well; add oatmeal and any added attractions; sift dry ingredients and add alternately with sour milk (and vanilla, if used). If dough is too stiff, add extra buttermilk. Roll out and cut with a cookie cutter and bake on greased cookie sheet in 375 degrees oven for about 10 minutes.

We always had an abundance of vegetables fresh from the garden or from jars on the pantry shelf. Father had started bringing home bushels of peaches, plums, tomatoes, green beans & field peas, and dozens of pineapples from the market plaza to can. He also purchased oranges, grapefruits and apples, and, oh yes, tangerines, by the giant sack-full when they were in season for us to eat fresh. Prices for those fresh vegetables and fruits in the bulk had gone down constantly until they were only about 50 cents to 75 cents a bushel or sack and the pineapples were unbelievably cheap.

A lot of our staples were purchased in bulk from the Chinese grocery store. Bulk items were much more economical than packaged items. There was always an abundance of rabbits and chickens to fry, stew and bake, and eggs, milk, butter and cream that came from our barnyard. And, oh yes, we always had plenty of honey from Father's bees. People were coming to our home less and less often to buy honey as they simply didn't have the wherewithal to pay for it and Father could no longer find anyplace else to sell it.

The things Mother did to stretch the food budget only made our meals better and tastier, as far as I was concerned, and I don't believe the Depression affected our diet at all, except maybe for the better.

When it came to our clothing, Mother had always made our dresses, slips, nightgowns and robes by choice, and we never had a shortage of any of them. As far as shoes were concerned we usually had whatever we needed, but no more. Mother never believed in purchasing anything frivolous, but only the necessary items. We also got new coats and sweaters only when we needed them. In fact, I might say that I really didn't know if we were wealthy or poor as we lived more or less the same in either instance, frugally and sensibly.

Father always seemed to have a new business suit fitted for him about once a year and all the dress shirts, neckties, and other clothing he needed. Mother had all the garments she needed also, but no more.

Our home was consistently comfortable. We had electricity for lights and appliances, including our electric refrigerator, which made all the ice we needed, and the electric stove, with which we cooked our food. We were on

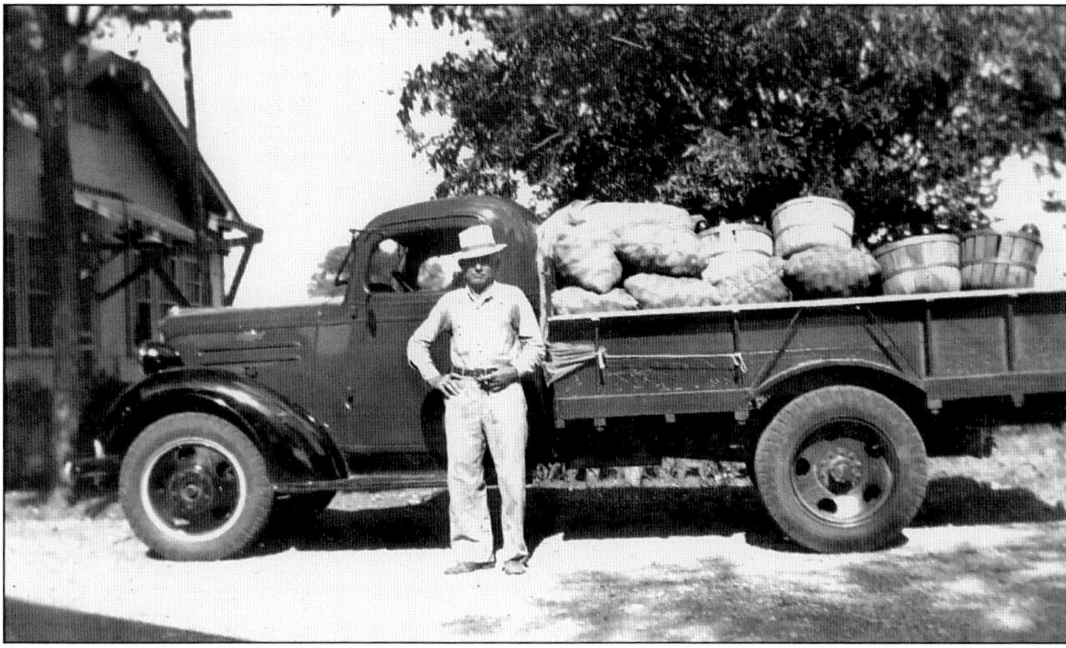

Belgian vegetable farmer Polidor Michiels stands ready to take his produce to market. The bags hold potatoes and the baskets are full of cabbages. (Photo courtesy of Tillie Persyn.)

a public water supply and always had plenty of water. Our home was heated in the wintertime with electric heaters, wood stoves, and a fireplace. Father always had an abundant supply of wood to keep them going all winter long.

I don't really know how much of a financial strain it was to keep our home and needs running smoothly, but when I read about some of the hardships endured by other people during the Depression, I almost feel guilty that we faired so well.

Nevertheless by the middle of the summer in 1935, I was beginning to get a sense of impending disaster descending on us precipitated by the Great Depression.

A lot of farmers had a devastating time because they couldn't find a market anywhere for the grains and livestock they raised. This was just as hard on them financially as having all their crops fail would have been. It was even worse, emotionally, because in many instances they had to stand by and watch their bumper crops just lie there in the field and rot.

The crisis was compounded for men operating small farms located a great distance from a metropolis, because they couldn't obtain employment elsewhere to help out when all else failed. In fact, things got so bad that Father's eldest sister Anna and her husband Harvey, who had always been well-off financially, decided to sell their farm and relocate in San Antonio, where her people lived and Uncle Harvey could find a job.

As soon as the farm was sold, they rented an apartment in San Antonio and Uncle Harvey started out on what was generally, in those days, a hapless mission: seeking employment. I remember Father worrying about them constantly, especially since Uncle Harvey was not trained for anything but farming.

Aunt Anna never expressed a negative thought about the situation. Instead, she was always ready to don a nice dress and one of the wide-brimmed oversized colorful hats that she always wore when leaving her home, and venture out to explore her new surroundings.

Those hats, which were decorated with large flowers, ribbons and lace, berries and fruits, or other things, were usually finished off with a large colorful feather, or plumage, and fastened securely to her hair with a decorative hat pin. They were sort of her "trademark" that made a statement to the effect that "all's right with the world" as she went forth to the grocer, butcher, church, a neighbor's, or wherever she chose.

Whenever Father expressed his concern to her about the situation, she always said, "Don't worry so much, Harvey will find a job."

And believe it or not, after several weeks of seeking employment, much to the joy and surprise of everyone (Father especially), Uncle Harvey announced that he'd found a job. He had acquired the position of custodian for a large north-side school wherein he immediately found that his farming experience had rendered him very capable in caring for and landscaping the school's grounds and that he had a natural aptitude for keeping all the utilities, and other things involved, functioning. He also liked being around the joyful carefree atmosphere of children. And, furthermore, he could do the job at the same slow laid-back pace he had become accustomed to on the farm.

All this culminated in Aunt Anna and Uncle Harvey purchasing a home on the north side of San Antonio not too far from his job. And I believe they were even better satisfied there than they had ever been on their farm. Especially since Aunt Anna was in the same town with her parents and brother (and his family) and surrounded by an endless number of people with whom she immediately became acquainted. Among other things, she joined a ladies club which met in a different home each week to play cards. She also developed the practice of going to a funeral any time she knew the deceased or any member of the deceased's family. Uncle Harvey continued in that position until he reached retirement age. Their son, Walton, went to Baylor University, married and became a Baptist minister. Their daughter, Marguerite, eventually married Paul Wiley and they acquired a fortune of their own by operating a dude ranch near Dallas.

Aunt Anna, pictured with her little sister, Ada, was the most popular young lady for many miles around. Six or eight suitors, many both handsome and prosperous, asked for her hand.

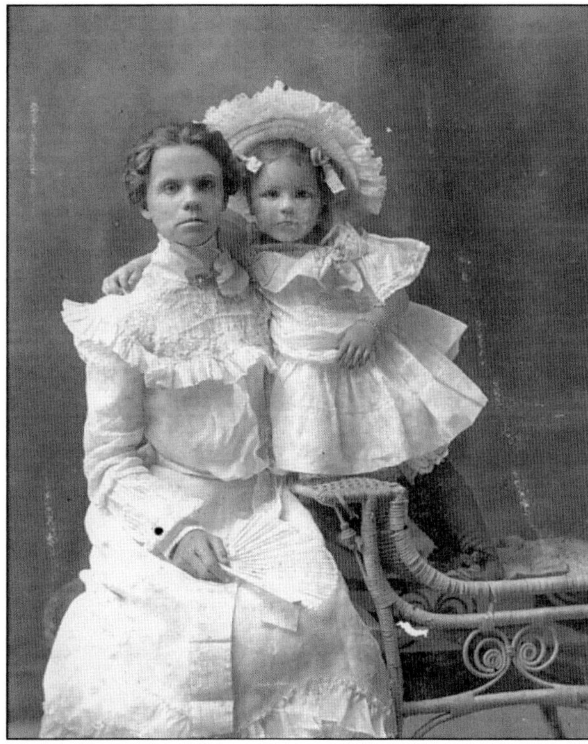

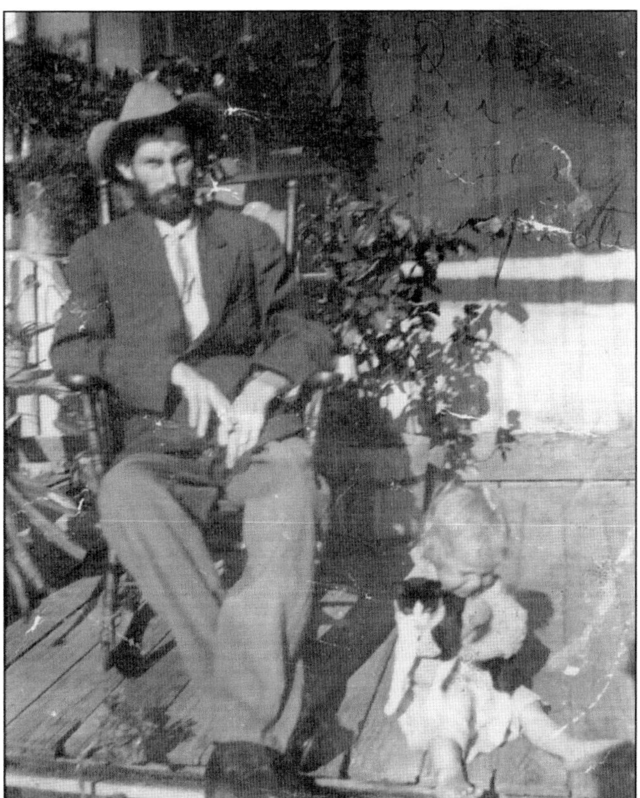

Aunt Anna turned down all the others and chose Harvey Robinson.

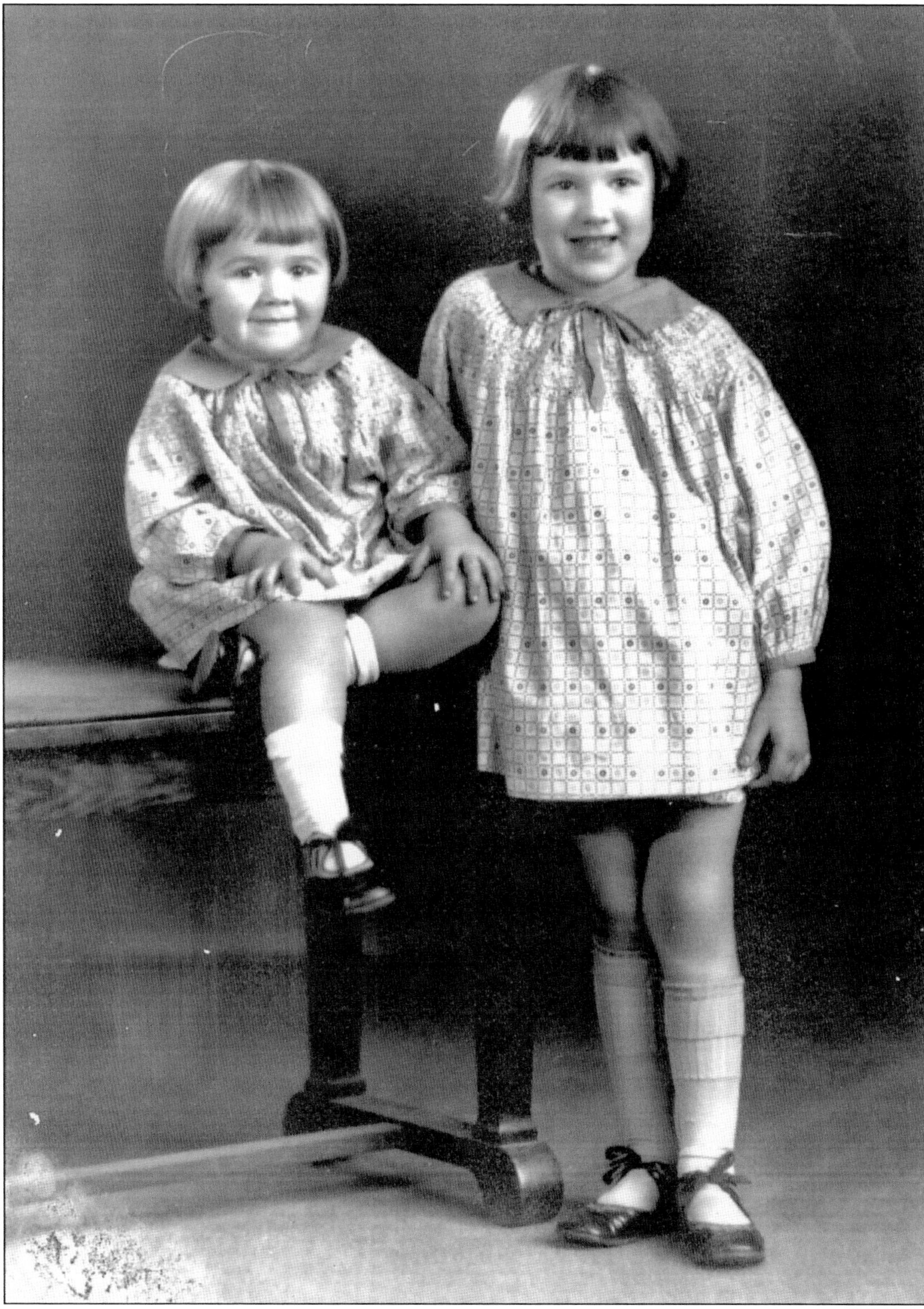

Jean and I pose here in some of our handmade dresses, which Mother sewed for us.

Chapter Seventeen
The Last Christmas at Mayfield Park

The last year we lived at Mayfield Park actually started in December 1934, shortly before Christmas, which was the last Christmas we celebrated there. It was, as always, a joyful occasion.

About two weeks before Christmas, Mother started playing carols on the piano. The ones I remember her playing the most were "Silent Night" and "Jingle Bells." She loved "Jingle Bells" and in no time she had me and my sisters singing along. As we sang we jumped around the living room and created a make-believe sleigh by arranging the sofa pillows on the floor. Mother told me many times that she had actually been on sleigh rides in the snow, when she was a very young girl in Sulphur Springs, and how much fun they were. She described the sleigh, the horse, and the horse's bell that rang as the sleigh went through the snow. I suppose that is why "Jingle Bells" seemed to be her favorite Christmas carol.

During the last eight or ten days leading up to Christmas day, Mother could always be found in the kitchen making several different kinds of candy, and 1934 was no exception.

The candies she usually made were chocolate fudge, divinity, Boston Creams, taffy and candied popcorn balls, all of which were made by standard recipes except the Boston Creams and perhaps the taffy. The Boston Creams were different from any other candy and they were made by a recipe Mother discovered somewhere that she never saw anyplace again. Once she lost the recipe for a time and couldn't find anyone else who had ever even heard of it. She couldn't remember the exact ingredients, and attempts to make the candy without a recipe were futile. When she finally located the recipe for Boston Creams, she made sure she never lost it again. I have included the recipe in this book on the following pages.

BOSTON CREAMS

3 cups granulated sugar
1-teaspoon vanilla
1 cup white corn syrup (Karo)
1 cup chopped pecans
1 cup sweet whole cream

Boil sugar, syrup, and cream to softball, stirring frequently throughout;
Remove from fire and beat long and hard until white and smooth,
Beat in nuts and vanilla. Put in a deep buttered pan and let stand for several days. Then cut in squares and serve.

The recipe also called for three squares unsweetened chocolate to be melted and poured over the pan of candy as soon as it cooled; then let stand for several days, cut into squares and serve. Mother left the chocolate off and it was still delicious.

Those Boston Creams were different from any other homemade candy I ever ate. They were indeed true to the "cream" in their name, being very creamy, with just a hint of a sweet buttery taste, but I thought three days was entirely too long to wait to taste the candy.

MOTHER'S TAFFY

1 cup granulated sugar
1/2 cup white Karo
1/4 cup water

Cook to 270 degrees; remove from heat and add:
1/4 teaspoon soda
1 tablespoon vinegar

Stir until mixed. Turn out on a buttered platter and round up; cool just enough to handle, then pick up with one hand on each side and pull hands away from each other, stretching the candy until you have a long rope, then bring hands together and take one hand and pick up free end of rope, then bring hands together and take one hand and pick up free end and stretch and pull out,
then bring hands back together and repeat that pulling, stretching operation until the candy begins to cool and has a light creamy look. Pull into a long rope; place on a surface covered with powdered sugar and cut into candy pieces.

Mother's recipe for taffy, which she learned when she was a girl in Sulphur Springs, is the only taffy recipe I ever made. When Mother lived there, taffy pulls were en vogue among the young folks in Sulphur Springs. They met in someone's home, made lots of taffy, divided into couples, and "pulled taffy" until it was ready to eat, all the while talking, singing and laughing. It was a popular way for young people to party.

Once in a while, Mother made sugared popcorn, which is still my favorite way to eat popcorn.

SUGARED POPCORN

Note: read instructions carefully all the way through before starting.

1/2 cup popcorn - pop and set-aside in an extra large bowl.

Sugared Coating:
2 cups granulated sugar
1/2 cup water
2 Tablespoons Karo (white)

Cook in open pan over direct heat until it spins a thread, stirring constantly until it boils, and only off and on after that, to see if it is spinning a thread.
Remove from heat and set pan on a cool surface.
Have all these measured ingredients ready to add at once as soon as syrup is removed from heat:

1/2 teaspoon vinegar
1 teaspoon vanilla
1 teaspoon soda
2 tablespoon butter

Add the above ingredients all at once and stir into syrup quickly, only until butter is melted and all are mixed,then pour over the popcorn, stirring constantly until it is all in and popcorn is coated. The syrup will become sugary. Coat all the popcorn with the delicious syrup.

The sugared popcorn was as much fun to make as it was to eat. I remember how the syrup foamed up and turned from the appearance of clear water to an off-white color and almost tripled in volume when the vinegar, vanilla, soda, and butter were added. Then it had to be poured over the popped popcorn quickly and stirred fast and constantly until the sugar set, or it would be one big lump of sugared popcorn, instead of in individual sugar-coated kernels.

As the candy making was all finished, Mother and I wrapped the individual pieces of candy in little pieces of waxed paper and packed three boxes with candy to be wrapped as gifts for Grandmother Templeton, Aunt Sissie, and Mrs. Huffor. Wrapping the candies and packing the boxes were a lot of fun for me. I had always been at school during that procedure in the past, as I was destined to be in the future. So that Christmas, candy making was special. Mother reserved the remainder of the candy for us to eat at home during the holidays.

As soon as the candy making was completed, I started looking forward to another big thrill of the Yuletide season, selecting the Christmas tree. Sometimes we purchased it from a local vendor and other times we went to the forest to cut our own tree, which was as much fun to me as anything else pertaining to Christmas. The day finally arrived (about three or four days before Christmas) when Father walked in and said "Come on, we are going after our Christmas tree." We all rushed to seat ourselves in the car and started out. When Father drove on by the local vendors and headed the car toward the hill country north of San Antonio, I knew I was in for a special thrill, we were going to chop down our own tree.

In those days there were acres and acres of unfenced cedar trees north of San Antonio and it was customary for anyone who so chose to chop down a tree and take it home for Christmas, free of charge.

I could tell that Father and Mother also received a special thrill from cutting their own tree by the way they rushed around excitedly through the cedar forest, which forevermore seemed to grow on the side of a small hill, until they found the exact tree they wanted. Father chopped the chosen tree down with the ax he had brought with him and then he tied it onto the top of the car and we returned home.

Decorating the tree was another highlight of the season. We had an assortment of colorful, almost paper thin, glass ornaments, about three or four inches in diameter, some of which were hand-painted, some had frosting on them, and some had bells dangling in them that actually made a tinkling sound when they were moved. There were strings of small red, silver, and blue ball-shaped ornaments that we circled the tree with, and shiny red and silver ropes to drape on the branches, and lots of silver icicles to hang all over the tree. Last, Mother had a large colorful ornament with a pointed white sphere on the top of it, which was placed on the very top of the tree with the sphere pointing straight up toward the ceiling.

After finishing the tree, we cut sheets of red and green construction paper into strips, then pasted the ends of a strip together to form a circle. Then we attached another ring to the circle to form a chain of alternating colors. We draped them across the windows, around the piano and over doorways and other things, adding Christmas cheer to the front part of the house.

Each Yuletide, Mother completed her Christmas candy making before the Christmas tree was in our home. This was almost a necessity as, since the birth of Frances in 1929, with the advent of the tree, she also had an unwanted, uninvited visitor, hay fever. In fact, within a few days after the tree was set up in our living room, Mother was deep in the throes of an acute attack of hay fever, which continued until the tree was removed.

In years to come she discovered it was the cedar Christmas tree that caused her to have the hay fever, but even though she knew what it would do to her, she still insisted for many years on having a real live cedar tree in her home every Christmas. When fir trees became popular in San Antonio, she consented to using one of them in place of cedar. The fir didn't bother her quite as much as the cedar and it was a real live tree, so she switched to them from that time on.

A day or two before Christmas, Grandmother Templeton always hosted a Christmas Tree Party. It was held early in the afternoon while all the menfolk were busy at their offices or jobs, thus, the only male in attendance was usually the butler/chauffeur, Alex, who didn't seem to mind at all being the only man there.

Mother brought several special gifts for Grandmother Templeton, Aunt Sissie, Mrs. Huffor, and in later years, Alex, and smaller gifts for some of the other guests. My sisters and I brought the gifts that Grandmother Templeton had bought for us at Winn's to give to each other and relatives who were at the party. In fact all of the guests usually brought gifts for almost everyone else in attendance, and needless to say, everyone received a lot of gifts.

For a good many years, Mrs. Huffor dressed up like Santa Claus and brought a sack of toys to the front door, rang the doorbell, came in and called out "Ho, Ho, Ho, Merry Christmas," and then she passed out the toys from "Santa's" sack. That was fun, even though I always knew that Santa was really Mrs. Huffor. Afterward we all gathered around the large Christmas tree and watched each other open gifts.

For lunch and dinner, they always had baked hen and more or less the same vegetables and other things that they usually ate on a Sunday. After the noon meal, Grandmother did handwork and Grandfather worked on legal briefs. That's the way they seemed to want it. Their children spent Christmas day at their own homes, or with their spouses' families.

Christmas Eve was always filled with excitement in anticipation of a visit from Santa Claus. At bedtime we hung our stockings on the mantle and then Mother usually read *A Visit From St. Nicholas* (we called it *The Night Before Christmas*). Then we went to bed so excited we couldn't go to sleep. I always thought for sure I would still be awake when St. Nicholas' sleigh and reindeer landed on the roof and he slid down the chimney (it was a large one) to fill our stockings. But I went to sleep in spite of myself, so I never saw him. But the next morning I saw what he had left for us.

Mother never believed in lavishing her girls with unnecessary expensive gifts, but always allowed "Santa" to bring each of us one "very nice gift," a few things to play with, and a stocking full of goodies. I can remember some of the "very nice gifts" Santa brought to me throughout the years. The first one I remember was a large brown teddy bear that I carried around with me until it fell apart. It was a throwback to those named for Theodore (Teddy) Roosevelt, and although it was soft and comforting to have around, it also exuded a sense of protection, just like its namesake. Another Christmas I received a baby doll. It had eyelids with long, dark brown eyelashes, which closed when I laid it down and opened when I sat the doll up, and when I pushed a certain spot on the doll's back (or was it the stomach?), it said "Ma—Ma." The next year I received a doll carriage and a doll suitcase for my baby doll, which I really enjoyed playing with more than the doll. Santa brought those things to me while we lived on Park Avenue.

One of the "nice gifts" I remember Santa bringing me at Mayfield Park was a very large set of Lincoln logs that I loved and built houses with over and over again.

Next, I remember that I walked into the garage one December day and looked up, for some reason, into the attic over the attached apartment and saw some toys that Mother thought were out of sight. One of them was a pastel ivory or pink colored sewing box on legs, made just like Grandmother Templeton's, but smaller.

I don't remember what the other toys were, but after thinking awhile I remembered Christmas was close at hand and decided not to mention the toys to anyone. I never even told Mother that I saw them.

Sure enough, when Christmas day arrived, Santa left me the sewing box. I was so proud of it. I put some sewing items in it and felt very grown-up. I learned later that Mother had induced Alex to apply his woodworking skills to make the sewing box, using Grandmother Templeton's as a model or pattern.

The few "things to play with" didn't vary much from year to year. There were always crayolas, watercolors, coloring books, construction paper, other art supplies, and maybe a ball, a jump rope or a top, and eventually jacks. That was the only time each year that we were allowed to have new crayolas and water colors.

Our "stockings" always contained pretty much the same things: oranges, apples, colorful hard Christmas candy, and lots of mixed nuts in the shell, such as pecans, almonds, hickory nuts, hazel nuts, and walnuts. It was fun to shell them and eat them. I must say that we always felt that we had received quite a few things from Santa Claus and we never complained because we didn't receive more.

Of course, children in the 1930s didn't have anything near the vast assortment of toys, games, and other things to choose from and want at Christmastime that children do today. It seems to me that in the 1930s we put more emphasis on getting one really nice gift and just being with family members at Christmastime than people do today. I know it is still important today to have the family around one at Yuletide, but it also seems to have become almost a necessity for most children to receive an enormous array of different gifts, in order for them to be happy.

Several weeks before Christmas, 1934, Mother started telling us we should ask Santa not to bring us many gifts that year, but to take them, instead, to children whose fathers were out of work. She finally convinced me to start thinking that way. I don't know if it affected my sisters or not, but by the time Christmas morning came, I was almost hoping that MOST of the gifts Santa had with my name on them had been taken to a poor child. After all, I was over 11 years old, and fully able to understand the state of our country, regarding the Depression. Therefore, when I went to see what he had left us, I was prepared for what I found. The only things there were the stockings, filled as usual, and the art supplies (fewer than usual) that I expected, but there were no large special gifts for any of us. I remember looking toward my sisters and hoping that they, especially Frances, wouldn't be too disappointed. If they were, they didn't let on, so Christmas day was a joyful occasion, just the same, as we were all together.

We spent Christmas day and ate Christmas dinner at Grandmother and Grandfather Rife's home, until he passed away in 1934. It was a boisterous celebration of Christmas centered around the gathering of the entire family. For Christmas dinner, Grandmother Rife always served a huge turkey, cornbread dressing, giblet gravy (ugh!), mashed potatoes, English peas, several vegetables, cranberry sauce, salads, many different kinds of pies, and one last thing that was considered an absolute necessity for the Christmas dinner to be complete—candied sweet potatoes, with marshmallows on top.

We didn't know in 1934, while we were going about the regular routine of celebrating Christmas, that that would be the last year we would celebrate it in Mayfield Park for 40 some-odd years.

No matter where we celebrated, Christmas was not merely a time of exchanging gifts, seeing relatives, and eating good foods, as I have related it up to now. It was actually our way of having a joyous celebration in commemoration of the birthday of Jesus. All of my family members felt the same way, being church-going Christians. But I have no intention of delving into religion at this time, so, enough said.

Chapter Eighteen

Father Seeks Something Better

By January 1935, Father had reduced his egg-laying business to one chicken house, not quite full of hens (probably about 200). Hard times had even caused the hotels and restaurants to stop buying eggs regularly, and he couldn't get enough for the eggs he did sell to break even.

But he kept the cows, and even bought another one now and then until he had acquired six milk cows and as many calves as he could find.

Shortly thereafter Father told the hired man he had to let him go because he no longer needed full-time help and couldn't afford to keep him in any event.

The hired man pleaded with Father to let him continue working in the scaled-down job for nothing more than a place to live plus eggs, milk, and butter for his family, until he could find other employment. He said he had no money and no place to move his family to. Father agreed and wished him luck in finding a job.

In no time Father reached the point where he couldn't find enough calves to handle all of the milk, so he started a "butter and egg" route on the south side of San Antonio.

A butter and egg route entailed a lot more than the gasoline and time involved in delivering the produce. Someone had to milk the cows twice daily. Mother strained the milk into ten-inch round pans about three inches deep, and set them in the refrigerator. Every 24 hours the cream was skimmed off and held in the icebox until about two gallons had accumulated, which usually took two or three days. The icebox was always full of those pans of milk and cream.

Next the cream was poured into the large three-gallon dasher churn. Mother, the hired man's wife (who had continued helping her), and sometimes me, worked hard making the butter. One of us plunged the dasher up and down churning the cream until golden yellow lumps of butter separated leaving buttermilk.

Mother had a large round wooden bowl, a wooden paddle, and a wooden butter mold. They were used to work and shape the butter into one-pound rectangles. Then they were wrapped in butter paper and stacked in the refrigerator. I think she usually managed to get five or six pounds of butter from each churning.

The hired man still sorted, brushed clean, and packed the eggs in cartons of one dozen each. Then they were stored in a cool place until delivery day.

Several times I rode along with Father on the butter and egg route. I remember it being a disaster of sorts. Almost everyone wanted to be included as a customer. All of them wanted eggs, but very few could afford to order butter. Most of them didn't have the money to pay for either the butter or the eggs when delivered.

I remember many "Mrs. So and So's" saying, "I need the eggs and butter so much. My children are hungry, but I don't have the money today. I'll pay you next time."

Father let some of the customers slide at first because he believed them and felt sorry for them. But then the next time a delivery was made, they not only couldn't pay for the last order, they started begging Father to leave some more eggs and/ or butter for them to pay for later. They would do anything to try to get their hands on something to eat.

Father dropped those customers fairly soon and wound up with only a few regular paying customers. The entire venture was rather grim, but my parents lumbered through somehow for quite a while.

Then toward the end of summer of 1935, even the regular paying customers started losing their jobs or something and they either canceled their orders or wanted to pay later. Shortly thereafter I heard Father say he couldn't go on with the butter and egg route because it was too depressing to hear so many people say they didn't have the money for food items, and furthermore, he couldn't afford to supply the neighborhood with free butter and eggs.

In the meantime, he had continued to sell a few hens from time to time, mostly to Polunsky's produce house on North Main Avenue. Now and then I watched him and the hired man cage several dozen hens in portable chicken coops and haul them off in the Model T Ford pick-up truck. On more than one occasion I went with him.

He was always devastated by the low price he received for his fine fat hens. But he said we couldn't eat all of them and he couldn't continue to buy feed for hens that didn't pay their way—he wasn't made of money. Then, late in 1935, it began to look as though Polunsky's wouldn't always take the hens, so he called them first and asked if they were buying hens that day. The answer was always the same, "If we aren't flooded with poultry before you get here." By November 1935, Father had sold all but 30 or 40 of the hens, which he kept back for our use.

The bees were still intact and self-sustaining, except for needing new frames when they were robbed of their honey, for which there was no market. Father wasn't about to part with his bees.

He also had no intention of parting with his beloved milk cows, or the horse or the donkey. He began to talk about needing more land and more cows. He said over and over again, "with enough land and cows, a person could ride out the Depression in comfort." But he had neither.

All he had was a seven-acre albatross draining any finances he could muster, and keeping him from any other endeavor. When he spoke of the situation, he had a worried demeanor about him, filled with stress and anxiety. I was old enough to realize that things were out of control.

At the same time the chicken and egg business was failing, the real estate business was also going downhill. When the Depression hit, Father was operating a very lucrative real estate and loan business, which he had established in 1920.

In addition to eight or ten full-time real estate salesmen working on commission, he had continually maintained a salaried office staff of four or five people that included a secretary, file clerk, errand boy, and bookkeeper. It was also common practice for him to have an apprentice Realtor working with him in exchange for experience (while being taught the real estate business) and a small salary. Father bore the full expense of operating the office. It had proven to be a very smooth operation with all parties well satisfied and earning a good living.

Father never discussed his financial situation with me, but I heard enough in remarks he made to Mother to know it was very expensive to operate a real estate office. Some of the expenses I heard mentioned were the rent for office space, charge for a business phone with extensions, and a large weekly ad bill for business ads in all the San Antonio papers: *The San Antonio Light, Morning Express, Evening News* and *La Prensa.* And of course, the salaries he paid office employees.

Sometime in the early thirties, Father started telling my mother about first one disparaging occurrence and then another. They went something like this: "One of the salesmen gave up today and took a small job somewhere." Or, "Another salesman left to try his luck in another city." And then, "I let the bookkeeper go. I need to keep my own books anyway." Next, "The errand boy offered to stay for half his salary." Finally, he came in one day and announced, "I let the file clerk go today as the secretary has time to do her job and his also." Eventually there wasn't enough work to keep the errand boy occupied so he let him go. Next, he had some of the telephone extensions disconnected.

This dwindling away of his large business office continued on a gradual scale over a period of several years. For instance, as the real estate business waned, the salesmen gradually left to seek a living elsewhere. Employees were dismissed when no longer needed and office space was reduced by the summer of 1935 to Father's private office, a reception room, and one room for salesmen. There was finally only one salesman left, clamoring for a periodic sale in order to exist.

When the last salesman gave up the ghost and left, Father reduced the office space a little more. Then there wasn't anything left to give up but one office, his secretary, and a telephone. Father let the secretary go, as there wasn't that much for her to do. He could run his loan brokerage business by himself and it didn't require as much space and other overhead as the real estate business. The loan business was still functioning to some degree.

The real estate business in general, nationwide (building, buying, and selling houses), had been in deep trouble and heading for a standstill since shortly after the stock market crash of 1929. First, construction had ceased. Next, hundreds of homes were repossessed as buyers lost their jobs and defaulted on their loans. Banks ceased to lend money to prospective buyers because of lack of job security and also because they were overloaded with repossessed real estate and short of funds. Since there were no buyers, the value of repossessed property had plunged to about one-third of its original appraisal. This contributed to the banks starting to fail altogether and closing.

During that same period (1930-1935) there were a number of wealthy individuals who didn't trust their money to banks (no FDIC), desiring to loan their capital to the people who were considered to be good financial risks, such as municipal, federal, and utility workers, to name a few. That covered a vast number of fields, including city, state, and county employees, postal workers, federal employees, railroad employees, schoolteachers, and water, electric, gas, and telephone employees. It's obvious that everyone wasn't out of work.

Father was a broker who brought the lenders (wealthy individuals) and the borrowers (good financial risks) together in exchange for a brokerage fee. He had a large clientele of wealthy men who relied upon his judgment and recommendations as to where to loan their money. He also engineered the selling of notes when an investor needed cash.

Then late in 1935, Father came up against "the last straw." The loan business was coming to a grinding halt. His last source of any income whatsoever was drying up. I heard him say to Mother, "The loan business is practically non-existent. My clients already have most of their money tied up in satisfactory loans. Times are bad. I have to find something to do until things get better." Father never failed to say, "until things get better." He never doubted for an instant that there would be an "end to the Depression."

The loan brokerage portion of Father's business helped out financially during the early thirties, but it certainly couldn't support his office, the chicken farm and his family all by itself. So what did he do? Well, no one ever actually told me, but from things I heard my parents discussing I have my own idea.

To begin with, Father had always in the past been self-supporting and had never been without sufficient funds to care for his family's needs. His real estate business had continuously been prosperous since its inception in 1920. In 1928 he and Mother sold their home at 630 East Park Avenue and invested the proceeds in the seven-acre chicken farm and home at Mayfield Park. Father had the balance of the Mayfield Park venture financed and retained his savings, (which were sufficient to cover same) to use for unexpected emergencies, fully expecting to pay the note off in two or three years from his flourishing business.

But instead, the Depression caused everything in the United States to come to a standstill in the early 1930s. Father, thinking it would be over soon, started digging into his emergency fund sometime in late 1930, or early 1931, in order to keep his businesses going. He thought things would get better soon. This continued over the next few years, until all reserve funds were exhausted.

After going this far, he negotiated a small personal loan from time to time from one of his investors, in order to continue. He still expected the Depression to be over soon, especially since President Roosevelt had started taking steps to end it in late 1933. But things only got worse until there was no way to continue supporting businesses that didn't pay for themselves. Actually, Father stayed ahead of the game a lot longer than most businessmen did during that era.

Finally, he decided he was fighting a lost cause and looked for something better to do until the Depression was over. But first (exclusive of the livestock, two automobiles and household furniture), he used every remaining asset he could find, including our home, to satisfy his creditors. I don't know the details of how he did it, but he wound up with his credit intact, fortunately.

Throughout the turmoil and disappointment of seeing all of his savings, prosperous real estate business, chicken farm, and home dwindle away, Father was undaunted. He never failed to look forward to "when the Depression lets up and things get better." But that didn't happen in time for him to keep the status quo.

During the summer of 1935, he started talking more and more about getting away from it all "until things get better." Each month when the utility bills for the home and office came due, Father said, "If we lived on a farm, we wouldn't have any of those bills to worry about." Mother didn't have much to say. She just listened to him and tried to run the house on as little as possible and keep everyone in good spirits at the same time.

For Mother, those last few months at Mayfield Park were filled with stress and fear. She was constantly worrying about whether Father had been able to pay the utility bills. It got to the point where she was afraid she would find the phone had been cut off when she started to make a call. On the other hand, she was loath to answer it when it rang lest it be a bill collector.

She was so nervous, she even thought that anyone who knocked on the door or entered the yard would turn off our lights, water, or phone. Having never been through such an experience before, she didn't know how a utility was cut off. But she needn't have worried, because no one ever cut anything off.

Worrying about utility bills was the closest I ever saw her come to bewailing the fact that our life at Mayfield Park was coming to an end. Otherwise, her spirits were very upbeat and filled with optimism. Never once did I see her cry one tear or grieve about leaving her dream house.

Father never conceded defeat to the Depression. To him it was only a temporary inconvenience that had to be endured until it "went away." Thus, he started looking toward something better to come as a result of it. And that's what he had in mind when he announced in November 1935 that he was closing his real estate office. By then, it was quite a simple thing to do. He had already disposed of most of the office furniture, except things used by him (desk, chair, file cabinets, Underwood typewriter, and a few other things). Those personal items were moved into our garage apartment.

Finally one day early in December 1935 when I came home from school, Mother said we were moving to a large farm. Father had leased the farm for one year with the intention of purchasing it when he made enough money to pay cash. He didn't want to buy another piece of property with a note on it.

I remember the evening when Father came in and said we were going to a place where we could exist off the land until "things got better." Instead of being sad, Father actually seemed to be excited and eager to get to the farm and live as he did when he was a lad. He started talking about all the things he could plant and the cows and calves he would raise and said he couldn't wait to get there. He even began talking about the hog he was going to buy to fatten and butcher. After all, Father's dream had always been to own a large farm or ranch with cattle in the pasture and crops in the fields.

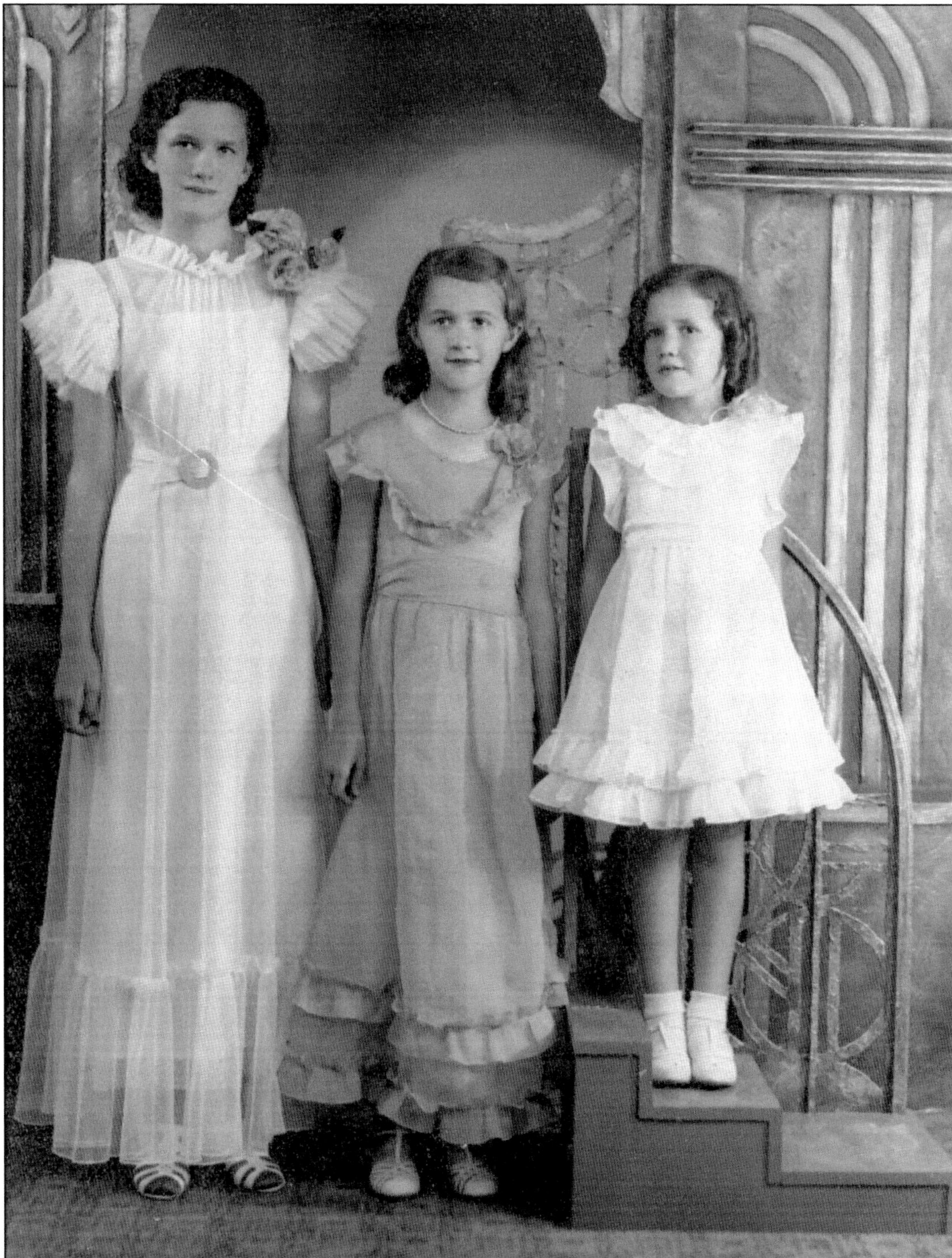

The three Rife girls are pictured as follows from left to right: Mary, Jean, and Frances. This is how we looked in 1935, about the time we moved away from Mayfield Park to begin our new life in Somerset.

Chapter Nineteen

Farewell to Childhood

During the first week of December 1935, Father told us we were moving to a large farm near Somerset. His excitement and exuberance about "living off the land until things got better" was contagious and almost immediately all of Father's womenfolk were ready to leave their nice home and follow him to the farm, sight unseen.

So far as I knew, Mother hadn't even seen the farmhouse we moved to before we arrived to stay. But nevertheless, she led me to believe there was something magical about moving to a place called "Somerset," that I had never heard of before, except in an English novel, and I knew we weren't going to England.

A few days before leaving Mayfield Park, I remember wondering about so many things. What would the new home and yard be like, and so on. Then I started thinking of all the things we were leaving behind that I had come to take for granted, for instance, the chicken houses, cow lot, honey separator, brooder house for baby chicks, vegetable garden west of the house, and Mother's flower beds and rose garden. I remembered our green lawn and wondered if there would be one where we were going.

Then I thought about the ligustrum trees and other shrubbery that enhanced the perimeter of our home, and the bees, butterflies, insects, and humming birds buzzing around them in spring and summer. I asked Mother if there would be any butterflies where we were going. She said she thought there were butterflies everywhere in the summertime.

Shortly after that, I heard the familiar strains of "The Glowworm" coming from the radio as someone played it on a piano and my mind wandered back to the first time I encountered fireflies. It was at Mayfield Park, on a lovely summer evening, just after dark. We were all outside watching the stars, trying to locate the big dipper, the little dipper, and maybe the evening star and the north star, when I noticed little blinking lights glimmering all-around us, close enough to reach out and touch. They were so pretty going on-off, on-off, flashing white spots of light with a hint of green or blue.

I asked Mother what those lightning bugs were. The way they flashed their lights reminded me of lightning. She said they were fireflies. I thought a while and then said, "What are fireflies?" Mother said glowworm was another name for them, like in the song, The Glowworm, that I liked so much.

Then I started catching the fireflies, which was really quite easy, as they didn't move very fast. They just sort of floated through the air with an ethereal aura about them, flashing their little lights as if to see their way.

Mother brought me a jar with holes in its lid and said, "If you're going to catch them, you might as well put them in this jar and watch them glimmer for awhile."

Jean and I ran around in the night chasing after and catching dozens of the pretty little fireflies. We put them in the jar and carried them around watching their glowing white lights flash and glimmer on and off until bedtime. Then we set them free and watched a little longer as they blinked their way off into the night. After that, we made a regular habit of playing with fireflies on summer nights.

Then, I started to pack some of my keepsakes. The first thing I came across was my invitation to an end-of-school party, which was held at Terrell Wells by the San Jose PTA for the fifth grade class in June 1934 (my class).

The invitation caused me to think about one more thing we were leaving behind—the Terrell Wells Swimming Pool. It was on Hutchins Avenue, probably less than a mile from our homE. I had always wanted to go swimming there but Father said, "No, it isn't sanitary." So imagine my surprise when he had a sudden change of heart during the summer of 1935, and announced, "Check out your swim suits, we're going swimming at Terrell Wells next Saturday."

What a thrill it was to finally get in the pool at Terrell Wells. I had been swimming only a few times in my life, once or twice in a pool at Brackenridge Park which was fed by freshwater springs, in a stream someplace in the hill county, and in the Gulf of Mexico on the Texas coast. But I had never been in a genuine public pool with many people around. And whenever I say anything about "going swimming," I am using the phrase loosely, as I certainly didn't know how to swim.

Mother and Father told my sisters and me to keep our heads out of the water and stay in the three-foot area. Then they, having learned to swim when quite young in rivers or creeks near their respective homes, swam toward the deeper part of the pool. I was tall enough to walk in the deeper water, so I started moving toward Mother and Father who were swimming in the shady area in five feet of water.

It wasn't as easy to walk in the five-foot water as I thought, and by the time I reached them I was stumbling around. I lost my balance and my head went under. As I came up gasping for air and grabbing for something to steady myself, I encountered Father. He was very unhappy that I had disobeyed him and left the three-foot area. But when he saw my head had been in that "unsanitary water," that was it. He could take no more. He cried out, "Come on, let's go home. We don't have any business in this public pool anyway, it isn't sanitary." And that was that, we went back home.

But nevertheless, I was happy because I had finally realized my ambition to go swimming in the Terrell Wells Swimming Pool. It really wasn't all that great though, as the water used to fill the pools came from a naturally warm sulphur well and it reeked with the horrible smell of sulphur. I didn't care at that time whether or not I ever went swimming there again, but I knew that I would miss the annual Fourth of July fireworks display, which I probably wouldn't see again.

My reflections were interrupted by Mother asking me to bring her some boxes, so I stopped packing my keepsakes and took them to her. Then I walked through our home and looked over all the familiar things I was leaving behind that I would miss. I couldn't generate any excitement at all about leaving the home I had spent most of my childhood in and around. The years spent there were crammed full with so much living. Outside the house, I had learned about all kinds of animals. Also, I had encountered the wonderment of watching vegetables, flowers, trees, shrubbery, and other plants grow.

Having watched the carpenters build the house, I actually felt I had a hand in creating it. And it was in that house that I learned so many things, such as needlework, canning, how to make butter, all about washing and ironing, how to clean and sweep, and how Mother prepared the foods we ate. Also, while living there, I had become acquainted with the medical profession, which played an important part during my adolescence in helping me to lead a normal life as an adult. And then I remembered that my baby sister had arrived in the front bedroom.

During the years I spent at Mayfield Park I learned all about our relatives and the many ways they affected our lives, including the grief involved when a close family member died. Then I thought about Grandmother and Grandfather Templeton, Grandmother Rife, and Aunt Sissie, all of whom I had seen regularly and frequently up to that timE. I called to Mother and asked her if we would be able to visit them very often after we moved. She said, of course we would, that we weren't really going that far away, only about 20 or 25 miles. And all of a sudden I wondered what Grandmother Templeton would have to say about our moving even further away from her. She never did like us being even seven or eight miles away.

I had enjoyed a happy, carefree, fun-filled, knowledgeable childhood, in and around that house, all in a time when the United States was in the midst of the worst Depression ever. But I was barely aware the Depression was all around me, as I never actually suffered from a lack of anything I needed because of it.

After a few more days of reminiscing, packing, and wondering what Somerset would be like, I finally went to bed for the last time in my room in my home at Mayfield Park, knowing full-well that the next day would be the start of a whole new chapter in my life—SOMERSET. And that's as far as my memories of childhood go, because the next night when I went to bed (at Somerset), I was a young adult. The mental transition from childhood to adulthood seemed to just happen somehow that day, during the move.

There were a lot of things I never experienced again after leaving Mayfield Park, which I only wondered about at the time we left. I am sure there are a lot of other things I never did again after leaving Mayfield Park. But the one single thing I left behind that I treasured the most, was my CHILDHOOD. From that time on, everyone, including myself, considered me, as being a young adult.

The End

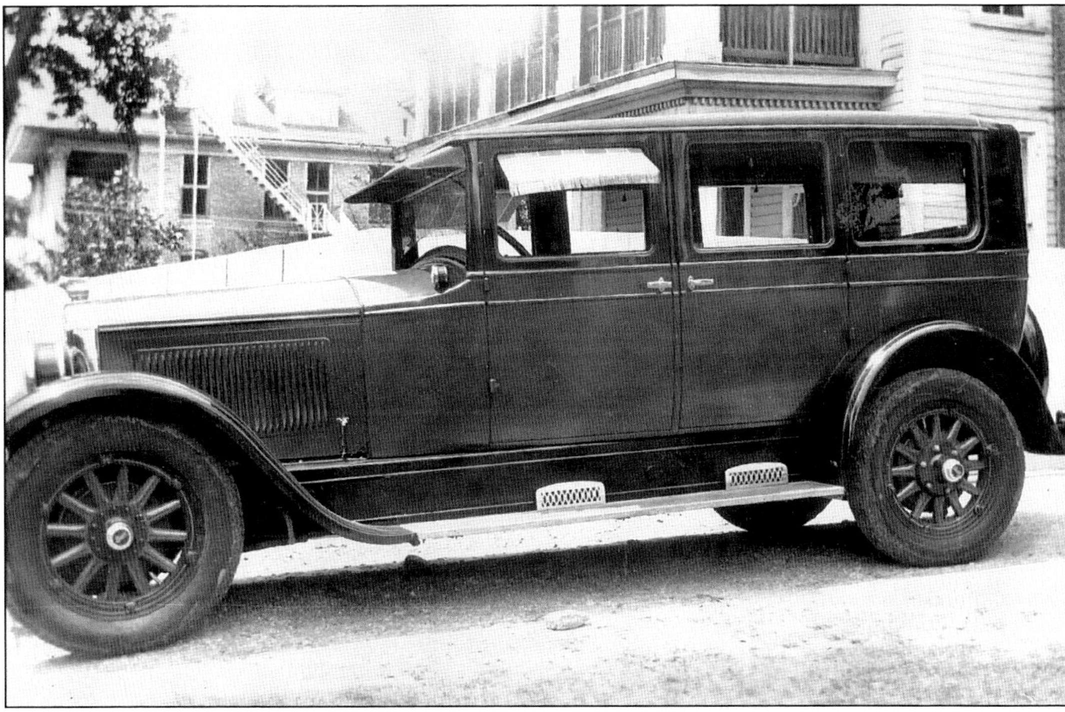

Grandfather Templeton bought a new car every year. This is one of his first luxury sedans.

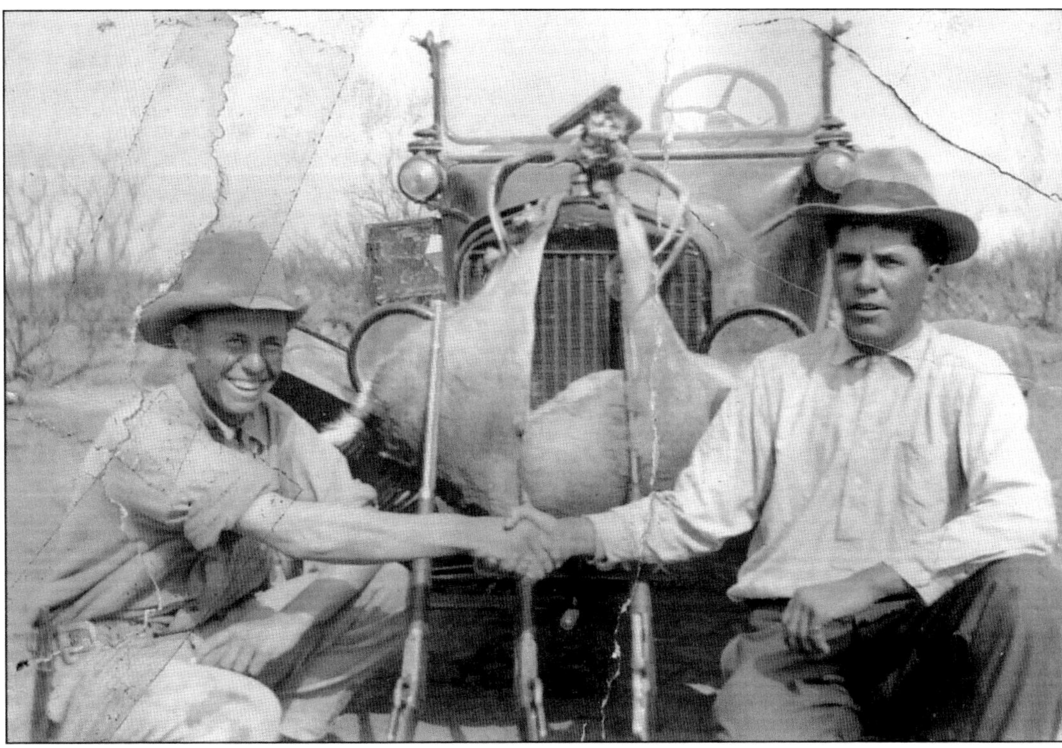

Father was quite a hunter. Here he is with a deer he shot near Del Rio.

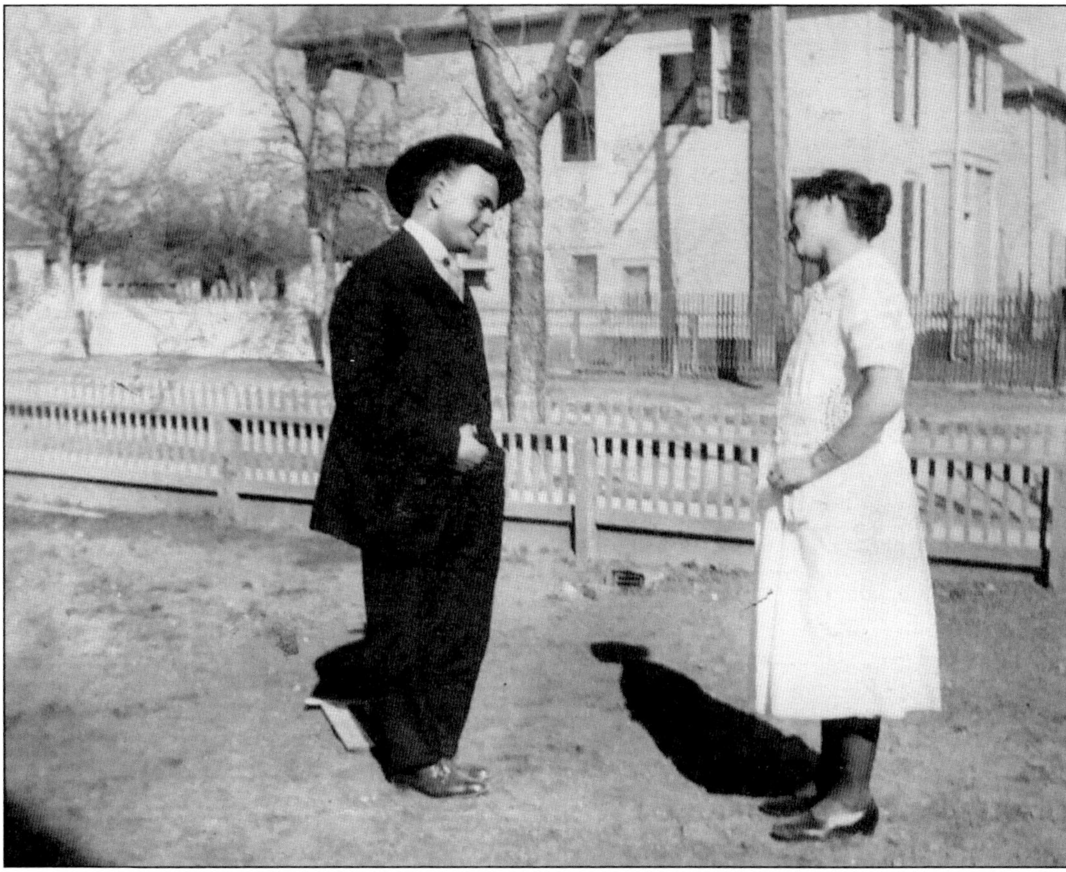

Alex and Aunt Sissie clowned around a lot!

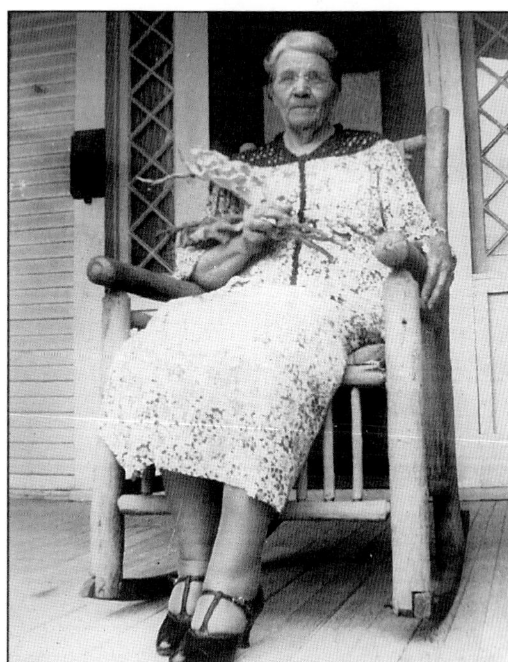

Grandmother Rife sits on her porch.

Other Titles in the *Voices of America* Oral History Series

Grant County, Indiana
B.J. Stevenson and the Grant County Historical Society

Lancaster County and the Great War, South Carolina
John Griffin

Rock Hill, South Carolina: Gateway to the New South
Dr. Edward Lee and Dr. Anne Beard

The Fagan Sisters: A History of Life in a New York County Village
Elinor Mettler